Proposal Planning and Writing
Third Edition

Lynn E. Miner and Jeremy T. Miner

An Oryx Book

GREENWOOD PRESS
Westport, Connecticut • London

Library of Congress Cataloging-in-Publication Data

Miner, Lynn E.
   Proposal planning and writing / Lynn E. Miner and Jeremy T. Miner.—3rd ed.
      p. cm.
   Includes bibliographical references (p.) and index.
   ISBN 1–57356–498–2 (alk. paper)
   1. Proposal writing for grants—United States.   I. Miner, Jeremy T.   II. Title.
HG177.5.U6 M56   2003
658.15′224—dc21   2002025791

British Library Cataloguing in Publication Data is available.

Library of Congress Catalog Card Number: 2002025791
ISBN: 1–57356–498–2

First published in 2003

Greenwood Press, 88 Post Road West, Westport, CT 06881
An imprint of Greenwood Publishing Group, Inc.
www.greenwood.com

Printed in the United States of America

The paper used in this book complies with the
Permanent Paper Standard issued by the National
Information Standards Organization (Z39.48–1984).

10 9 8 7 6 5 4 3 2

Contents

Preface

He from whose lips divine persuasion flows.
Alexander Pope

For most organizations, today's reality presents a gap between what they want to do and the resources available to do it. To close this gap, many are seeking outside sources of financial support through grants.

Normally, people don't just give money away. They do, however, invest in causes in which they deeply believe. Sponsors will invest in your cause when you can persuade them that you actually share the same values. Persuasion is a key element to successful grantseeking.

Grantwriting is a form of persuasive writing. Beginning grantwriters sometimes assemble a collection of facts and present that information to grantmakers, hoping to receive support. Successful grantseekers know that persuasion, not information, attracts funding. They know that winning proposals must systematically respond to the needs of the sponsor.

This book helps you successfully traverse the grants gauntlet in an era of increased competition by suggesting many persuasive writing techniques. It begins with a list of questions frequently asked by both inexperienced and experienced grantseekers and then offers answers to these questions as directly as possible to provide efficient and effective strategies for successful grantseeking. The book guides you through a systematic, step-by-step approach to developing persuasive and successful grant proposals.

The content of this book is based, in part, on our grantseeking experiences over the past three decades in writing successful proposals, conducting grant workshops nationwide, and reviewing proposals and critiquing application guidelines for government agencies and private foundations. The ideas and procedures described in these eighteen chapters are applied on a daily basis in our grants offices and at thousands of schools, colleges, universities, hospitals, clinics, agencies, research institutes, and foundations. The book is heavily sprinkled with examples taken directly from successful proposals that have generated more than $25 million in grant funding.

Your successful grant proposal should show the uniqueness, underlying resources, and potential benefits of your proposed idea—benefits that match closely with the interests of potential funding sources. This book presents specific guidelines and examples designed to maximize the likelihood of a match between the two.

COMPUTERIZED GRANTSEEKING

Computers play a significant role in today's society, and the grants arena is no exception. This book shows how computers can simplify the grant development process. And you don't have to be a computer guru to take advantage of electronic information sources that will help you to quickly identify appropriate funding sources. Many of the existing computer programs are "user-friendly" and "idiot-proof." By using computers to develop your grant proposals, you will be able to submit more proposals in less time, thereby increasing your chances of getting funded.

If you have not had much computer experience, particularly on the Internet, details concerning Web site addresses or search engines can be almost blinding. Fortunately, if you can point and click your mouse, you will comfortably manage the electronic grantseeking information offered in this book. Chapters 2 and 3 identify a number of Web addresses that will help you find funding sources for your projects; Chapter 17 describes how to use search engines to develop better proposals. This online information is easy to use—so much so, in fact, that some sponsors disseminate grant information or receive proposals only electronically. You will find in this book many practical guides that will lead you to these sources, a rewarding experience for you and your organization.

The book contains hundreds of Web addresses. The ones we selected are based on content, design, and ease of navigation. None of these sites paid to be included. All facts and Uniform Resource Locators (URLs, also known as Web addresses) were accurate at press time, but because the Internet is constantly changing, you may need to periodically update your address book of Web sites.

TARGET AUDIENCES

The people who have attended our grant workshops and who are currently using the ideas presented in this edition represent a wide variety of professions and disciplines. Seven major categories stand out.

- **Education**: Day care programs, adult education, public and private schools, special education departments, colleges and universities, English as foreign language programs.
- **Social Services**: Sociolegal, mental health, community development, rehabilitation agencies.
- **Health Care**: Physicians' offices, hospitals, nursing homes, public health organizations, Veterans Administration.
- **Religions**: Churches, synagogues, mosques, and other houses of worship; their administration offices, schools, and development offices.
- **Philanthropy**: Foundations, charitable organizations, service clubs.
- **Government**: Local, state, federal agencies, courts, human services, agencies, law enforcement agencies.
- **Economic Development**: City planning, land use, urban revitalization, and job creation offices.

Other groups include the fine and performing arts, senior citizens' advocates and agencies, and special interest groups. Because grantseekers are such a diverse group, you must present your ideas clearly to the public and private organizations that fund worthy recipients. Health care systems, universities, and agencies that are involved with the development and submission of numerous grant proposals will find the information in this book useful in setting up an institutional grants office.

STRUCTURE AND CONTENT

This book discusses funding sources from the federal government, private foundations, and corporations. There are eighteen chapters and a bibliography, arranged in a logical order—developing ideas, identifying and qualifying potential funding sources, setting up systems and procedures to support grantseeking activities for the present and future, developing the components of the proposal, budget forecasting, submission procedures, and follow-up techniques. You will find specific examples, models, and step-by-step instructions throughout the text. Additionally, you will find many helpful Web site addresses throughout the chapters. These Web addresses will provide you with further vendor information, including mailing addresses, telephone numbers, and fees, when appropriate.

The computer information provided assumes that the readers have only a nominal level of computer sophistication—namely, access to the Internet and the understanding that all Web site addresses begin with *http://*. (Because all Web site addresses begin with *http://*, we have not listed this information within the addresses. Further note that most, but not all, of the Web addresses listed in this book begin with *www*. Not all Web addresses require the *www*.) Beyond that, no further computer skill is required. If you enter the address exactly as listed, you should establish a link unless the server is down or the address was changed recently.

NEW TO THIS EDITION

This third edition presents scores of concrete writing examples and many time-saver tips drawn from successful grantseekers. The following five changes to this edition are designed to better meet the emerging needs of today's grantseekers in an era of increased competition for limited resources.

- **More Web Sites of Public and Private Funding Sources**: More than three hundred Web sites are included to help you identify potential funding sources. Targeted approaches to these different sponsors are presented, including perspectives on the elusive world of corporate philanthropy.
- **Detailed Discussion of Preproposal Contacts**: Preproposal contact is one of the most important things you can do to increase your chances of getting funding. The process involves a strong opening statement to pique interest, followed by asking four different types of questions to qualify potential

funding sources and fine-tune your proposal so it more closely matches the sponsor's priorities.

- **New Presentation of Evaluation and Outcomes**: As grant dollars become increasingly competitive, accountability is key. Project evaluations and outcome measures, fuzzy areas for many grantwriters, demonstrate to the sponsor that project funds are being spent wisely and that the project is making a difference.
- **Expanded Information on Budgets**: Your budget is as much a credibility statement as your project narrative. A fresh and expanded discussion of direct costs, indirect costs, and cost sharing is presented, including a complete example of a budget and budget narrative.
- **Current Approaches to Managing Site Visits and Grant Decisions**: Some sponsors may wish to visit your organization firsthand before making a funding

decision. Before they do, view a sample timeline and questions posed during a site visit from a national private foundation. And learn to better manage grant decisions by taking a long-term view to grantseeking.

THE INFAMOUS BOTTOM LINE

Successful grantseekers are often individuals who are so dedicated to their ideas that they will find the means to carry them out with or without outside support. Sponsors have clear objectives and expectations that they hope to realize by providing financial support to such dedicated persons. A persuasively written grant proposal is the link between them. This book helps you forge that link.

Let's begin planning your best grant ever!

PART I
Finding Sponsors and Planning Proposals

Thousands of grantmakers give away billions of dollars. How do you find those sponsors who would fund your projects?

Part I gives you the basic print and electronic information sources to identify a list of public and private sponsors who might fund your projects. With a little research time, you can determine those grantmakers who are your potential financial supporters.

Just like salespeople must qualify their potential customers to see who is likely to buy their products, grantwriters must qualify their potential sponsors to see which ones have the greatest likelihood of providing grant dollars. This is done through a process of pre-proposal contact. The last chapter in this section provides a four-step process that will significantly increase your likelihood of getting funded.

CHAPTER 1
Introduction to Grantseeking

*There is nothing more uncertain in its success than to take
the lead in the introduction of a new order of things.*
Machiavelli

Grantseeking is a multibillion-dollar-a-year business—and growing annually!

Following a 500-year-old Machiavellian maxim, your challenge, as a grantseeker, is to introduce a new order of things with no guarantee of outcomes. This book will help you to get your share of those grant dollars by providing time-tested answers to frequently asked questions:

1. How do I find grant money?
2. What are my chances of getting a grant?
3. Is it easier to get government or private grants?
4. Do I have to know the "right people" to get a grant?
5. How big a grant can I get?
6. What can I do with my grant money?
7. How hard is it to get my first grant?
8. Should I talk to grantmakers before submitting a proposal?
9. What do grantmakers look for in a proposal?
10. Is it all really worth it?

To begin with the last question, "Yes, it really *is* worth it." At least those organizations that receive grant dollars each year think so. To find out how you can access those dollars and answer many questions along the way, we begin by looking at some attitudes—and misconceptions—about grants.

ATTITUDES ABOUT GRANTSEEKING

Individual Attitudes

What does the word "grants" mean to you? Frankly, for some people the term generates negative reactions, such as "professional begging," "futility," "risk taking," "mystique," "hustling," or "con job." To such people, pursuing grants is risky because positive outcomes aren't guaranteed. These people steer clear of grants for many negative reasons: lack of motivation, lack of skills, lack of confidence, fear of failure, fear of change, fear of success, lack of time, unrealistic expectations, and laziness. Such individuals, who are a "quart low on attitude," are destined to fail if they pursue grants. Skeptics will say, "Grants, why bother?" Grant winners, on the other hand, will answer, "For many reasons." People write grants to

1. Earn money
2. Finance crucial projects
3. Gain job security
4. Achieve recognition
5. Break the regular job routine
6. Solve problems creatively
7. Have fun

What brings you job satisfaction? Certainly, money—a decent salary and the security it brings—is a very important factor on the job. More broadly, employee satisfaction fluctuates with the circumstances in each organization. Nevertheless, most job satisfaction studies show that employees desire the following:

- Interesting work
- Recognition for work performed
- A feeling of being "in" on things

Grantseeking can satisfy all three components of a rewarding job. If you are responsible for mustering grant support from others on your staff, you must show how grants will meet these needs.

Perhaps the most critical element in your ability to pursue successful proposal planning and writing is your sense of self-worth, the picture you have of yourself in your mental photo album, your self-esteem. Those with high self-esteem have a feeling of competence and believe in their ability to cope with the challenges of life. The value you place on yourself ultimately dictates your performance.

If you approach proposal planning and writing with a positive attitude and are willing to persist, you will succeed. If you doubt success from the start, you will fail. The applicable behavioral principle is the notion of the "self-fulfilling prophecy." In essence, it says, "What you believe will happen." We believe you can be a successful grantseeker.

Organizational Attitudes

Grant Myths. Many nonprofit organizations harbor misconceptions about grantseeking, attitudes that serve as formidable internal barriers to winning grants. Some common myths that need to be debunked include the following.

Myth: People will fund my needs. Sponsors fund their needs, not yours. When writing proposals, you must show that you can become a change agent to solve a problem important to them. For example, as a school official you may want a new computer laboratory. Sponsors are apt to be much less interested in your perceived needs than in an opportunity to support a project that will train computer-literate children in the new century. Put differently, sponsors care more about innovative ways to teach children than they do about buying computers.

Myth: Proposals are funded by the pound. Little relationship exists between the length of a proposal and its probability of getting funded. Although government proposals are usually longer than private proposals, there is no relationship between the number of pages you write and the amount of money you receive.

Myth: You can run a program on grants forever. Sustained grant support over many years is difficult to obtain. Start-up project support is the easiest to find, and operating support is the most difficult. Although project support can be successfully parlayed over many years, it is usually segmented into different phases or is periodically redefined if it is to be sustained.

Myth: Use the weasel words that people want to hear. There are no magic buzzwords to sprinkle in your proposal. "In" words today go "out" tomorrow. Don't be concerned about using vogue words. The simple, honest, direct approach is best.

Myth: Always plead poverty. Pleading poverty is a poor grant strategy. Sponsors will not give you money just because you are poor. Sponsors may conclude that you are poor because you lack good ideas, management, or community support. Instead, base your funding rationale on the fact that you propose to solve an important need for the sponsor.

Organizational Benefits. Seeking grants offers a huge plus side. Organizations pursue grants for many financial and administrative reasons. For instance, grants will provide budget relief through the direct and the indirect costs they provide. Often, grant money can be leveraged to attract additional funds from other sources. Beyond these fiscal considerations, receiving grants can have considerable public relations value for your organization. This, in turn, can bring zest to your recruitment program, making it easier to attract new talent to your organization.

Organizational Barriers. Agencies entering the grants arena must recognize and respond to one very important principle of behavior: *organization prevents reorganization.* That is, the fact that you are organized one way makes it difficult to organize another way; yet commitment to a successful grants program means that organizational priorities may need to change. Time and resources will be allocated differently. New systems and procedures will be implemented.

Resistance to change is natural and can be minimized by showing individuals how their job satisfaction will increase. As noted above, perhaps the best motivators for employees are the achievement, the recognition, the work itself, and the responsibility. One of people's greatest needs is the ability to achieve, and through achievement, experience psychological growth. Your task is to control and increase the effectiveness of the motivators within your organization that induce growth.

Motivating Others within Your Organization. Work smarter, not harder. Encourage others to join your grantseeking activities. These suggestions will help you secure "buy-in" from your colleagues:

- Have a central administrator issue a policy memo indicating that grantwriting is encouraged, indeed expected, within the organization.
- Give people time, resources, and training to write grants.
- Recognize and reward grant activities within the organization. For instance, writing grants should be one of the factors considered when awarding promotions and raises.

- Use the in-house newsletter or letters from a central administrator to praise grantwriters on their efforts.
- Share your grant knowledge with others in your organization. Remember, enthusiasm is contagious.
- Start small and build. Pick a few people to become the in-house grant experts. As they develop and experience success, others will also want to get involved.

As you work with others in your organization, help them build realistic expectations about grantseeking; otherwise, their false expectations will produce disappointments and disincentives for pursuing grants. For instance, supervisors must recognize that it takes approximately six to nine months to find out if a federal grant has been awarded. If bosses expect a decision soon after submitting a proposal, they will be needlessly disappointed.

Sponsor Attitudes

Grantmakers (sponsors) have a particular view of the world. They are vitally concerned about specific problems, injustices, or inequities. They are so concerned, in fact, that they are willing to commit their money to solve these problems. In essence, they see a gap between what is and what ought to be. Their mission is to close this gap. Another name for "gap" in grant parlance is "need," perhaps the most crucial section of your proposal; see Chapter 7 for further details. The gap represents how they view the problems that interest them.

Successful grantwriters understand the sponsor's view and express that view in the proposal. Successful proposal writers are able to reflect the "priorities" of the sponsor. Too often, proposal writers focus on their own need for funds instead of matching their project's goals with a sponsor's priorities. You should select sponsors that share your view of the world and tailor proposals to them. (See Chapter 4 for specifics.) Sponsors view grants as investments in an improved future. Proposals are funded when they express the priorities shared by the sponsor. Projects are rejected when they do not match a sponsor's priorities.

GETTING STARTED

Attitudes healthy? Ready to take the plunge? Great! We'll guide you through the five main steps to become a successful grantseeker.

1. **Select your grant ideas**. Look internally to your staff and volunteers for suggestions. Hold brainstorming sessions. Ask colleagues, "If we had a million dollars, what would we do with it?" Look externally to citizens, clients, and advisory boards. What suggestions would they have? For now, compile your list of grant ideas. Don't worry about which ones are the most fundable; that'll come shortly, in Chapter 4. Regardless of the idea you select for possible funding, your proposal should persuade its reviewers that your project shines with three kinds of merit: conceptual innovation, methodological rigor, and significant content.

2. **Identify possible funding sources**. Examine print and electronic funding sources for both public (Chapter 2) and private (Chapter 3) grants. When finished, you'll have a list of sponsors who *may* be interested in funding your projects.

3. **Conduct preproposal contacts**. Following the four-step process in Chapter 4, you will find out which sponsors are *most* likely to fund your proposals. Grantseeking is a contact sport. You will want to contact program officers, past grant winners, and past grant reviewers—all before you decide *if* and *what* you should write.

4. **Write your initial proposal draft**. Following the application guidelines and reviewer's evaluation form, quickly write your first draft. Remember: the first draft is for getting down, not for getting good. Experienced grantseekers spend approximately 25% of their time writing the first draft and 75% of their time rewriting and editing, your next step (Chapters 5–14).

5. **Edit your initial proposal draft**. Cycle through your draft many times, continually looking for one feature to improve at a time (Chapters 15–16). Examples: make sure you provide all of the requested information, check for spelling and grammar errors, and design a visually appealing document (Chapter 17).

Time Management

Why do we all complain about the lack of that precious commodity—time?

Effective time management enables you to

- Be more in control of what you do
- Be productive and secure in your job because you are in control
- Enjoy what you are doing

Very few people have grantwriting as their only job responsibility. Usually it is one of many responsibilities that also include such things as project administration, training, research, advising, public relations, other fundraising, personnel management, budgeting, phone answering, envelope stuffing—and more.

Planning proposals requires time. Planning is not a luxury; it is a necessity. We wrote this book assuming you are superbusy. Successful—and busy—grantseekers tell us that effective time management is a matter of controlling four factors:

- Procrastination
- Interruptions
- Procedures
- Priorities

Accordingly, we conclude this chapter, and the sixteen others as well, with concrete time management suggestions. Look for the clock symbol; it signals another time management tip.

 Time-Saver Tip #1
Common Sense Ideas

1. Set priorities daily.
2. Do first things first.
3. Remember, you don't "find" time, you "make" time.
4. Recognize there is always time for important things.
5. Recall long-term goals while doing small tasks.
6. Eliminate unproductive activities quickly.
7. Focus on one thing at a time.
8. Establish deadlines for yourself and others.
9. Delegate whenever possible.
10. Handle each piece of paper only once.
11. Keep things organized.
12. Don't fret when time is spent on activities beyond your control.

These dozen practical time management tips are things that you are probably already doing, but they are good common sense reminders for all of us.

Next, let's focus on more specific grant time management tips.

 Time-Saver Tip #2
Computers

Computers can simplify and expedite the grantseeking process. Of course, computers can also compound and lengthen proposal development, if used inefficiently. The key is to use the computer as an efficient information management tool. This book presents three ways in which the computer can strengthen your grantseeking skills.

- To identify funding sources, many Web site addresses are presented (Chapters 2 and 3).
- To strengthen document design, desktop publishing is reviewed (Chapter 15).
- To develop proposal content, search engines are discussed (Chapters 17).

Used efficiently, computers can scan the more than ten billion Web pages, find persuasive proposal information, and present your information in a distinctive way.

 Time-Saver Tip #3
Clip Files

Beyond efficient computer usage, you need to have effective grant systems and procedures in place to save time when hunting for and organizing information. If you could cut down the amount of time you spend managing information, you could write more proposals or work on other responsibilities. Successful grantseekers adopt efficient systems and procedures to simplify the proposal planning and writing process. We recommend using the "clip file" for organizing and managing grant information. With it, you "chunk" the grant process into small, manageable units and distribute your information into those categories.

The clip file theme runs throughout the book. We'll cite some examples below to get you started; additional tips are spread throughout the book as they apply to pertinent portions of the grant development process.

To begin, create a system of file folders, notebooks, or electronic files that contain the following labels.

Clip File Labels

Developing Grant Ideas (Chapter 1)	Goals and Outcomes (Chapter 8)
Refining Grant Ideas (Chapter 1)	Methods (Chapter 9)
Uniqueness (Chapter 1)	Evaluation (Chapter 10)
Advocates (Chapter 1)	Dissemination (Chapter 11)
Finding Public Grants (Chapter 2)	Budget (Chapter 12)
Finding Private Grants (Chapter 3)	Appendices (Chapter 13)
Proposal Introduction (Chapter 6)	Summary/Abstract (Chapter 14)
Statement of Problem (Chapter 7)	Dealing with Funding Decisions (Chapter 18)

We'll give examples of the first five clip files here to familiarize you with the concept; the remaining topics are discussed in the appropriate chapters, as indicated in parentheses. Whenever you see the *clip and save* symbol in this book, get out your kitchen (or electronic) scissors, clip the action item, and add it to your *clip* file; you'll *save* time when you write your next grant. In fact, the best time to build your clip file is when you are *not* writing a grant.

Clip File Action Item #1
Developing Grant Ideas

This notion should sound very familiar, for it was step 1 of the five-step process for successful grantseeking cited above. In essence, assemble your wish lists of organizational needs. Beyond the internal and external sources cited earlier, where else can you get grant ideas? Consider reports from commissions or government offices citing pertinent needs, consultant reports, grant idea worksheets, lists of recently funded grants, and lists of requests for proposals. Every time someone says, "We ought to do this if we had the money," write "this" on a piece of paper and add it to your clip file. Experienced grantseekers have found they can sometimes combine ideas and craft them into a bigger—and more fundable—idea.

Clip File Action Item #2
Refining Grant Ideas

In essence, you can take four different approaches to redefining your project. You can identify alternatives

- Subject matter areas
- Project locations
- Constituency groups served
- Types of grants

The more ways you can describe your grant ideas, the better chance you have of getting funded. Why? Because different sponsors fund different types of projects serving different populations in different locations. For instance, assume you work for an inner-city elementary school. How else might you describe your school? A model school for language immersion? A demonstration center for parental involvement in education? A cross-cultural community center? A school-industry partnership location? Each description presents your school in a different light and could attract different sponsors.

As another example, assume you work for a rural health care agency. How else might you describe yourself? A regional one-stop health shopping service? A countrywide multispecialty health clinic? A rural life-care health center? A federal health demonstration

center? Again, different focus points could appeal to different sponsors.

Each variable—subject matter, location, constituency, grant type—gives you some choices in the way you might describe your project. For example, suppose you want to create an information clearinghouse for the homeless. You might redefine your project as follows:

Subject Matter Area: In broad terms, your project might be described as one dealing with "education," "social welfare," or "social justice." In more narrow terms, keyword phraseology might include *"low-cost housing," "information dissemination,"* or perhaps *"minority education."* As further examples, keyword terms in the broad area of medical diseases might include the following: *"accidents," "AIDS," "Alzheimer's disease," "asthma," "breast cancer," "cardiovascular disease," "cystic fibrosis," "diabetes," "mental health," "HIV infection," "Parkinson's disease,"* and *"sudden infant death syndrome."*

Project Location: Your project impact area could range from the neighborhood to the city, region, county, state, or even national level, depending upon the scope of your efforts.

Constituency Groups Served: While you might want to make your information clearinghouse available to all those who need its service, you might wish to specialize in serving the needs of one or more populations, e.g., "minorities," "the elderly," "disadvantaged," "single parents with low income," or "poor families." Other target groups might include the following: "children and youth," "the disabled," "refugees," "veterans," and "women."

Type of Grant: Keywords for different types of grants include the following: "research", "equipment and instrumentation," "exhibitions," "fellowships," "workshops," "travel," and "social service delivery." Since many different types of grants are available, you could choose to cast your information clearinghouse for the homeless project to emphasize any of these categories.

Putting some of these choices together, you might describe your project as follows:

- A low-cost housing dissemination project for minorities in your city
- A housing demonstration information project for the disadvantaged poor in the Midwest
- A housing training project for the elderly in the state
- A seed project for an information clearinghouse on housing in the region

Use "out-of-the-box" thinking to identify different ways to appeal to potential sponsors. What can you adapt, modify, magnify, minify, substitute, rearrange, reverse, or combine to come up with a distinctive project?

Clip File Action Item #3
Uniqueness

Include the following in your clip file: your mission statement, mission statements from other organizations like yours in order to enable you to identify your distinctive differences, endorsements from experts, bibliographies, resumes, and organizational self-assessment tools.

One starting point in identifying your uniqueness is to examine (or brush off the dust and reexamine) your organizational mission statement. Typically, it describes your reason for being. It should encompass all the activities of your organization while distinguishing you from other, similar institutions. More precisely, the mission statement is a brief, clear summary of your organization's goals. Ideally, it contains no more than one hundred words. It provides a context for formulating the specific grant activities that you will pursue. It sets the arena in which you will compete. It determines how resources will be allocated. It guides the general pattern of growth and direction you will follow in the future.

What makes your organization unique? What is your special niche? One hospital identified its unique characteristics as follows: the only self-sufficient laboratory in the state with administrative support for the project, a strong community reputation, a centralized location, a solid partnership program with physicians, an open-heart surgery center, and an active research program.

Consider this mission statement from an alcoholism rehabilitation agency named Return:

> The mission of Return is to help individuals regain an active, productive life without the use of alcohol. Recovery comes through rehabilitative support and a self-desired change rather than from prescription. Return is a hospital-based program that emphasizes keeping the alcoholic in contact with family, employer, church, community, recreation, and cultural activities during the recovery process. (56 words)

Still having trouble determining your organizational uniqueness? Ask yourself and answer these questions:

1. What is your agency "known" for?
2. What are you recognized as being "the best" at?
3. What will make you more unique in the future?

4. What separates you from your grant competition in the eyes of grantmakers?
5. What do the leading grantmakers say about your agency?

Clip File Action Item #4
Advocates

List the types of services that your organization needs but is unable to provide with internal staff (e.g., legal, financial, management, or personnel); contact external service providers who know your organization and may be able to advocate on your behalf. List specific services you might use but lack access to (e.g., telephone credit card, data entry, desktop publishing, and travel); perhaps your organizational friendraising can identify people who can assist with these services. For example, a corporate executive may authorize use of the company telephone credit card by a nonprofit organization. Include brief resumes of key advocates in your clip file; see Chapter 13 for an example.

To build your clip files, invoke the help of your colleagues. Have staff members, for example, bring one addition to your clip file at each staff meeting. Further, make full use of so-called idle moments. Whether you are reading the evening newspaper, waiting in a doctor's office, or scanning the in-flight magazine on an airplane, develop a habit of continually being on the lookout for printed ideas that may be useful someday in developing a proposal.

What about politicians? Are they good advocates? Should you use them to help get grants? The answer is like Thanksgiving dinner: yes, but in moderation. Local, county, state, and federal government officials can be of some help in getting grants. Among the appropriate ways to network with politicians:

1. Keep them posted on your grant priorities.
2. Meet periodically with staffers in charge of congressional liaison in your specialty area—education, health, social services, environment.
3. Invite them to share new reports with you (for your clip file).
4. Write draft support letters you'd like to receive from them for major (not all) proposals you submit, if the sponsor would see value in it. If you are unsure about this, ask the sponsor as part of your preproposal contact (Chapter 4).
5. Invite them to visit your organization and see for themselves the good work you are doing.

Finally, to jump-start using clip files, contact your local newspaper and ask to see and copy their files on

---

the topics that interest you, e.g., drug abuse, adolescent pregnancy, teen smoking, environmental pollution, battered women and so forth. Most local newspapers microfilm or clip their publications and file stories by topic in an archive they refer to with a vinegar philosophy as "the morgue." Review these newspaper clip files, and you will find ready additions to your own. The larger national newspapers maintain online editions that can be searched electronically for valuable clip file additions.

Clip File Action Item #5
Electronic Newspapers

To quickly build your clip files, search the larger regional and national newspapers for stories that pertain to your interest area. For instance, if you live in Atlanta, Georgia, and you are seeking grant funds in the area of "school violence," electronically search your metropolitan newspaper for school violence–related stories and then, to see how Atlanta compares with other major cities, conduct similar searches in other city circulations as well. This information will help you document the frequency and severity of the problem (Chapter 7). Some pertinent newspaper Web addresses follow for the 25 largest cities in the United States.

Atlanta: www.accessatlanta.com/partners/ajc
Austin: www.auschron.com

Baltimore: www.sunspot.net
Boston: www.boston.com/globe
Charlotte: www.charlotte.com
Chicago: www.chicagotribune.com
Columbus: www.dispatch.com
Dallas: www.dallasnews.com
Detroit: www.detnews.com
El Paso: www.mondotimes.com
Houston: www.houstonchronicle.com
Indianapolis: www.starnews.com
Jacksonville: www/jacksonville.com
Los Angeles: www.latimes.com
Memphis: www.memphisflyer.com
Milwaukee: www.jsonline.com
Nashville: www.tennessean.com
New York: www.nytimes.com
Philadelphia: www.philly.com/mld/inquirer
Phoenix: www.phoenixnewtimes.com
San Diego: www.signonsandiego.com
Seattle: www.seattletimes.com
San Jose: www.mercurycenter.com
St. Louis: home.post-dispatch.com
Washington, DC: washpost.com/index.shtml

Most newspaper home pages contain a search engine to expedite your query. See Chapter 16 for suggestions on using search engines.

CHAPTER 2
Finding Public Funds

The art of government consists in taking as much money as
possible from one class of citizens to give to the other.
Voltaire

OVERVIEW OF PUBLIC FUNDING

Consistent with the two-hundred-year-old Voltaire observation, federal and state governments award billions of grant dollars each year. This chapter focuses on finding public grant funds at the national and state levels. Although no one single source of information covers all government grants, many agencies have some type of grant-making program, usually found on a World Wide Web site or in an agency publication. Since so much information is available on the Web, we begin by looking at the interagency references and then focus on agency-specific print and electronic sources of information, at both federal and state levels.

FEDERAL GOVERNMENT INFORMATION

Three global reference sources transcend any individual agency: the Catalog of Federal Domestic Assistance, the Federal Register, and FedBizOpps. These sources disseminate grant and contract information for all federal agencies in both print and electronic format.

Catalog of Federal Domestic Assistance

The most comprehensive document to identify federal funding opportunities is the Catalog of Federal Domestic Assistance (CFDA), available at a nominal charge from the Superintendent of Documents, Washington, DC 20402, or free at www.cfda.org. The CFDA is published annually in the spring, with a fall supplement. To many grantseekers, it represents a "Christmas Wish Book" of grant possibilities and in-

cludes over 1,000 pages of federal grant programs. The CFDA contains useful browsing features that will save you time in identifying potential grant opportunities.

CFDA Browsers

Experienced grantseekers find four browsers particularly useful: agency program index, applicant eligibility index, deadline index, and functional area index. Each is discussed below.

Agency Browser. Although numbers vary slightly from year to year, the Agency Browser typically lists 1,500 grant programs, distributed among 50 different federal grantmaking agencies. In essence, the Agency Browser lists every program in the catalog by the agency that administers it. For instance, if you suspect the Department of Health and Human Services (DHHS) might fund a project in your area, you could look under DHHS in the Agency Program Index to identify all of the programs it administers. To illustrate, CFDA number 93.145 identifies the National AIDS Education and Training Centers program administered by the Health Resources and Services Administration in DHHS. The "93" identifies DHHS and the "145" refers to the specific program within DHHS. The Agency Browser is most useful if you want to find all of the programs administered by a particular agency. One click on a program number, and you are presented with its detailed description.

Applicant Eligibility Browser. The Applicant Eligibility Browser lists the programs for which a particular type of applicant is eligible: individual, local, nonprofit (or for-profit), state, U.S. territories, and federal tribal governments. This index is most useful if you want to find all of the federal programs to which you might theoretically apply, based on your type of organization. To use this browser, you first indicate your functional area of interest and then click on the type of organization you represent, e.g., state government, hospital, nonprofit organization, Indian tribe. For instance, if you represent a local city government and are interested in the area of communications, you are one click away from identifying all of the communication grant opportunities for which local governments might apply. However, recognize that many federal dollars flow through to the states. You could check the Applicant Eligibility Index to find the location of federal dollars in your state government; after identifying these sources, just call the federal program officer and ask who the point of contact is at the state level to pursue the flow of funds.

Deadline Browser. The Deadline Browser lists those programs in the CFDA that have firm application deadlines. The programs are listed in ascending date order for each date or month in which the applications must be received by the federal agency administering the program. Programs that do not have a submission deadline are not listed in this index, since those applications can be submitted at any time. Recognize, however, that deadlines do change, so you should verify those that are important to you.

Functional Area Browser. The Functional Area Browser classifies roughly 1,500 federal grant programs into 20 broad categories, ranging from agriculture, consumer protection, education, and health to transportation. Many grant programs are cross-listed under multiple functional areas. Use the Functional Area Browser when you want to conduct a broad topic search regardless of sponsoring agency.

Exhibit 1 shows the home page for the CFDA. A click on the "Find Assistance Programs" phrase will lead you to the browsers cited above—and others too.

You have many search options to find federal grant programs. Besides using the browsers noted above, you can search by program number or key words or phrases. If you know the CFDA number, enter it in the "View Program" box. If you don't know it, you can enter an appropriate single keyword or phrase in the "Keyword Search" box. Sometimes beginning grantseekers get frustrated because their key words find no grant programs. Experienced grantseekers have learned several efficient search tips for the CFDA, as the following examples indicate.

CFDA Search Tips

1. Begin searching by using narrow terms, and broaden them on subsequent searches until acceptable "hits" are found. For example, if you are seeking funding for a youth violence prevention program, begin with narrow terms like "youth crimes" and if that search is unsuccessful, use broader terms like "juvenile justice," "dispute resolution," "gangs," and "anti-crime."

2. Select some terms from the Functional Area Browser to begin your search. More than likely, you'll come up with too many options, and some won't be relevant to your situation. It's time to narrow your search.

3. Skim several relevant grant programs identified in step two. Look for the key words used in those grant descriptions and use them to search further. For example, we were once looking for funds for a "community development" project. Use of the phrase "community development" revealed very few hits. Conclusion: Our search was too narrow. Looking for broader terminology, we read some grant descriptions and saw repeated use of the phrase "economic revitalization." When that phrase was entered into the search engine, it yielded the types of grant programs we were seeking.

4. When using phrases, enclose them in quotation marks; otherwise, the search engine will look for occurrences of each word singly rather than the literal string phrase.

5. To further narrow your search you can use Boolean Operators, words like AND, OR, NOT (all in capital letters). Named after a famous British mathematician, George Boole, you can string words and phrases together. Examples follow:
   - "highway construction" AND noise
   - "drug abuse" AND "battered women"
   - "dispute resolution" AND NOT international
   - "community development" OR "economic revitalization"

   Note that the CFDA uses AND NOT as a Boolean Operator, whereas most search engines simply use NOT. Note also that phrases—but not single words—must be enclosed in quotation marks.

6. Use "wild cards," the asterisk symbol (*) for root words. For instance, bio* will include search for such words as biological, biomedical, and bioinformatics.

7. Remember, the CFDA is not only a source of information about federal funds, it also identifies

The Catalog of Federal
Domestic Assistance

FAQ |Privacy |Feedback |About The CFDA Website |Search

 The Events of September 11th:
- Assistance Programs relating to recovery/response.
- U.S. Government Resources for the events of September 11th.

Features

Types of Assistance

Applying for Assistance

Writing Grant Proposals

Top 10% Program List

All Programs Listed
Numerically

Formula Report

Historical Index

Featured Links

Firstgov

Federal Commons

FedBizOpps

The Catalog of Federal Domestic Assistance (CFDA)

First Time User's Guide
What this website can and cannot do for you.

Browse The Catalog
Additional resources for applying for assistance.

Find Assistance Programs
Find assistance programs through a variety of search mechanisms.

CFDA June 2002 Print Edition.

The online Catalog of Federal Domestic Assistance gives you access to
a database of all Federal programs available to State and local
governments (including the District of Columbia); federally-recognized
Indian tribal governments; Territories (and possessions) of the United
States; domestic public, quasi-public, and private profit and nonprofit
organizations and institutions; specialized groups; and individuals.

After you find the program you want, contact the office that administers
the program and find out how to apply.

CATALOG OF FEDERAL DOMESTIC ASSISTANCE (CFDA) HOME PAGE

EXHIBIT 1

state-level sources via flow-through dollars. Use the Applicant Eligibility Browser to identify those grants that state governments are eligible to receive. Contact the federal program officer to identify precisely where those funds end up in the state government.

Beyond its Internet version, the CFDA can also be accessed through diskettes or a CD-ROM. The CD-ROM version includes a new feature that enables you to query a Bureau of Census database (Federal Assistance Award Data System) that provides funding history information, including awardees, amounts, and project descriptions; these details are particularly useful in developing proposal solicitation strategies. For more information on all print and electronic versions of the CFDA, call the Federal

Domestic Assistance Catalog Staff at (202) 401-8233.

Sample CFDA Web Pages

Assume you want to enter 93.145 as the CFDA program number. You would enter this number in the "Program Number" box and then click on the "View Program," as indicated in Exhibit 2. Several further clicks will lead you to a description of the grant program, as shown in Exhibit 3.

As you scroll down the screen, some sections will be more useful to you than others. The ten major CFDA sections of interest to experienced grantseekers are described below.

Federal Agency. The U.S. Health Resources and Services Administration administers this program,

The Catalog of Federal Domestic Assistance

Home | FAQ | Privacy | Feedback | Tips on Searching for Programs

Browse The Catalog

By Functional Area

By Agency

By Sub-Agency

Alphabetically by Program Title

By Applicant Eligibility

By Beneficiary

By Program Deadline

By Type of Assistance

By Programs Requiring Executive Order 12372 Review

By Budget Function Code (App. III)

By Programs Having Assistance Formulas

Lookup Programs

Go Directly to a Program Number
If you know the program number you wish to view, enter it here.

Program Number:
93.145   View Program

Keyword Search
Search for words or phrases in program text.   (Search Tips)

Keyword:
_____   Search

Find a Grant
Search the Catalog for only grant programs.

Advanced Search
Run your own SQL-like queries against the CFDA database.

All Programs Listed Numerically
Shows a complete listing of all programs (BIG page).

Top 10 Percent of Programs
A list of the top 10% by number of viewings.

SAMPLE CFDA SEARCH BY PROGRAM NUMBER: 93.145

EXHIBIT 2

The Catalog of Federal Domestic Assistance

Home | FAQ | Privacy | Printer Friendly Version of 93.145

93.145 AIDS Education and Training Centers

FEDERAL AGENCY:

HEALTH RESOURCES AND SERVICES ADMINISTRATION, DEPARTMENT OF HEALTH AND HUMAN SERVICES

AUTHORIZATION:

Public Health Service Act, Title XXVI, Part F, Public Law 106-345; Ryan White Care Act Amendments of 2000.

OBJECTIVES:

To: (1) Provide education and training to primary care providers and others on the treatment and prevention of acquired immunodeficiency syndrome (AIDS), in collaboration with health professions schools, local hospitals, and health departments; (2) disseminate new and timely information about human immunodeficiency virus (HIV) infection and its treatment to primary and secondary health care providers; and (3) serve as the support system for area health professions through AIDS Hotlines, clearinghouses, and referral activities.

TYPES OF ASSISTANCE:

Project Grants.

USES AND USE RESTRICTIONS:

Grants will be awarded for the establishment of AIDS Education and Training Centers.

PARTIAL CFDA DESCRIPTION OF PROGRAM 93.145

EXHIBIT 3

93.145, which is a part of the Department of Health and Human Services. As you prepare to write your proposal, familiarize yourself with the mission statement of the agency, usually found on the home page of its Web site. Study the authorizing legislation, available from your senator or congressional representative. When you write, you should reflect the agency values in your proposal narrative.

Authorization. This section identifies the federal law that authorizes the grant program. Although most people scan this section rather quickly, experienced grantwriters recognize that it contains useful information. More precisely, it specifies the intent of Congress in authorizing the legislation. Some granting agencies include it in their application kits; others don't. You can request a copy of the authorizing legislation from your congressional representative. In some instances, you may be able to locate this document on the Internet at www.access.gpo.gov/congress/cong009.html. Backtrack on the authorizing legislation by reading the Senate and House discussion of the bill before it was enacted. This information is found in the *Congressional Record*, available in most major libraries, or at www.access.gpo.gov/su_docs/aces/aces150.html. You can often find useful information worthy of emphasis in the writing of federal grants, such as keywords or needs documentation—words and references you will include in your proposal.

Objectives. While this section is supposed to spell out program purposes so you can see how well it fits with your needs, the descriptions are often too general to be of precise value; that is, the CFDA definition of "objectives" more closely matches what grantseekers define as "goals." (See Chapter 8 for a distinction between "goals" and "objectives.") Typically, you need more information to determine if their priorities match yours, information that is obtained from a federal program officer, as discussed later in this chapter and in Chapter 4.

Types of Assistance. This section describes the fifteen different types of assistance you can obtain from federal grants. They include formula grants; project grants; direct payments for specified use; direct payments with unrestricted use; direct loans; guaranteed insured loans; insurance; sale-exchange-donation of property and goods; use of property-facilities-equipment; provision of specialized services; advisory services and counseling; dissemination of technical information; training; investigation of complaints; and federal employment. In most cases, you will be looking for project grants, money awarded to your organization for a specific project. Note that you can

also receive technical assistance as well as money in some cases. The technical assistance pathway is worth considering for organizations that are just getting started with federal grants. It can help you build a relationship with federal grantmakers and establish your organization's credibility. Use the Applicant Eligibility Browser to identify sources of both financial and non-financial support.

Eligibility Requirements. This portion describes which applicants can and cannot receive funding under the program. Recall, however, that some funds flow directly to state governments. While you may not be eligible to apply for federal funding under a particular program, you may be eligible for state dollars. Thus, studying the CFDA can help you find state monies as well as federal monies, especially in those instances involving formula grants.

Application and Award Process. Pay particular attention to the preapplication coordination section, because it identifies the individuals you should contact before proposal submission. (See Chapter 4 for preproposal contact details.) Some proposals may require prior approval from your state government before submission. This step requires extra proposal preparation time. Local or state agencies that supposedly would be affected by your proposal may write comments to be included with the proposal when submitted to the federal government. In actual practice, they often choose to make no comment because your proposal will have no impact that will affect local or state government. Verify deadline information and find out whether it is a receipt date or a postmark date. Deadlines occasionally change after appearing in CFDA.

Financial Information. This section provides basic budget information for the past two years and a current estimated program budget. Unfortunately, this information is notoriously inaccurate because budgets change frequently in Washington, DC. Further, there is often a discrepancy between the authorization and appropriation legislation. What was requested may be different from what is actually awarded. Again, verify this information before starting to write a grant.

Information Contacts. This portion will direct you to key federal personnel who are sources of further details. It pays to establish preproposal contact with these officials. Often, they can provide valuable informal feedback that will strengthen the competitiveness of your proposal. Equally important, this section provides the Web address for the program.

Related Programs. This section presents you with a crosswalk to other similar programs. Although the listing is not comprehensive, it does identify other programs to which you should also consider submitting proposals. Often similar proposals can be submitted to more than one federal agency at a time, see "Multiple Submissions" in Chapter 18 for further details.

Criteria for Selecting Proposals. This section will indicate the yardstick used to evaluate your proposal. It is important to know how your proposal will be rated as you begin writing, so that you can emphasize your proposal in proportion to the evaluation scheme.

The information contained in the CFDA is so massive that one is apt to conclude that it is exhaustive, but it isn't. The Office of Management and Budget (OMB) publishes the CFDA on the basis of information received from other federal agencies. Some agencies are more thorough than others in providing timely, accurate, and detailed information. Because some information may be dated, use the CFDA as a starting point, but verify key details from the contact individual, which it identifies, before preparing a grant proposal. Finally, the CFDA does not contain information about new grant programs that were created after the last catalog edition was published. To find out about new grant opportunities, turn to another information source: the Federal Register.

Federal Register

The *Federal Register* is the government's "daily newspaper." Among other things, it lists rules, regulations, and application deadlines for new grant programs from federal agencies. Successful grantseekers have established systems and procedures to gain early access to grant information, rather than responding to a grant opportunity at the last minute. Regularly monitoring the *Federal Register* is a valuable way to receive an "early alert" about new grant programs. Here's how.

Before a new grant program becomes law, an agency notice of intent to create a new grant is usually, but not always, published in the *Federal Register*. It is listed as a "Notice of Proposed Rulemaking" (NPR). The NPR describes the planned program and invites public comment. Once the public comments are received, they are summarized in a later issue of the *Federal Register*. The sponsoring agency will summarize and respond to the public comments and then issue revised guidelines. Although the duration of this process varies considerably, it commonly takes six to nine months from the first publication of the NPR until the deadline for the formal application. Using this feature is an excellent way to find out about new grant pro-

grams and have sufficient lead time to prepare a quality proposal. Besides introducing new programs, the *Federal Register* announces changes, expansions, or clarifications of programs already in existence. Occasionally, it also includes the names of recent grant recipients.

Like the *Catalog of Federal Domestic Assistance*, the *Federal Register* is available in both print (available at twice the cost of the typical annual newspaper subscription) and electronic (available free) versions. Exhibit 4 shows the *Federal Register* home page at www.access.gpo.gov/su_docs/aces/aces.140.html.

Scrolling down the home page screen for the *Federal Register* will take you to the box you can check to look at NPRs, as indicated in Exhibit 5, lower left-hand column.

Scrolling further down the home page screen for the *Federal Register* takes you to the key word and date search, as indicated in Exhibit 6, which seeks *Federal Register* entries after May 1, 2001 that include the phrase *"child abuse" AND adoption.*

From the phrase search "child abuse" linked with the Boolean operator AND to the single word "adoption," the following grant opportunity was revealed; Exhibit 7 shows the summary portion of a lengthy description about the grant program from the Department of Health and Human Services. The entire listing is available on the Web.

You have a choice of three different ways to display your *Federal Register* hits: (1) HTML format, a complete Internet on-screen display announcement, (2) PDF, a Portable Document Format that opens up in your Adobe Acrobat Reader, and (3) a text summary of the program announcement.

Federal Register *Search Tips*

Successful grantseekers have found the following tips useful to save time and improve search efficiency.

1. Monitor the *Federal Register* (FR) regularly. Bookmark this address: www.access.gpo.gov/su_docs/aces/aces140.html. Scroll down to browse the current issue twice a month.
2. Once you click on the current FR issue, open it up in the HTML format. Then open up your search command and enter the word "grant" to find all grant-related entries in the table of contents. This will save you considerable search time.
3. Use "wild cards," the asterisk symbol (*), for root words. For instance, child* will include searching such words as child, child's children, childhood, and childproof.

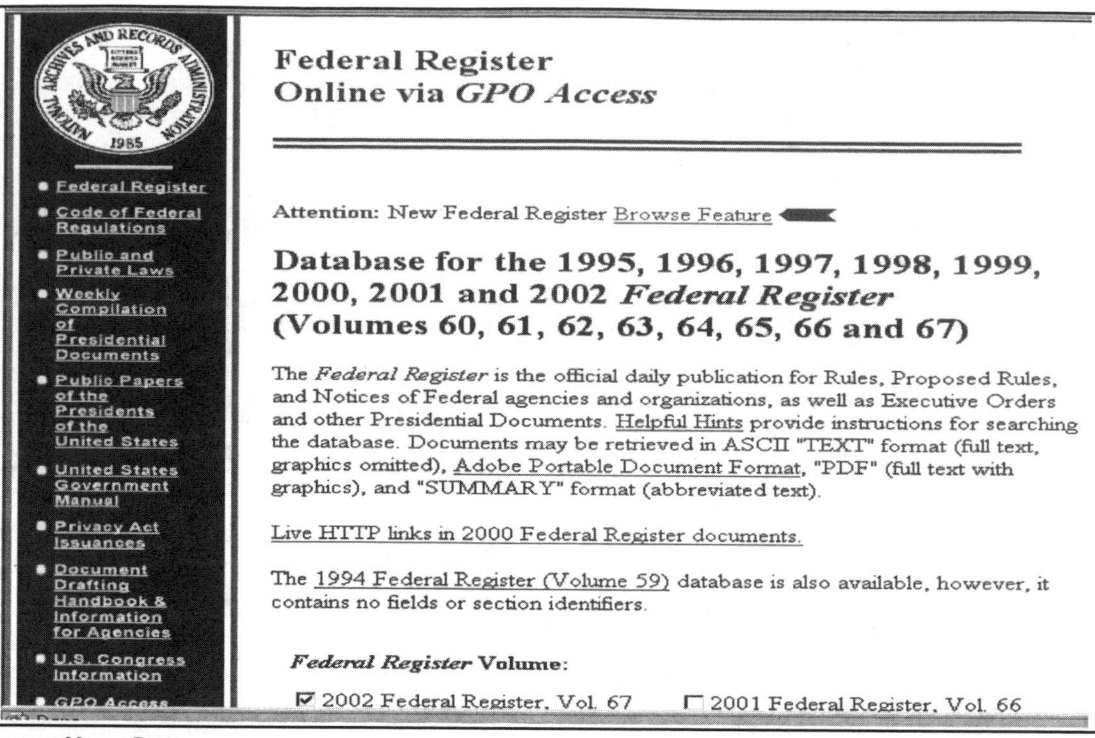

Federal Register
Online via *GPO Access*

Attention: New Federal Register Browse Feature ◄

Database for the 1995, 1996, 1997, 1998, 1999, 2000, 2001 and 2002 *Federal Register* (Volumes 60, 61, 62, 63, 64, 65, 66 and 67)

The *Federal Register* is the official daily publication for Rules, Proposed Rules, and Notices of Federal agencies and organizations, as well as Executive Orders and other Presidential Documents. Helpful Hints provide instructions for searching the database. Documents may be retrieved in ASCII "TEXT" format (full text, graphics omitted), Adobe Portable Document Format, "PDF" (full text with graphics), and "SUMMARY" format (abbreviated text).

Live HTTP links in 2000 Federal Register documents.

The 1994 Federal Register (Volume 59) database is also available, however, it contains no fields or section identifiers.

***Federal Register* Volume:**

☑ 2002 Federal Register, Vol. 67   ☐ 2001 Federal Register, Vol. 66

Sidebar navigation:
- Federal Register
- Code of Federal Regulations
- Public and Private Laws
- Weekly Compilation of Presidential Documents
- Public Papers of the Presidents of the United States
- United States Government Manual
- Privacy Act Issuances
- Document Drafting Handbook & Information for Agencies
- U.S. Congress Information
- GPO Access

FEDERAL REGISTER HOME PAGE

EXHIBIT 4

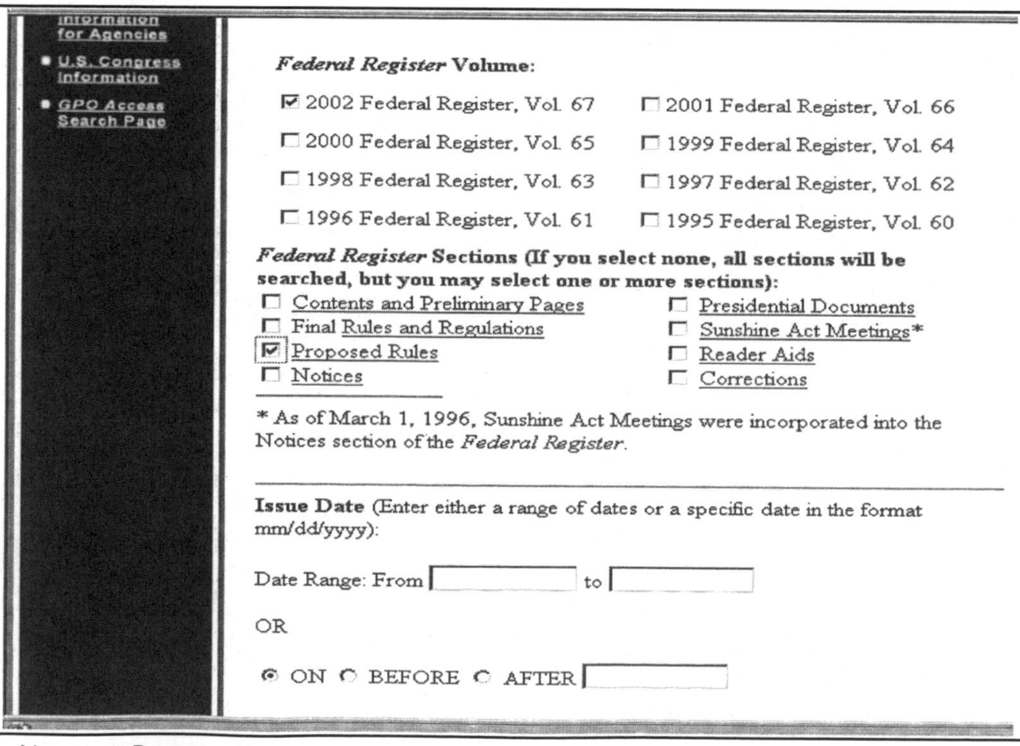

Sidebar navigation:
- Information for Agencies
- U.S. Congress Information
- GPO Access Search Page

***Federal Register* Volume:**

☑ 2002 Federal Register, Vol. 67   ☐ 2001 Federal Register, Vol. 66

☐ 2000 Federal Register, Vol. 65   ☐ 1999 Federal Register, Vol. 64

☐ 1998 Federal Register, Vol. 63   ☐ 1997 Federal Register, Vol. 62

☐ 1996 Federal Register, Vol. 61   ☐ 1995 Federal Register, Vol. 60

***Federal Register* Sections (If you select none, all sections will be searched, but you may select one or more sections):**

☐ Contents and Preliminary Pages   ☐ Presidential Documents
☐ Final Rules and Regulations   ☐ Sunshine Act Meetings*
☑ Proposed Rules   ☐ Reader Aids
☐ Notices   ☐ Corrections

* As of March 1, 1996, Sunshine Act Meetings were incorporated into the Notices section of the *Federal Register*.

Issue Date (Enter either a range of dates or a specific date in the format mm/dd/yyyy):

Date Range: From [＿＿＿＿＿] to [＿＿＿＿＿]

OR

⦿ ON ○ BEFORE ○ AFTER [＿＿＿＿＿]

FEDERAL REGISTER NOTICE OF PROPOSED RULEMAKING

EXHIBIT 5

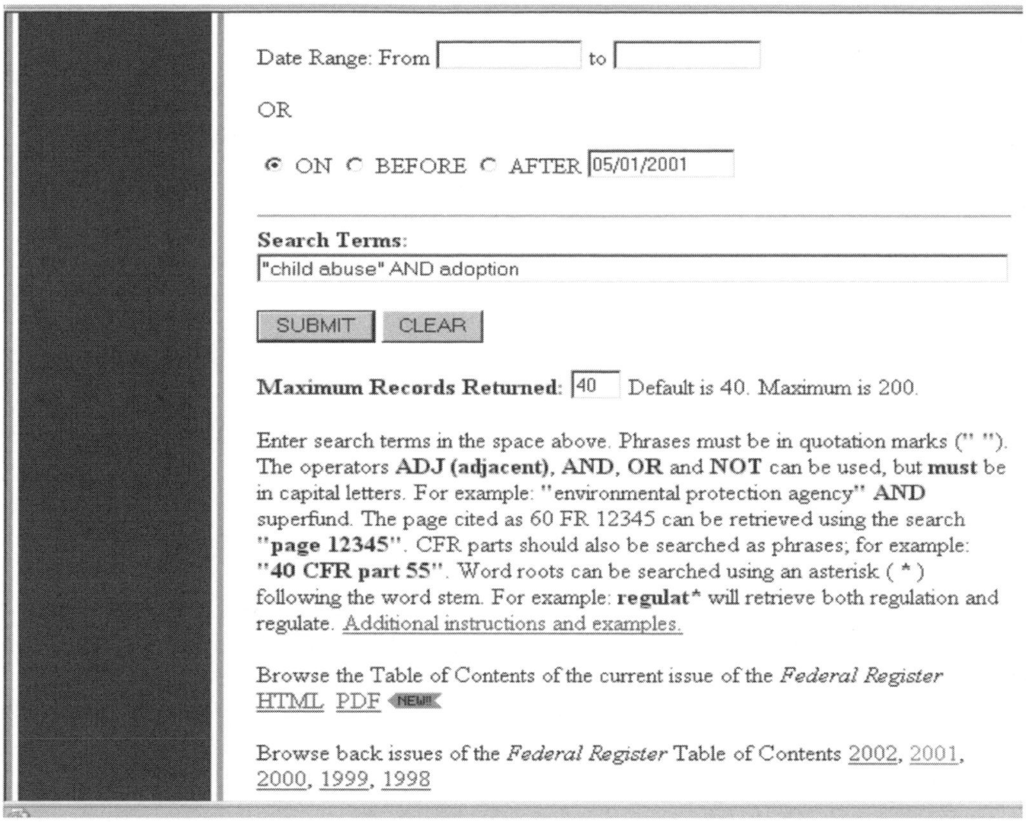

Date Range: From [ ] to [ ]

OR

ON BEFORE AFTER 05/01/2001

Search Terms:

"child abuse" AND adoption

SUBMIT CLEAR

Maximum Records Returned: 40 Default is 40. Maximum is 200.

Enter search terms in the space above. Phrases must be in quotation marks (" "). The operators **ADJ (adjacent), AND, OR** and **NOT** can be used, but **must** be in capital letters. For example: "environmental protection agency" **AND** superfund. The page cited as 60 FR 12345 can be retrieved using the search **"page 12345"**. CFR parts should also be searched as phrases; for example: **"40 CFR part 55"**. Word roots can be searched using an asterisk (*) following the word stem. For example: **regulat*** will retrieve both regulation and regulate. Additional instructions and examples.

Browse the Table of Contents of the current issue of the *Federal Register*
HTML PDF NEW!

Browse back issues of the *Federal Register* Table of Contents 2002, 2001, 2000, 1999, 1998

FEDERAL REGISTER **KEY WORD SEARCH: "CHILD ABUSE" AND ADOPTION**

EXHIBIT 6

The *Catalog of Federal Domestic Assistance* and the *Federal Register* both provide information about federal *grants*. In addition there are also opportunities for *contract* dollars. The following section discusses the differences between grants and contracts before citing contract information sources.

Grants versus Contracts

The *Catalog of Federal Domestic Assistance* and the *Federal Register* contain information about grants. In addition, the federal government uses contracts to procure services. Several major differences exist between grants and contracts. One difference regards the outcome expectations. Grants are awarded to conduct projects or do experiments that may or may not produce a tangible outcome. The agency outlines general priorities that it hopes to achieve by awarding a grant. In contrast, contracts have a very specific goal in mind. Contracts award funds to individuals or groups to generate a service or product within the contract period. Put differently, a grant is a mechanism to support a project whereas a contract is an instrument to procure a project.

Another element that distinguishes grants from contracts is the budget. Generally, grant programs allow considerable flexibility in determining the way in which a project can be administered and in allocating expenditures among staff and supplies. With a contract, less budgeting flexibility is available. Funds are spent as projected in the budget.

A further grant contract difference concerns the selection process. Multiple grants are usually awarded as the result of a peer review process that identifies the most meritorious proposals. Contracts usually go to the lowest bidder, often after internal staff review, and may include an external peer review as well.

Contract support, as opposed to a grant, concentrates on the practical, often immediate benefits. Often, the Project Director has a slightly different role in contracts than in grants. The solicitation describes

[Federal Register: May 1, 2001 (Volume 66, Number 84)]

Department of Health and Human Services

Administration for Children and Families

Announcement of the Availability of Financial Assistance and Request for Applications To Support Adoption Opportunities Demonstration Projects, Child Abuse and Neglect Discretionary Activities, Abandoned Infants Assistance Awards and Projects To Build the Analytical Capacity of State Child Welfare Programs

AGENCY: Administration on Children, Youth and Families (ACYF), ACF, DHHS.

ACTION: Notice.

SUMMARY: The Children's Bureau (CB) within the Administration on Children, Youth and Families (ACYF), Administration for Children and Families (ACF) announces the availability of fiscal year (FY) 2001 funds for competing new Adoption Opportunities Program, Child Abuse and Neglect Discretionary Activities, Abandoned Infants Assistance and projects to build the analytical capacity of state child welfare programs. Funds from the Adoption Opportunities Program are designed to provide support for demonstration projects that facilitate the elimination of barriers to adoption and provide permanent loving homes for children who would benefit from adoption, particularly children with special needs. Discretionary funds from the Promoting Safe and Stable Families Program support research, training and technical assistance and evaluation efforts to preserve families. Funds from the Child Abuse Prevention and Treatment Act support knowledge-building research and service demonstration projects designed to assist and enhance national, State and community efforts to prevent, assess, identify and treat child abuse and neglect. Funds from section 101 of the Abandoned Infants Assistance Act, as amended (42 USC 670 note) are to establish a program of comprehensive service demonstration projects to prevent the abandonment in hospitals of infants and young children, particularly those exposed to a dangerous drug and those with the human immunodeficiency virus or who have been perinatally exposed to the virus.

DATES: The closing time and date for receipt of applications is 4:30 p.m. (Eastern Time Zone) on June 15, 2001.

Note: The program announcement, including all necessary forms can be downloaded and printed from the Children's Bureau web site at www.acf.dhhs.gov/programs/cb. Hard copies of the program announcement may be requested in hard copy by writing or calling the Operations Center (see phone number and address below) or sending an email to cb@lcgnet.com.

FOR FURTHER INFORMATION CONTACT: ACYF Operations Center at: 1815 N. Fort Myer Drive, Suite 300, Arlington, Virginia 22209 or 1-800-351-2293.

SAMPLE *FEDERAL REGISTER* ENTRY

EXHIBIT 7

Grants	Contracts
• Initiated by project sponsor	• Initiated by Project Director
• Project Director determines direction	• Sponsor determines direction
• Little sponsor oversight	• Much sponsor oversight
• Project Director keeps equipment	• Sponsor may keep equipment
• Upfront or drawdown payments scheduled	• Payment after expenditures scheduled
• Unsolicited project announcement	• Competitive bidding announcement

GRANTS VERSUS CONTRACTS

EXHIBIT 8

the project objectives and many of the methodological details. It may even prescribe the instruments and statistical analyses to be used. The agency prepares the solicitation, which usually contains a fairly rigid timeline. Once you begin, continual pressure is exerted to complete the project on time. While grants and contracts are both written legal documents the differences are summarized shown in Exhibit 8.

FedBizOpps

FedBizOpps (www.fedbizopps.gov) is the single source for federal government procurement opportunities that exceed $25,000. All federal agencies must use *FedBizOpps* to tell the public about these contract opportunities. It replaces notices that were formerly published in the *Commerce Business Daily* (CBD).

On a typical federal workday, the government publishes Uncle Sam's official shopping list of 500–1000 procurement notices. More precisely, federal agencies use *FedBizOpps* to post any and all relevant procurement information on the Internet, including procurement notices, solicitations, drawings, and amendments. Grantseekers can sign up to automatically receive procurement information by solicitation number, selected organizations, and product service classifications. *FedBizOpps* is maintained by the U.S. General Services Administration. A visit to the *FedBizOpps* home page reveals the screen as seen in Exhibit 9.

As you review a contract solicitation, you may wonder if it is truly open for competition; that is, does someone else already have the "inside track?" It's possible they do. One way to tell is to look at the length of the announcement. The longer the announcement,

the greater the likelihood it is "wired." If it refers to prior work conducted by another organization, that group may have an advantage on the bidding.

If you are interested in a solicitation, begin your preproposal contacts (as described in Chapter 4). Tell your program officer about you, your organization, and the kind of projects that you are interested in. Through your preproposal contacts, you will be able to judge whether you want to do business with this agency. One caution: contract support is relatively complex and certainly not for the uninitiated.

GOVERNMENT-SPONSORED FEDERAL AGENCY WEB SITES

The *Catalog of Federal Domestic Assistance*, the *Federal Register*, and the *FedBizOpps* are the three federal government grant and contract information sources that globally cut across all agencies. In addition to these primary source documents, most federal grantmaking agencies maintain robust and frequently changing Web sites.

For convenience, the common federal Web sites are listed on the inside back cover of this book. As you would expect, these Web addresses are quick and easy reference tools for identifying grant opportunities and deadlines. However, these Web addresses contain many other types of information as well, as the 19 examples in column two Exhibit 10 exemplify.

Obviously, not all agencies provide all of the column two information. However, with the rapid changes occurring in Web-based information dissemination, the

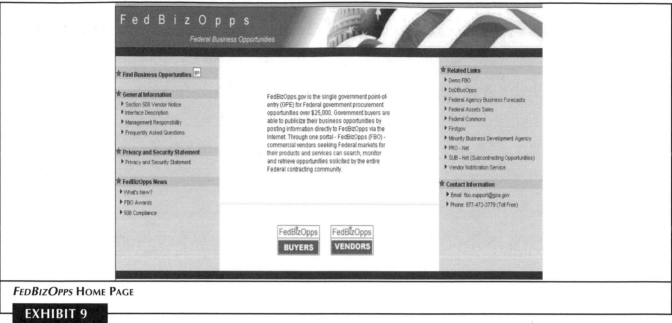

***FedBizOpps* Home Page**

EXHIBIT 9

trend is to expand. As a result, the future will see more agencies providing more detailed information.

ONE-STOP SHOPPING FOR FEDERAL FUNDS

Rather than jump from one federal Web site to another in search of grant-related information, you can explore one federal Web site that pulls together more than 20,000 existing government home pages. Visit FirstGov (www.firstgov.gov), which the Office of Management and Budget hopes will be your first stop in seeking government information. It is an easy-to-search, free-access Web site designed to give you a centralized place to find information from local, state, and U.S. government agency Web sites. A helpful list of frequently asked questions provides more details.

PRIVATE-SPONSORED FEDERAL AGENCY GRANT INFORMATION

Beyond the print and electronic newsletters and bulletins published by federal agencies, a few private companies also provide grant information. To remain competitive, all are expanding the services they provide. Brief descriptions follow of eight commercial vendors along with their Web addresses for additional information.

GrantSelect. GrantSelect, maintained by The Oryx Press, is widely recognized as a premier resource for grantseekers. GrantSelect, the online version of the GRANTS Database, compiled and edited by The Oryx Press, contains over 10,000 funding opportunities provided by more than 4,000 public and private sponsors and is applicable to a broad range of organizations interested in such things as health care, educational institutions, social welfare, environment, the arts, and religion.

Each record includes the following:

- Contact information
- Sponsor name and address
- Subject terms for related searches
- Type of sponsor (federal agency, foundation, corporation, etc.)

Each record also includes, where available, this information:

- Web addresses to more information on the funding opportunity
- Deadline date(s)
- Restrictions on who may apply (including geographic restrictions)
- Lists of previous awards
- Amount(s) of grant or award

Agency Name	Type of Information	Web Address*
Administration on Aging	Latest Agency Press Releases	www.aoa.dhhs.gov
Centers for Medicare and Medicaid Services	Grant Opportunities	Cms.hhs.gov/contracts/default.asp#grantopportunities
Environmental Protection Agency	Grant Writing Tutorial	www.epa.gov/seahome/grants.html
Health Resources and Services Administration	Progress Report Forms	www.hab.hrsa.gov/tools/data/dataform.htm
National Endowment for Democracy	Home Pages of Grantees	www.ned.org/grants/grants.html
National Endowment for the Humanities	Grant Deadlines	www.neh.gov/grants.html
National Endowment for the Humanities	List of Recent Grant Awards	www.neh.gov/news/recentawards.html
National Endowment for the Humanities	Evaluation Criteria	www.neh.gov/grants/guidelines.milschools.html
National Historical Publications and Records Commission	What We Do/Don't Fund	www.archives.gov/nhprc_and_other_grants/administering_a_grant/what_we_fund_and_what_we_don't_fund.html
National Institutes of Health	Names of Current Reviewers	grants.nih.gov/grants/peer/peer.htm
National Institutes of Health	Abstracts of Awards	www-commons.cit.nih.gov/crisp
National Science Foundation	Mission Statement	www.nsf.gov/home/about/creation.html
National Science Foundation	Staff directory	www.nsf.gov/staff
US Department of Agriculture	Sample Grant Awards	www.usda.gov/rus/telecom/dlt/awards.htm
US Department of Education	Number and Size of Awards	www.ed.gov/offices/OCFO/grants/grntawd.html
US Department of Health and Human Services	Organizational Chart	www.dhhs.gov/about/orgchart.html
US Department of Housing and Urban Development	Standard forms and assurances	www.hud.gov/adm/grants/nofa/stdforms.html
US Department of Justice	Downloadable application kits	www.ojp.usdoj.gov/fundopps.htm
US Department of Transportation	Grant Management Regulations	www.dot.gov/ost/m60/grant/regs.htm

TYPES OF WEB-BASED GOVERNMENT GRANT INFORMATION

EXHIBIT 10

Contact Address	For Information at your Desktop...
www.nsf.gov	Select "Custom News Service" at bottom of home page, free
www.nih.gov/grants/guide/listserv.htm	Select table of contents and URLs, free
www.grantselect.com	Select key words, subscription fee
www.sciencewise.com	Select request e-mail delivery for funding opportunities, subscription fee

GRANT INFORMATION SOURCES SENT AUTOMATICALLY

EXHIBIT 11

- *Catalog of Federal Domestic Assistance* number, when appropriate
- Populations encouraged to apply (e.g., women, minorities, disabled)
- Request for Funding Announcement and Program Announcement numbers for NIH grants
- Program numbers for NSF grants

Funding opportunities range from pure research grants to arts programs, biomedical and health care research, community service programs, children and youth programs, and K–12 education funding.

Sponsoring organizations consist of federal government agencies (including the National Institutes of Health, National Science Foundation, Centers for Disease Control and Prevention), foundations and other nonprofit organizations, corporations and corporate foundations, research institutes, state agencies, and universities. Additionally, GrantSelect includes over 300 grants provided by Canadian private sources and more than 175 by Canadian government sources.

One unique feature of GrantSelect is that users can purchase a portion of the database that is most germane to their interests. For example, if your interest is in the area of community welfare programs, you could purchase that portion and not have to purchase the entire grant database, much of which would not be applicable to your interests. For subscription information and a free trial, visit www.grantselect.com.

FEDIX. FEDIX is an outreach tool that provides grant information to educational and research organizations from participating federal agencies, including the U.S. Agency for International Development, U.S. Department of Agriculture, U.S. Department of Defense, Air Force Office of Scientific Research, National Aeronautics and Space Administration, U.S. Department of Transportation, and portions of the National Institutes of Health. The grant and contact information is primarily targeted to universities, research institutes, and oth-

ers engaged in research and development activities. No registration fees or access charges are assessed for using FEDIX. While traversing the available information among the participating agencies, you will find details regarding such things as equipment grants, faculty student exchange programs, procurements, and special notices, including broad agency announcements (BAAs) and requests for proposals (RFPs); proposal and award guidelines; elementary school programs; science curriculum programs; and minority education opportunities. Visit www.sciencewise.com.

The Grant Advisor Plus. The Grant Advisor Plus publishes electronic information about grant and fellowship opportunities, especially targeted for faculty in U.S. institutions of higher education. An online newsletter covers grant opportunities from federal agencies (except NIH) as well as many independent organizations and foundations. Published monthly (except July), each issue contains 20–25 program reviews with descriptions, eligibility requirements, special criteria, funding amounts, and contact information (including phone and fax numbers, e-mail and Web addresses). The remainder of the newsletter is composed of the Deadline Memo with more than 300 listings of grant and fellowship programs for the coming four months, organized into eight academic divisions: fine arts, humanities, sciences, social sciences, education, international, health related, unrestricted/other. For more details, visit www.grantadvisor.com.

Illinois Research Information System (IRIS). The Illinois Researcher Information Service (IRIS) is a unit of the University of Illinois Library at Urbana-Champaign. The IRIS database of funding opportunities contains records on over 8,000 federal and private funding opportunities in the sciences, social sciences, arts, and humanities. The IRIS database is updated daily and is available in Web and Telnet versions. In addition to its database, the IRIS office also maintains

SAMPLE STATE GOVERNMENT HOME PAGE: NORTH CAROLINA

EXHIBIT 12

the IRIS Alert Service and the IRIS Expertise Service. The alert service allows users at subscribing institutions to create personal IRIS search profiles and receive funding alerts automatically. The expertise service enables faculty members to create detailed electronic CVs ("biosketches") and post them on the Web for viewing by colleagues at other institutions, program officers at federal and private funding agencies, and private companies. For details, visit gateway.library.uiuc.edu/iris.

Federal Grants and Contracts Weekly. The *Federal Grants and Contracts Weekly* (FGCW) is a weekly newsletter published by Capitol Publications, Inc. It provides summary information on many programs announced in the *Federal Register* and *FedBizOpps*. Occasionally, foundation information is published in the FGCW as well. They also publish diskette versions of the CFDA and private grant opportunities. More information is available at www.grantscape.com.

Federal Assistance Monitor. The *Federal Assistance Monitor* (FAM) is a semimonthly newsletter featuring reports on federal and private grant opportunities. It includes comprehensive reviews of federal funding announcements, private grants, and legislative actions affecting community programs, in-

cluding education, economic development, housing, children and youth services, substance abuse, and health care. For foundations, it indicates areas of interest and projected grant awards as well as funding priorities for both national and regional organizations. Proposal writing tips are often included. To view a sample online newsletter, visit www.cdpublications .com.

InfoEd. InfoEd, International, Inc. is a commercial firm that spun off from a grant information system developed at the State University of New York. Its primary product is called the Sponsored Programs Information Network (SPIN). This database provides comprehensive grant information on research and development, international projects, collaborative projects, fellowships, academic programs, exchange programs, travel, endowments, equipment, outreach and service delivery projects, and so forth. Other grant products are in various stages of development. For more information, visit spin.infoed.org.

Community of Science. The Community of Science (COS) provides rapid access to information about the funding of science. It is a global registry designed to provide accurate, timely, easy-to-access information about what new funding opportunities

CRIS provides information about grants and loans administered by North Carolina state agencies. Some technical assistance programs are also described. The Office of State Budget and Management is the coordinator of the CRIS project. Please visit the CRIS home page regularly.

Text Menu

- **Welcome to CRIS**
- **Learn about CRIS**

SAMPLE HOME PAGE FOR STATE GRANTS: NORTH CAROLINA

EXHIBIT 13

exist, and who is working on what subject, and where. Their Web site address is www.cos.com.

"PUSH" VERSUS "PULL" FUNDING INFORMATION

All of the public grant sources discussed to date have one thing in common—you must proactively seek the funding information; that is, you have to "pull" the information to you. There is an alternative. You can let the information come to you; that is, you can let someone else "push" the information your way. More precisely, there are some reference sources that you can subscribe to (many are free) that will automatically send you grant information on a regular basis. Some of these reference sources allow you to select key words or topics in your interest area; others just send out thumbnail sketches from which you pick and choose.

The advantage of the "push" approach is that it may save you valuable time; you don't have to search for grant information. The disadvantage is that you may get too much irrelevant information, such that "e-mail" becomes "eeek mail." Decide for yourself as you subscribe or unsubscribe to the following "push" approaches to finding grant funds, public and private, indicated in Exhibit 11.

STATE GOVERNMENT FUNDING

The discussion so far has focused primarily on federal grants and contracts, although some state dollars can be identified by use of the Applicant Eligibility Browser in the *Catalog of Federal Domestic Assistance*. These funds are essentially federal "pass-through" dollars targeted for state distribution. Unfortunately, no state-level equivalent of the CFDA exists. Generally, states are just beginning to come online with basic grant information, although it is still sparse for many states. As a result, specific state-level funding opportunities must be searched out through electronic sources and personal contacts as opposed to print directories.

Electronic Information Sources for State Government Funding

As a starting point to find state grant information, visit the generic address www.state.xx.us, where the XX represents your two-letter postal abbreviation. For instance, if you live in North Carolina, you would surf www.state.nc.us. It would take you to the state government home page for North Carolina, as Exhibit 12 reveals.

A little probing on the state government home page will lead you to existing grant opportunities at www.cris.state.nc.us, as shown in Exhibit 13.

State Government Home Page Search Tips

Search Engine. Most home pages contain a search engine. Initially enter a narrow term—like "frail elderly grants"—to see what results you obtain, then begin to broaden your search with more inclusive terms until some desired hits are found. For more tips on using search engines, see Chapter 17.

Technology Development Funds. Most state agencies have a technology development fund, designed especially to create new jobs through technology transfer and economic development projects within the state. Often, a state agency like the Department of Development, Department of Administration, or the Department of Commerce will administer those funds. Explore those agency Web sites if you are seeking technology-related support. For example, the Technology Development Fund for the state of Wisconsin is found at commerce.state.wi.us/MT/MT-FAX-0803.html.

Office of Attorney General. One relatively unknown source of state grant funds is the Office of the Attorney General. Because of lawsuit settlements, AGs have brought billions of dollars into their states, as tobacco companies and car manufacturers can testify. As a result of the tobacco and car settlements, grant funds are available in some states for health and transportation safety. See if funding options exist in your state by exploring its Web site, starting with your state home page, or going to the National Association of Attorneys General site at www.naag.org. In some states, the AGs have regranted their award funds to other agencies for administration.

Human Information Sources for State Government Funding

Legislative Officials. Your state legislative officials can help identify pathways to grant programs, if you let them know your interests. To identify your legislative officials at both the state and federal levels, visit congress.org. One main job of legislators, of course, is to provide constituency services. As one of their constituents, it is appropriate for you to request their assistance, especially since they have access to comprehensive information networks and a support staff to help "dig" for information.

Agency Mission Statements. Review the mission statements of those state agencies whose broad interests match your needs. The Department of Health and Social Services might be interested in your approach to adolescent pregnancy prevention. The Department of Transportation might be interested in your ideas on improving highway resurfacing. The Department of Public Instruction might welcome your ideas on teaching geometry to middle school students. A few persistent phone calls or a walk down a few corridors in the state capitol building should identify existing grant opportunities in your area of interest, whether it is in education, health, social services, or technology development.

Clip File Action Item #6
Finding Public Grants

Build your Finding Public Grants clip file by including such information as the following:

- Copies of pertinent *Catalog of Federal Domestic Assistance* and *Federal Register* pages
- Lists of past grant winners
- Model letters requesting application forms and guidelines
- Web pages from federal and state grantmaking programs
- Copies of successful public grant proposals

Time-Saver Tip #4
Procrastination

Procrastinators are skilled at rationalizations. You may be a procrastinator if you've ever said the following:

- It takes too much time to prepare for grant writing.
- I can't bothered with preproposal contacts.
- It's easier to let things go with the flow.
- If I get organized, it'll kill my creativity for good grant ideas.
- My situation is different from others; trust me.
- I don't know how to do it; someday I'll learn—right after I get organized.
- I'll start my proposal writing tomorrow.

 **Clip File Action Item #7**
Finding Public Funds

Set aside five minutes each day and explore the government Web sites listed on the inside back cover of this book. When you find sponsors who might fund your projects, copy that information and paste it in your Finding Public Funds clip file.

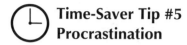 **Time-Saver Tip #5**
Procrastination

To stop procrastinating, do something—anything—to overcome inertia. It'll be easier to keep going once you get started. Why not start by identifying possible federal and state funding sources for your next proposal?

CHAPTER 3
Finding Private Funds

*The impersonal hand of government can never replace the
helping hand of a neighbor.*

Hubert H. Humphrey

OVERVIEW OF PRIVATE FUNDING

Vice President Humphrey recognized the importance
of private philanthropy: nongovernmental philanthropy is crucial. Private grant funding comes primarily
from foundations and corporations. Although wealthy
individuals also provide private funding, those dollars
are seldom available for competitive grants since they
are usually given at the sole discretion of the philanthropist. (Some information sources for seeking individual philanthropy are found in the Bibliography.)
Accordingly, this chapter restricts itself to finding
foundation and corporation grants. Specifically, this
chapter discusses the multiple resources for locating
foundation and corporate sponsors; you will want to
use more than one information source to gather background information for your initial funding list. The
Web addresses in this chapter and on the back inside
cover of this book will help you find private funding
sources for your projects. See Chapter 17, Search Engines, for ideas on how to conduct efficient searches.

Compared to public grants, private grants are usually shorter in length and less background information
is available for prospect research. Private funds sometimes provide support in areas not extensively funded
in the public sector, e.g., religion. Private proposals
may take less time to prepare and, in many instances,
offer a quicker funding decision. However, your choice
is not necessarily between public or private funding;
often, both can and should be solicited.

This chapter begins with a general discussion of
foundations and their roles in society, followed by
sources of print and electronic information about finding funds. Next, it describes the five different founda-

tion categories and their outlooks on giving: national
foundations, community foundations, family foundations, special purpose foundations, and corporate
foundations. While the corporate foundation is legally
an independent tax-exempt organization, it conducts
business more like a corporation than a foundation.
The discussion of corporate foundations midway
through this chapter serves as a segue into corporations: their cultures, funding options, and reference
sources.

Basic Foundation Characteristics

A private foundation is a tax-exempt philanthropic
organization concerned about injustices or inequities. In 2002, more than 65,000 private foundations were registered in the United States. Annually,
they award more than $24 billion. While the figures
vary slightly from year to year, the 10,000 largest
foundations have 90 percent of the assets and make
80 percent of the awards. By federal law, foundations
must give away five percent of their market value assets or interest income each year, whichever is
greater. This law means, for example, that the W. K.
Kellogg Foundation with $4.8 billion in market as-
sets must award at least $240 million annually. Foun-
dations must follow the five percent rule or risk
losing their tax-exempt status.

Foundation Roles

Foundations see themselves in multiple roles, to
which proposal writers should appeal, as suggested in
the examples.

As grant-makers, foundations provide direct financial resources that target immediate or emerging concerns.

As a grantmaker, you perform an incalculable service by helping groups and individuals foster lasting improvement in the human condition.

As catalysts, foundations help mobilize leaders and constituencies.

An extraordinary convergence of community need and immediate opportunity motivates us to seek your investment in triggering an overdue change—the primary reason for our special request. From a broader perspective, this proposal is a catalytic change agent to impact the lives of a vulnerable population through fierce dedication and warm compassion.

As community resources, foundations provide services to donors, nonprofit organizations, and the community-at-large.

Our proposal concentrates on assisting people to build just and caring communities that nurture people, spur enterprise, bridge differences, foster fairness and promote civility.

As resource developers, foundations build a permanent unrestricted endowment.

This proposal develops crucial resources to build better futures to more effectively meet the needs of today's vulnerable children and families. The project outcomes will strengthen the support services, social networks, physical infrastructure, employment, self-determination, and economic vitality of our target community.

As stewards, foundations receive and distribute community resources.

You and I share something in common—a profound stewardship responsibility to the local community. Accordingly, this proposal invites your shared partnership in making a difference.

To help determine which roles your target foundation deems most important, read their "About Us" description on their Web site or mission statement in their annual report. Next, use your preproposal contacts (Chapter 4) to validate your first impressions and base your appeals on those roles, for they represent the psychological needs of foundations.

With these orienting perspectives on foundations, we now turn our attention to print and electronic in-

formation sources that explain funding priorities, application protocols, and, often, grant histories.

THE FOUNDATION CENTER

The Foundation Center is an independent national organization that provides information about philanthropic giving. National collections exist in New York City and Washington, DC. Field offices are found in San Francisco, Cleveland, and Atlanta. Each location contains extensive reference materials and tax records. Further, each state has one or more regional foundation collections to service people in its area—free. To find the location of the collection nearest you, visit http://fdncenter.org or call the Foundation Center toll free at (800) 424-9836.

Each regional collection contains basic grant-related print and electronic reference materials as well as tax records for its state and perhaps an adjacent state. The tax records (Form 990) provide information about a foundation's income, annual disbursements, expenses, employees, and, most important, a list of all grants made or approved during the year.

The following sections discuss the Foundation Center print and electronic primary source materials. The print materials can be either purchased or read in your nearest regional foundation library. The electronic references are available on CD-ROM or through an online service, both for a fee. Details are available at the Foundation Center Web site. Our discussion of private foundation reference materials then turns to information sources distributed by others, including The Oryx Press and Taft publications.

The Foundation Directory

The *Foundation Directory* is the private foundation equivalent of the *Catalog of Federal Domestic Assistance;* that is, the *Foundation Directory* is a primary starting point to identify the larger foundations. For instance, the 24th edition (2002) lists the 10,000 largest grantmaking foundations. Collectively, these foundations donate more than $21 billion annually. Each entry identifies the foundation name, address, and telephone number. It usually lists the names of officers and directors. It often includes a statement of purpose and notes any giving limitations or restrictions. Web addresses are included where they exist. Brief application information is included. It is published biannually in odd-numbered years, with updates

Big Bucks Foundation

Texas Center for Healing, Houston, TX, $100,000 toward start-up operating expenses and staff costs for development of Center that provides peer support groups for children suffering catastrophic or life-threatening illnesses.

Texas Lighthouse for the Blind, West Houston, TX, $15,000 toward purchase of equipment for establishing Low Vision Optical Aid Clinic to aid in restoring residual sight to the visually handicapped.

SAMPLE ENTRIES FROM FOUNDATION GRANTS INDEX

EXHIBIT 14

in even years. Approximately one-third of the foundation entries include sample information about recipients of recent grants.

In addition to its basic descriptive information, the *Foundation Directory* contains some useful indexes. For example, a Donor-Officer-Trustee Index identifies the names of all of the people listed in the book. This information is valuable in two different ways. First, tracking the names may identify a connection with your organization; that is, someone in your organization may know an individual listed on the board of directors of a foundation that you might approach. Second, a person involved in philanthropic activities is often a member of more than one foundation board. For every foundation you plan to approach, you should cross-check the names in this index; frequently, you will discover another foundation you might solicit but have otherwise overlooked. If not, this cross-linkage will at least help you assess the priorities or values of your target foundation. Other indexes include a subject index that notes local vs. national giving, and another that records giving patterns by fields of interest, e.g., aging, alcoholism, buildings and equipment, cultural programs and so forth. Another index specifies types of grants awarded, e.g., project support, operating support, equipment grants, and so forth.

Although the 10,000 largest grantmaking foundations represent less than 25 percent of the total number of existing foundations, they control more than 90 percent of all foundation assets and make more than 90 percent of all foundation grants. The *Foundation Directory* has been a basic prospect research tool for many years. Individuals who want information about smaller foundations should explore a companion publication: *The Foundation Directory: Part 2*. This research guide provides information on the next largest 10,000 grantmaking foundations. The information format is the same as the *Foundation Directory*, with obvious content differences. Collectively, both volumes present information on a little less than 50 percent of all private foundations.

Foundation Grants Index

The *Foundation Grants Index* is the companion publication to the *Foundation Directory*. The 2001 edition lists more than 102,000 grants of $10,000 or more that were awarded by the major foundations. Since the *Foundation Directory* is limited in the sample awards it can list, the *Foundation Grants Index* contains a substantial supplementary list of awards. Some hypothetical entries are provided in Exhibit 14.

This foundation funding history information is important in your prospect research because it indicates precisely where a foundation is spending its money. Occasionally, you may note a discrepancy between what sponsors say they fund and what they actually fund. Or you may note that while a sponsor says it provides funding in five (or two or six) different areas, most of the money really goes to one topic. These insights are helpful in deciding which foundations to approach for funding.

The *Foundation 1000*

Within the private foundation arena, substantial interest lies in the larger foundations because they, obviously, have the most money to distribute. The *Foundation 1000* provides detailed information about the 1000 largest U.S. foundations on the basis of total grants awarded; for instance, the 1000 foundations listed in the 2001 edition accounted for 67 percent of all foundation grants awarded. Each entry may be several pages long and includes contact information, purpose, limitations, key personnel, background information, analysis of giving patterns, types of support provided, types of recipients, partial listings of grants, application guidelines, and funding cycles. It is one of the most comprehensive di-

RAMSEY CHARLES FOUNDATION

Address: 505 Madison Avenue   Telephone: (212) 506-9867
New York, NY 10222   Contact: Sharon Belanger, VP

Purpose: Principal source of philanthropy for Ramsey Charles Corporation and its subsidiaries; scope is national, emphasizing support for institutions and projects in the areas of health care, social welfare, minority education and the arts. Aid to local communities provided primarily through the United Way.

Limitations: Giving primarily in areas of company operations. No grants to individuals or for religious organizations for sectarian purposes; local chapters of national organizations, elementary schools, medical or nursing schools; disease-related health associations, or for operating expenses. No support for operating budgets or endowments. Does not purchase advertisements or donate equipment.

Officers:

Ronald Lewis, President
Jane Griff, Vice President
Arne Johnson, Vice President
Sharon Belanger, Vice President
Michael Fredricks, Secretary
June Smythe, Treasurer

Financial Data: (FY 02)

Assets $68,647,921
Gifts Received $1,947,837
Expenditures $17,221,933
Grants Paid $16,032,149
Number of Grants 943
High Grant $500,000
Low Grant $100
General Range $9,000–50,000

Trustees:

Randall Block, Chairman
Debra Jones
Ray Lazarus
Frank Abramoff
Susan Burch
Thaddeus Porter
Roy Clayton

Number of Staff: Eight full-time and three part-time professional, four full-time support

Sponsoring Company: Ramsey Charles Company

Business: Oil

Employees: 24,500

Sales: $37.81 billion

Fortune 500 Ranking: 2002-3rd in sales, 6th in assets, and 10th in net income

Corporate Locations: New York City (headquarters); Houston, New Orleans, Galveston, Tampa

Background: The Ramsey Charles Foundation was established in 1968 in New York with some of the proceeds from the sale of substantial quantities of oil. Their philanthropic giving has reduced during periods of oil shortages. Historically they have provided substantial support for worthy institutions and causes.

Ronald Lewis, president of the foundation, was formerly vice president for corporate communications at the Ramsey Charles Company. He has also served on the Community Services Agency of New York. In the academic world, he has served as an adjunct assistant professor in Lehman College's Department of Political Science.

Grants Analysis: In 2001, the foundation contributed $16,032,149 in grants. The largest portion (37 percent) was distributed to United Ways through the country. Educational organizations accounted for 33 percent of the allocations, including $100,000 or more to the University of Texas at Austin, Florida Atlantic University, and the Massachusetts Institute of Technology. The remaining 30 percent was dispersed throughout a wide range of social welfare and arts organizations; each received approximately $10,000.

SAMPLE ENTRY FROM *FOUNDATION 1000*

EXHIBIT 15

Type	No. of Grants	Amount	Percent	Range
Health Care	168	1,603,215	10	5,000–50,000
Social Welfare	79	1,282,571	8	1,000–20,000
Education	212	5,290,609	33	1,000–500,000
Arts	32	1,923,859	12	100–100,000
United Way	452	5,931,895	37	100–300,000
Total	943	$16,032,149	100	

Corporate Contributions Program: Through other corporate programs, Ramsey Charles gave further grants of $7,322,945 to nonprofit organizations. Most of it went to areas of company operations. A few selected universities received computer surplus equipment that was not open to applications.

SAMPLE ENTRY FROM *FOUNDATION 1000*

EXHIBIT 15 (Continued from page 30)

rectories available and is extremely valuable if it lists your foundation of interest. A hypothetical example from *Foundation 1000* is shown in Exhibit 15.

The Foundation Center—Electronic Resources

The Foundation Center makes some grant information available free on the Internet, and, for a fee, on a CD-ROM. Each is described briefly.

Internet Access. Foundations have lagged behind the federal government but are beginning to come online. Rather than go hunting for each foundation at its own Web site, the Foundation Center maintains a central directory of foundations with Web sites, including active links to them. Further, the Foundation Center Web site (http://fdncenter.org) has an active search engine that permits you to electronically scan all linked sites to find keywords of interest to you. The Web site includes annotated links to private foundations, corporate grant makers, grantmaking public charities, and community foundations.

Since the Web addresses are only links to Web sites developed by the various types of foundations, the quality and quantity of information will vary. At a minimum, you will find demographic information, fields of interest, and application protocol. These links represent a good starting point if you are looking for a larger foundation; many smaller foundations lack the time and resources to develop viable Web sites.

CD-ROM Access. Beyond the Internet information, the Foundation Center also publishes several CD-ROMs that are periodically updated. The 2001

version of the *Foundation Directory* includes information on more than 53,000 private grantmakers and 200,000 grants. This database can be searched on 21 different parameters, including fields of interest, total assets, and contact information. Similar CD-ROMs are available for the *Foundation Directory: Part 2*, the nation's larger and midsize foundations, the *Foundation Grants Index* and *Foundation Grants to Individuals*.

ORYX PRESS PUBLICATIONS

In contrast to the Foundation Center grant information that deals primarily with foundation funding, The Oryx Press disseminates information about both public and private funding sources in print and electronic form, including an e-mail alert service.

Directory of Research Grants

The annual edition of the *Directory of Research Grants* is a basic reference tool containing information about 6,200 private and public funding sources. Each program includes a description, deadline date, *Catalog of Federal Domestic Assistance* program number for federal programs, restrictions or requirements, contact names and addresses, telephone number, and funding amounts. A subject index contains over 2,000 subject terms to help you identify sponsors you may wish to approach. From these initial listings, you will want to continue gathering further information to conduct a complete prospect search. A new edition appears annually from The Oryx Press. A sample entry is provided in Exhibit 16.

How to Use This Directory

The *Directory of Research Grants 2002* is designed to allow the user quick and easy access to information regarding funding programs in a researcher's specific area of interest. This *Directory* is composed of a main section, Grant Programs, which lists grant programs in alphabetical order, and four indexes: the Subject Index, the Sponsoring Organizations Index, the Grants by Program Type Index, and the Geographic Index.

GRANT PROGRAMS

Each listing in this section consists of the following elements: an annotation describing each program's focus and goals, requirements explaining eligibility, funding amounts, application and renewal dates, the *Catalog of Federal Domestic Assistance* program number (for U.S. government programs only), sponsor information, contact information, and Internet address.

GRANT TITLE —— **American College of Surgeons Resident Research Scholarships** 320 —— ACCESSION NUMBER

ACS scholarships will be awarded each year to encourage residents to pursue careers in academic surgery. Priority will be given to residents beginning full-time investigative activities, with no clinical responsibilities, for the two-year period of the scholarship. Study outside the United States or Canada is permissible. The scholarship is for the personal use of the recipient and is not to diminish or replace the usual or expected compensation; award is made directly to the scholar and not to the institution. Renewal for the second year is contingent upon acceptable progress and study protocol for the second year. Requests for application forms will not be accepted after July 1. —— GRANT DESCRIPTION

REQUIREMENTS —— *Requirements* The applicant must have completed two postdoctoral years in an accredited surgical training program in the United States or Canada at the time the scholarship is awarded and shall not complete formal residency training before the end of the scholarship. Approval of the application is required from the administration (dean or fiscal officer) and the head of the department under whom the recipient will be studying.

RESTRICTIONS —— *Restrictions* Only in exceptional circumstances will more than one ACS scholarship be granted in a single year to applicants from the same institution.

APPLICATION/ RENEWAL DATE —— *Amount of Grant* $20,000 per year —— FUNDING AMOUNT

Date(s) Application Is Due September 1. Receipt of application satisfies deadline date requirements.

Contact Administrator, Scholarships Division, (312) 664-4050 —— CONTACT

INTERNET ADDRESS —— *Internet* http://www.facs.org/about_college/acsdept/fellow_dept/research.html#2

Sponsor American College of Surgeons —— SPONSOR INFORMATION
633 N Saint Clair St
Chicago, IL 60611-3211

SAMPLE PAGE FROM DIRECTORY OF RESEARCH GRANTS

EXHIBIT 16

Beyond this comprehensive reference document, The Oryx Press periodically extracts special sections and republishes portions that concentrate on special topic areas, as noted below. As always, funding circumstances change after publication and should be verified before submitting a proposal.

Directory of Grants in the Humanities

The annual *Directory of Grants in the Humanities* contains brief descriptions of more than 4,000 funding programs that support research and performance in literature, language, linguistics, history, anthropology, philosophy, ethics, religion, and the fine and performing arts including painting, dance, photography, sculpture, music, drama, crafts, folklore, mime, and other areas. These programs fund research, travel, internships, fellowships, dissertation support, conferences, and performances in the United States and Canada. Each listing includes deadline dates, contact name and address, restrictions, and amount of money available.

Directory of Biomedical and Health Care Grants

The annual *Directory of Biomedical and Health Care Grants* offers concise descriptions of over 3,000 funding programs concerned with human health and biomedicine, including the application of the natural sciences—especially the biological and physical sciences—to clinical medicine. Funding programs range from laboratory investigations to those designed to study the needs of society in health care delivery. Special efforts have been made to increase coverage of such areas as clinical and programmatic studies in gerontology and mental health; clinical studies of the cause, detection, and elimination of cancer; health care delivery and maintenance; and all areas relating to acquired immunodeficiency syndrome (AIDS). Each listing includes deadline dates, contact name, restrictions and requirements, and amount of money available.

Funding Sources for Community and Economic Development

This publication guides local organizations and individuals to more than 3,200 funding sources that describe such programs as special school needs, health care, business development, civic affairs, and arts and humanities projects. Samples of previously awarded grants are included.

Computer Access to Oryx Publications

The Oryx Press maintains a comprehensive database of over 10,000 grant programs available from approximately 4,000 different foundation, private, local, and federal funding sources. It includes listings of previously awarded grants. It is available in a wide array of formats: the Internet, CD-ROM, tape, or diskette.

In essence, these 10,000 grant records, updated every two months, are available to anyone wishing to conduct their own searches. The database subject areas encompass more than 90 academic disciplines and topics as well as social service and performance programs. The use of Boolean Logic (Chapters 2 and 17) enables you to quickly narrow funding prospects to those grant programs that meet your subject, funding type, or geographic needs.

Several attributes of the database capability deserve special comment. The database is the largest that is commercially available. Its search capability is very fast. Thousands of documents can be checked within seconds to locate those that meet your search criteria. You know your wants, interests, and capabilities better than anyone else. When someone else conducts a computerized funding search for you, the matches are not always on target; that is, too many or too few "hits" are revealed. Since you have the entire database under your control, you can easily and quickly research or fine-tune your initial funding list. The end result is that you quickly identify potential funding sources.

An effective search of a database starts with narrowly focused terms and then shifts to broader ones until you find the options that meet your needs. The database provides you with a number of useful search options, including type of grant, type of sponsor, key words, geographic restrictions, dollar amounts, and deadlines. In just a few minutes, you can target potential sponsors and be well on your way to pursuing good leads.

For more information about accessing the Oryx Grants Database, visit www.greenwood.com.

TAFT PUBLICATIONS

Foundation Reporter

Currently in its 33rd edition (2002), the *Taft Foundation Reporter* profiles 2,800 leading private foundations with assets in excess of $10 million. Entries include foundation type, giving levels, assets, contact points, types of grants, officers and directors, application procedures, grants analyses, areas of interest, and sample grants. It presents more detailed information than is found in the Foundation Directory but less information than contained in the *Foundation 1000*.

The *Foundation Reporter* includes background information about major foundation officers, e.g., year and college of graduation, major corporate and noncorporate affiliations—mini "who's who" information that can be very useful when trying to adapt a proposal idea to a particular audience. Seven foundation indexes—by state, grant recipient location, types of grants, field of interest, donor, list of foundations, and application deadlines—arrange foundations by the nature and distribution of their grant support and application deadlines. The *Foundation Reporter* is also available for licensing on magnetic tape or diskette in a fielded format. For more details, visit www.galegroup.com or call (800) 877-TAFT.

America's New Foundations

Roughly one thousand new foundations are created each year. Since they don't have a lengthy history of giving to the same organizations, you may have a competitive chance of getting a grant from a newly created foundation. As the title of this Taft publication implies, *America's New Foundations* profiles the new foundations, including their applications procedures, officers and directors, and fiscal circumstances. The 14th edition (2000) identifies and profiles more than 3,000 private, corporate and community foundations created since 1989, including 600 new to this edition. It also contains a variety of cross-indexes.

State Foundation Directories

Most states publish a directory of their private foundations. These directories customarily present the basic identifying information for all statewide foundations, small and large. This document is particularly useful when you are seeking support for local or statewide projects because many of the small- to mid-sized foundations concentrate their support on projects that serve their locale. The Foundation Center can identify where to obtain the directory for any given state. For example, the Wisconsin Foundation Directory is available through Memorial Library, Marquette University, Milwaukee, WI 53233. More details are available at www.marquette.edu/fic.

OTHER GRANTS PUBLICATIONS

Annual Register of Grant Support

Some reference sources include information on all types of grantmakers: foundations, government agencies, and corporations. *The Directory of Research Grants* (Oryx Press), discussed earlier, is one such publication. Another reference book containing information from different types of sponsors is the *Annual Register of Grant Support* (R. R. Bowker, a division of Reed Elsevier, Inc.; www.bowker.com). The 34th edition (2001) details 3,408 grant programs from public and private sources. Because it lists so many different types of sponsors, it, like the *Directory of Research Grants,* is a good starting point for prospect research. Entries are arranged by field of interest and are cross-indexed. Entries include valuable information on how the grants are made, the ratio of applications to grants awarded, and application procedures and deadlines.

The *Grants Register*

The *Grants Register* is another prospect research tool that contains information about private and public funding sources. It differs from other reference works in that it contains information on international grant programs as well as those in the United States. More precisely, it provides information about (1) scholarships, fellowships, and research grants; (2) exchange opportunities and travel grants; (3) grants-in-aid; (4) grants for all kinds of artistic or scientific projects; (5) competitions, prizes, and honoraria; (6) professional and vocational awards; and (7) special awards. A new edition appears every two years from Palgrave Macmillan, Ltd. Visit www.palgrave.com.

Chronicle of Philanthropy

In addition to the books and newsletters that provide grant-related information, one biweekly newspaper publishes information about a wide range of philanthropic activities. The *Chronicle of Philanthropy* contains information about governmental, foundation, corporate, and individual grants. It describes new grant trends and changes in personnel within the philanthropic community. Because it publishes information so frequently, it is an effective way to monitor subtle changes in the philanthropic scene or to obtain early access to information about new grant opportunities. Electronic updates are posted regularly at www.philanthropy.com, which is available free to regular print subscribers.

SPECIAL PURPOSE REFERENCE SOURCES

A number of grant information references provide funding-source information about a particular topic area, e.g., religion, health, or aging. Some of these directories are briefly listed on the following pages. Most provide similar information for their topic area, e.g., contact name and address, funding interests, and basic fiscal data. These publications are available at the nearest Regional Foundation Collection Center. The titles indicate the focus area of the books.

1. *Fund Raiser's Guide to Human Service Funding,* Taft
2. *Fund Raiser's Guide to Religious Philanthropy,* Taft
3. *International Grantmaking II,* Foundation Center
4. *National Guide to Funding for Children, Youth and Families,* Foundation Center
5. *National Guide to Funding for International and Foreign Programs,* Foundation Center
6. *National Guide to Funding for Libraries and Information Services,* Foundation Center
7. *National Guide to Funding for the Environment and Animal Welfare,* Foundation Center
8. *National Guide to Funding in Aging,* Foundation Center
9. *National Guide to Funding in AIDS,* Foundation Center
10. *National Guide to Funding in Arts and Culture,* Foundation Center
11. *National Guide to Funding in Health,* Foundation Center
12. *National Guide to Funding in Higher Education,* Foundation Center
13. *National Guide to Funding in Religion,* Foundation Center

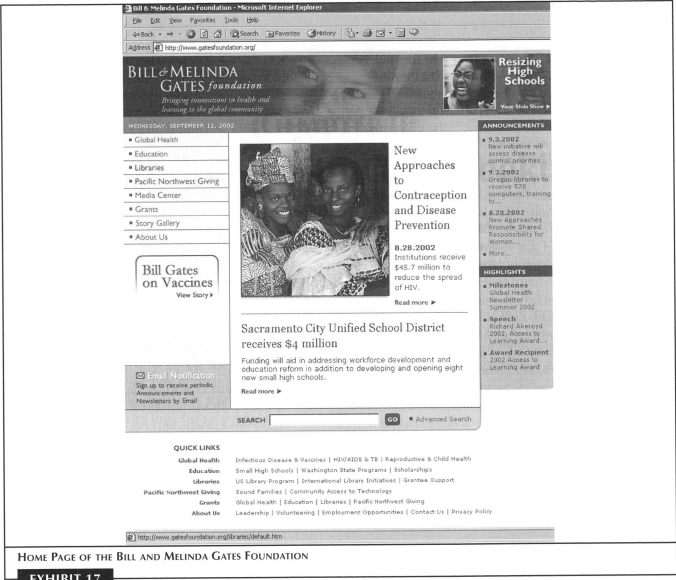

HOME PAGE OF THE BILL AND MELINDA GATES FOUNDATION

EXHIBIT 17

Private Foundation Web Sites

At present, a small but growing percentage of the private foundations have Web sites available to disseminate grant-related information. At least three Web sites monitor private foundation activity and establish links to those Web sites once they are created.

- Foundation Center: www.fdncenter.org/funders
- Council on Foundations: www.cof.org/links
- Grant Advisor: www.grantadvisor.com

Although the lists do overlap, most sites are clearly organized and easy to navigate. For instance, study the home page for the Bill and Melinda Gates Foundation (Exhibit 17). To locate grant information, you would click on "About Us" to learn more about one of the largest foundations in the world.

List of Cumulative Organizations

Finally, after searching available references you may discover that you are unable to find information about a potential sponsor, although you have reason to believe it does provide some type of financial support. When all else fails, consult the Internal Revenue Service, Department of Treasury publication, *List of Cumulative Organizations*. This reference tool is available from the IRS or the Superintendent of Government Documents; additionally you can find it in most Regional Foundation Collection Centers. It gives a comprehensive list of different types of organizations. For example, the organization you are attempting to track down may not be a private foundation but rather a public charity or trust. The term "foundation" in an organizational name is no guarantee of its legal tax status.

ANALYZING TAX RETURNS

From the reference sources listed so far, you will identify several potential sponsors that might be interested in supporting your organization. An important next step is to determine precisely where these sponsors have spent their money in the past. Some publish annual reports or list recent grant winners on their Web site; that information is very valuable in analyzing giving patterns. The *Foundation Grants Index* also provides such information for some of the larger foundations. In some instances, however, lists of grant recipients are simply not published by your target foundation. To gain additional financial and funding information about all foundations, large or small, you can review their tax records.

By law, foundations are required to submit IRS 990-AR (Annual Reports) or 990-PF (Private Foundation) returns. The 990s are the private foundation equivalents of your individual 1040 income tax records; the 990s are inching their way onto the Internet, thus inviting a new era of public scrutiny. Here are some Internet sites worth exploring.

- *www.form990.org*. A site showing nonprofits how to electronically send and receive tax information. This is a demonstration site only; watch for changes.
- *www.guidestar.org*. A charity group working with the IRS to post 850,000 nonprofit tax records.
- *www.muridae.com/publicaccess/index.html*. A site that both helps nonprofits post their tax records and provides links to other organizations with 990s on individual Web sites.
- *www.nonprofits.org*. Provides online information for and about nonprofit organizations. Information on these sites may not be current; bookmark them and watch for any changes in the future.
- *fdncenter.org/funders/grantsmart/index.html*. You'll be able to locate and download (via PDF, portable document files) the tax records on more than 60,000 private foundations—and the number is growing regularly. By looking at sections on the tax records that list giving patterns, award amounts, board

members and so forth, you can help decide if a foundation is a good match with your needs.

As you review these tax records, pay particular attention to three important pieces of information.

1. *Net assets of the foundation*. If you multiply this value by five percent, you will know the minimum amount of money the foundation dispersed during the reporting year.
2. *Names of key foundation personnel*. Circulate that list within your organization to identify possible linkages or networks.
3. *Recipients of grants for the reporting year*. Study the list and see if you can identify organizations similar to yours that received foundation dollars.

Finally, remember that the vast majority of all foundations do not have any paid staff. Even among the larger foundations—those giving away more than $100,000 annually or with assets of at least $1 million—approximately 15 percent have any paid employees. As a result, the 990 serves as the only source of information on activities of most smaller foundations.

APPEALING TO FOUNDATIONS

Foundations award grants to organizations that can help them reach their long-term goals. Your proposal appeals can assume several different forms. Some foundations make their money available for *specific purposes*, e.g., building funds, operating support, equipment, or seed capital. Other foundations target their funds for *specific populations*, e.g., frail elderly, minorities, or homeless. Still other foundations concentrate their dollars on *specific types of organizations*, e.g., hospitals, universities, or youth organizations. As another alternative, some foundations make their money available to *specific geographic areas*, e.g., a city, a county, a state, or a region. Finally, certain foundations have their own *specific priorities* and interests that determine the types of programs they support. With these considerations in mind, you will want to cast your project in a way that appeals to their self-defined mission.

TYPES OF FOUNDATIONS

Foundations vary considerably in market assets, staff size, funding priorities, review protocols, geographic giving patterns, and preferred approach. Some are eager to share information about themselves; others

$175,000 to Arkansas State University for a tourism development program for minority and distressed communities.

$1,250,000 to Center for Puppetry Arts Inc. (Atlanta) to advance exemplary artistic initiatives by increasing permanent capital, expanding the individual donor base, and enhancing board leadership.

$75,000 to Los Angeles Alliance for a New Economy to increase government and corporate accountability regarding job subsidies and tax incentive programs.

SAMPLE FORD FOUNDATION GRANTS: A NATIONAL FOUNDATION

EXHIBIT 18

take a very constrained approach to information dissemination. As you search for private foundation funding sources, it is essential to understand the five different types of foundations. Note in particular the differences in types of projects funded by each type of foundation, as evidenced by actual funding examples.

National Foundations

National foundations are the largest and most familiar funding sources because they control a significant percentage of the philanthropic assets and make more than 50 percent of all foundation awards. Ten of the larger national foundations are listed below. Note that Lilly does not presently have a Web site, although it may in the future. The larger national foundations (in terms of assets and giving) include the following.

1. Bill & Melinda Gates Foundation: www.gates foundation.org
2. The David and Lucile Packard Foundation: www.packfound.org
3. The Ford Foundation: www.fordfound.org
4. Lilly Endowment Inc.: no Web address
5. J. Paul Getty Trust: www.getty.edu/grants/index .html
6. The Rockefeller Foundation: www.rockfound.org
7. The Pew Charitable Trusts: www.pewtrusts.com
8. W. K. Kellogg Foundation: www.wkkf.org
9. John D. and Catherine T. MacArthur Foundation: www.macfdn.org
10. The Andrew W. Mellon Foundation: www.mellon.org

Because they are national in scope, such foundations prefer impact programs with high visibility. They are not good sources of requests for operating income or grants to extend old projects into new areas. "New

ideas with national impact" are the watchwords for attracting national foundation dollars. Fortunately, information about national foundations is generally quite accessible. For example, a visit to the Ford Foundation Web site will list examples of recently funded projects. Three examples are shown in Exhibit 18.

National foundations are looking for projects that address national needs, or at least very widespread issues. Methodologically, they are interested in unique, cost-effective approaches. Decisions are usually made by an independent board of directors.

Community Foundations

Community foundations are the best places to go for strictly local support. They are very responsive to programs serving local or community needs. They seek creative solutions to community problems. Their focus is on long-term community betterment. They are generally available to all nonprofit organizations regardless of their program area. They are quite willing to disseminate information about their programs and priorities. Examples of community foundations include the following:

1. The New York Community Trust: www.nycommunitytrust.org
2. Houston Endowment: www.houstonendowment.org
3. The Cleveland Foundation: www.clevelandfoundation.org
4. Marin Community Foundation: www.marincf.org
5. The Chicago Community Trust and Affiliates: www.cct.org
6. The San Francisco Foundation: www.sff.org
7. The Columbus Foundations: www.columbusfoundation.org
8. The Saint Paul Foundation: www.saintpaulfoundation.org

$120,000 to Asian Pacific Health Care Venture, Inc., Los Angeles, CA, to expand prenatal care services for pregnant, Asian Pacific Islander women in Los Angeles.

$140,860 to Centinela Valley Juvenile Diversion Project, Hawthorne, CA, to support mental health services and medical referrals for at-risk youth residing in Hawthorne, Inglewood and selected areas of South Los Angeles.

$100,000 to Children's Dental Center, Inglewood, CA, to continue preventive and basic dental care treatment for low-income children residing in Hawthorne, Inglewood and selected areas of South Los Angeles.

SAMPLE CALIFORNIA COMMUNITY FOUNDATION GRANTS: A COMMUNITY FOUNDATION

EXHIBIT 19

9. California Community Foundation: www.cal-fund.org
10. Greater Milwaukee Foundation: www.greatermilwaukeefoundation.org

As an example, the California Community Foundation, established in 1915, was Los Angeles's first grantmaking institution and is the country's second-oldest community foundation. The Foundation makes grants to organizations serving the greater Los Angeles region in the following areas: human services, children and youth, community development, civic affairs, community health, community education, arts and culture, the environment, and animal welfare.

Visitors to the California Community Foundation's Web site will find a range of useful information, including grant guidelines, a downloadable version of the Foundation's grant application form, a list of recent grants, brief bios of selected donors, a list of Foundation-sponsored publications, and a calendar of upcoming Foundation-related events. Exhibit 19 lists examples of three grants among many recently made by the California Community Foundation for fall 2000.

Contacts with community foundations are essential. If you can demonstrate credibility and project need, you can overcome the lack of prior grant experience. A board of directors representing the diversity of the community typically makes decisions.

Family Foundations

Family foundations are generally small and controlled by the donor or the donor's family. The special family interests determine their granting priorities. Often, geographic limitations are apparent in their giving patterns. Networking through preproposal contacts (Chapter 4) discloses top funding priorities. Examples of family foundations include the following. Note

again that not all foundations have Web sites, but more are coming online all the time.

1. William and Flora Hewlett Foundation: www.hewlett.org
2. Hall Family Foundation: no Web address
3. The Henry J. Kaiser Family Foundation: www.kff.org
4. The Ford Family Foundation: www.tfff.org
5. Walton Family Foundation: www.wffhome.com
6. The Joseph C. Nugent Family Charitable Trust: no Web address
7. Roberts Family Foundation: no Web address
8. The Hulston Family Foundation: no Web address
9. Wood Family Memorial Trust: no Web address
10. Helen Bader Foundation: www.hbf.org

One example of a family foundation is the William and Flora Hewlett Foundation. The Palo Alto industrialist William R. Hewlett; his wife, Flora Lamson Hewlett; and their eldest son, Walter B. Hewlett, incorporated it as a private foundation in the state of California in 1966. The Foundation concentrates its resources on activities in education, performing arts, population, environment, conflict resolution, family and community development, and U.S.–Latin American relations. In its grantmaking decisions and its interests and activities, the Hewlett Foundation is wholly independent of the Hewlett-Packard Company and the Hewlett-Packard Company Foundation. Three sample grants recently made by the William and Flora Hewlett Foundation are shown in Exhibit 20.

Special Purpose Foundations

Special purpose foundations serve very precise purposes. For instance, the Whitaker Foundation restricts its support to biomedical research. The Research Corporation supports projects primarily in the physical

SAMPLE WILLIAM AND FLORA HEWLETT GRANTS: A FAMILY FOUNDATION

EXHIBIT 20

and life sciences. Many special purpose foundations are health-related and concentrate on a specific medical conditions, e.g., cancer, heart or lung problems. Other are more academically focused and support faculty in particular disciplines, e.g., chemistry or philosophy. Examples of special purpose foundations follow.

1. Robert Wood Johnson Foundation: www.rwjf.org
2. Whitaker Foundation: www.whitaker.org
3. Research Corporation: www.rescorp.org
4. American Philosophical Society: www.amphilsoc.org
5. American Chemical Society: www.acs.org
6. American Heart Association: www.americanheart.org
7. American Diabetes Association: www.diabetes.org
8. American Council for Learned Societies: www.acls.org
9. American Psychological Association: www.apa.org
10. Ronald McDonald House Charities: www.rmhc.org

Perhaps the best known special purpose foundation is the Robert Wood Johnson Foundation, which specializes in funding health care. More precisely, about three-quarters of the Foundation's $370 million in annual grantmaking (1999 figure) takes the form of national programs—organized, multisite efforts to implement a proven strategy or develop new approaches to a problem. The remaining one-quarter of grants are awarded to a single site in response to an unsolicited proposal or at the Foundation's initiation.

The Robert Wood Johnson Foundation supports research, training, and service demonstrations. They like to field-test promising ideas and evaluate the results; take proven ideas and approaches to scale; give heightened visibility to an issue, idea, or intervention; cause coalitions of like-minded or disparate individuals and groups to form and act around a problem or issue; and reach and engage organizations and institu-

tions that would not otherwise seek philanthropic support. Three examples of recently funded projects appear in Exhibit 21.

Your needs statement should be documented in terms of their priorities. Your methodology should be viewed as unique in this area. Networking with people who are experts is especially important. The board of directors usually makes funding decisions.

Corporate Foundation Funding

Corporate foundations represent the philanthropic arm of their corporate parents. Generally, corporate foundations are especially interested in funding programs in communities where their companies have plant operations. As a result, they are particularly responsive to the needs of their workers in those communities. To attract corporation foundation dollars, specify what you have to offer that will affect their workers, products, or corporate concerns. Networking through your contacts can help to reveal funding priorities. Examples of major corporate foundations follow.

1. Ford Motor Company Fund: www.ford.com
2. Bank of America Foundation: www.bankofamerica.com/foundation
3. Wal-Mart Foundation: www.walmartfoundation.org/
4. AT&T Foundation: www.att.com/foundation/
5. GE Fund: www.ge.com/community/fund/index.html
6. Verizon Foundation: foundation.verizon.com/
7. Chase Manhattan Foundation: www.chase.com/cdg
8. UPS Foundation: www.community.ups.com/community/resources/foundation/index.html
9. Procter & Gamble Foundation: no Web address
10. Merck Company Foundation: no Web address

$1,993,698 over three years to State of North Carolina Department of Health and Human Services Raleigh, NC, for statewide youth-led program to prevent tobacco use by young people.

$74,708 to Oregon Pacific Research Institute, Eugene, OR, for surveying changes in spit-tobacco use among Major and Minor League Baseball players.

$994,697 over four years to Child Welfare League of America, Inc., Washington, DC, for technical assistance to promote health and social services in distressed public housing.

SAMPLE ROBERT WOOD JOHNSON GRANTS: A SPECIAL PURPOSE FOUNDATION

EXHIBIT 21

Example of Corporate Foundation Funding

An example of a corporate foundation is the Toyota USA Foundation. One of its major priorities is to build bridges that lead to improvements in mathematics and science education, as Exhibit 22 indicates.

Prior grant experience is important when seeking corporate funds. Corporate foundations give money to those organizations they trust. A board of directors, who are usually corporate officials as well, makes funding decisions. Study the corporate culture to understand how to approach the corporate foundation.

Corporate Foundation Profiles

Foundation 1000 was well received in the philanthropic community because of its emphasis on larger foundations. As a result, the Foundation Center now publishes a companion document that focuses exclusively on corporate foundations. Called the *Corporate Foundation Profiles*, it contains the same information as the *Foundation 1000* but only for corporate foundations.

The 11th edition provides carefully researched, multipage profiles on the more active corporate funders. More precisely, it presents information on 207 of the largest corporate foundations in the United States—grantmakers that each give at least $1.2 million annually. Its grants analyses allow you to find out immediately how much grant money is earmarked for your subject area, or how much money a foundation gives to recipients in your category. You can also discover the amount of grant money a foundation directs to specific population groups such as children and youth, minorities, or the elderly. It also categorizes funders' philanthropic activities by geographic area and types of support awarded. The volume also includes a special appendix that lists quick-reference financial data on an additional 1,300 smaller corporate grantmakers.

Corporate foundation funding represents one of three different sources of corporate-related money. The remainder of this chapter shifts its focus from the nonprofit world of foundations to the for-profit world of corporations and offers concrete tips on securing their dollars.

PERSPECTIVES ON CORPORATE PHILANTHROPY

Overview

In larger corporations—those with net annual sales in excess of $10 million and more than 200 employees—grantseekers can usually find three different "pots of money."

1. *Corporate Foundation Funding.* Some corporations establish separate foundations for social and legal purposes. Technically, these funds are independent of the parent corporation and are legally classified as a foundation. In reality, they behave like corporations and they are best approached from the corporate perspective. Suggestions for securing corporate foundation funding were cited above.

2. *Corporate General Philanthropy Funding.* Some corporations establish a pool of pretax corporate earnings to distribute for general philanthropic purposes. Depending on the health of the economy, those philanthropic dollars represent 1 to 3 percent of pretax profits. Usually, the grants are made to those projects for which the corporation can also benefit.

3. *Corporate Research and Development (R&D) Funding.* Some corporations rely on outside organizations like universities and research institutes to develop new products or services, especially in those instances when corporations lack the in-house expertise or equipment to conduct the needed R&D. Usually, strong collaborations need to be established before funding is secured.

$185,000 over two years to Santa Fe, New Mexico public schools to develop a Rainforest Exploration curriculum for fourth and fifth graders. The curriculum and teachers' guide will include inquiry-based activities and experiments related to the rainforest ecosystem.

$400,000 over three years to the University of Southern California's Integrated Media Systems Center to study, evaluate and develop interactive visualization content materials and tools for high school biology. These interactive modules will utilize manipulative 3-D representations of biological objects and processes.

$390,000 over two years to WNET New York to assist schools in integrating environmental education in their science programs. Entitled "What's Up in the Environment," this multimedia program will enable educators and students to make connections with the natural and social sciences, as well as mathematics, arts, and humanities.

SAMPLE TOYOTA USA GRANTS: A CORPORATE FOUNDATION

EXHIBIT 22

This chapter concludes by offering practical tips on the basic approaches to both general and R&D corporate funding, including pertinent examples and electronic and print corporate information sources.

Corporate General Philanthropy Funding

Approach to Corporate General Philanthropy Funding

Because corporations award shareholder profits as they make grants, corporate officials are particularly selective in identifying their recipients. When corporations award grants, they follow a concept of "profitable philanthropy"; that is, they often fund those projects that will bring them better products, happier or healthier employees, lower costs, or good public relations—all things from which they can benefit, the "What's in it for me?" syndrome. As a corporate grantseeker, your challenge is to describe your project in terms that will benefit the corporation.

Example of Corporate General Philanthropy Funding

Organizations can attract corporate funding by making it a "win-win" situation for all. Recently, the Healthy Baby Agency was concerned generally about the high incidence of adolescent pregnancy in its inner city, and it specifically was alarmed at the low birth weight and poor nutrition of the newborns. Visiting nurses reported that mothers were cutting off the end of the nipples on baby bottles so the infants could consume their nourishment faster; additionally, the nurses observed that the infant formula consisted of sugar water instead of healthy nutrients. The problem:

these new mothers lacked information on the benefits of good infant nutrition. The Healthy Baby Agency went to a manufacturer of baby food formula and gained $25,000 to develop a video on infant nutrition that would be played for mothers of newborns while they were still in the hospital. What was in it for the corporation? Two things: their products were prominently displayed during the filming of the view (but not commercially plugged) and the corporation was generously acknowledged during the credits at the end of the video. This project was so successful, in fact, that the corporation later sponsored additional videos in languages other than English.

The Healthy Baby Agency found that crucial point of connection with the corporation: an innovative project that underscored the importance of the corporate mission—namely, developing healthy babies. The corporation was able to secure substantial publicity from this project, letting others know what a good corporate citizen it is. What is your point of connection with a corporation? These organizations found "hot buttons" with corporations and were successful in obtaining philanthropic support.

- A university approached a corporation that hires many of its engineering graduates and obtained funding for minority student scholarships.
- A museum first loaned paintings to help decorate a new corporate office and then later received funding for an art restoration project.
- A hospital received support for a diabetes research project from a corporation whose CEO had a family history of diabetes.

The way to find your corporate "hot button" is through prospect research.

Corporate Research and Development (R&D) Funding

Approach to Corporate R&D Funding

Corporations are "for-profit" firms. This descriptor pretty well sums up the major purpose of any corporation—to make money for its owners, who range from the sole owner and entrepreneur of a small company simply looking to support a family, to a large publicly traded company holding millions of shares of stock. Corporate R&D funding represents the pinnacle of profitable philanthropy. Corporations fund those projects for which they believe a long-term—but often a "more immediate"—gain will be received.

Example of Corporate R&D Funding

Profitable philanthropy worked for both parties recently when a university laboratory was conducting cutting-edge research on sensors and their use in liquid environments. The laboratory director approached an automobile manufacturer and explained how the sensors could detect when it was time to change the oil in an automobile; that is, instead of changing the oil automatically every 3,000 miles, as most people do, an automobile owner could rely on this sensor to determine when the oil became dirty and should be changed, regardless of the number of miles driven. This could efficiently reduce engine wear. The corporation supported the R&D project and now includes the sensors in all automobiles it manufactures. The research laboratory received funding for its R&D project as well as continuing revenue from royalty sales and patents. It was a win-win situation for both parties.

Corporate R&D Funding through Collaborative Relationships

The ultimate structure for corporate funding is not in short-term project support, but rather in building long-term collaborative relationships. Typically, successful project support can be leveraged into sustained collaborations if—and it's a big "if"—both parties understand their cultural differences and move beyond them to forge new relationships. Building successful corporate collaborations takes time, trust and talent. Although industries and nonprofits may appear to be unlikely partners because their institutional objectives are so dissimilar, cooperation can occur and mutual interests can be served. Recognizing these cultural differences becomes an important first step in seeking corporate support for nonprofit projects.

Understanding the Corporate Culture

A corporation succeeds by meeting the needs of its customers. Accordingly, to seek funding from a corporation, you must understand the needs of that firm, which are very often the needs of the company's customers. Corporations exist to furnish a service or product to be sold for a profit, which sustains their operations. A board of directors, elected by shareholders, runs the company. Industries benefit from interactions with nonprofit organizations in a number of ways. They have access to the following:

1. A source of trained workers
2. Special expertise, e.g., university faculty or medical personnel
3. Unique facilities and instrumentation
4. New ideas and developing technology
5. Continuing education of staff

Successful interactions are the product of "arrangement champions" at high levels in each organization. Informal and formal linkages are needed to obtain knowledge of each other's resources. Written guidelines, policy statements, and sample contracts will facilitate negotiations of grants and contracts. Ultimately, your corporate activities should return something of value to the marketplace.

Understanding the Nonprofit Culture

Nonprofits are in the service industry. They all provide some sort of specialized service. Universities, for example, are in the knowledge business. Hospitals are in the health care business. Both provide unique services. More broadly, nonprofit organizations gain the following benefits from industrial interaction:

1. Gain access to industry as a new source of money
2. Expose staff and clients to real-world research problems
3. Have better trained personnel later going into industry
4. Avoid the bureaucracy associated with government grants
5. Gain access to company facilities and equipment

Obviously, any successful relationship must be a "win-win" situation for all parties at all levels, including the institutions and the individuals within them.

Your existing networks can often provide important insights into a company. For example, universities can contact alumni employed by a company to better understand that company's philosophy, especially if those employees are highly placed within the organization. Those alumni can also suggest forms of support other than outright gifts, e.g., donations of unused equipment or patents. Unused or underused patents and other intellectual property held by a company represent a particularly valuable gift if your organization has a program for commercializing technology, such as a technology transfer program for making research developed commercially available. Patents donated by a company can be combined with your organization's research to make a "technology package" that is more attractive to potential licensees.

Recipes for Successful Industry/ Nonprofit Collaborations

How can industries and nonprofits work together successfully? To begin, representatives of both sectors must get to know each other and develop a mutual trust. The methods are obvious: personnel exchanges, joint seminars, and site visits. These collaboration activities must be seen not only as a means of meeting specific needs but also as opportunities for people to get to know each other—to better understand personalities and motivations. The most fruitful form of collaboration is often a "bottom-up" approach with one-on-one relationships, rather than "top-down" management decisions for collaborative arrangements. A solid working relationship is crucial to recognize a potential product or a goal, assess the appropriate time frame, identify the risk and "marketability" of an idea, and judge the credibility of the personnel involved.

Types of Industry Nonprofit Collaborations

Is collaboration right for your organization? If your needs outstrip your resources, the answer may be "yes." There are several models of implementation that characterize the structure of ongoing collaborative partnerships.

1. *Informal Collaborations.* Casual unwritten agreements to work together on a program or project of mutual interest, often sealed with a handshake. Participants may be geographically dispersed.
2. *Consortia.* Formal project-specific written agreements to work together on a program or project of mutual interest. Agreements spell out rights and responsibilities of all parties, e.g., programmatic, fiscal, and administrative arrangements. Participants are geographically dispersed.
3. *Interdisciplinary Teams.* Clusters of specialists who share complementary interests. Interrelationship among specialists is at least interdisciplinary and often interinstitutional as well. Participants may

be geographically dispersed or co-located in common physical quarters and conduct programs or projects of mutual interest.
4. *Centers or Institutes.* A center or institute represents a substantial administrative and financial commitment of resources to managing formally structured relationships among its staff. Units may be freestanding or affiliated with a larger entity.

In all of these collaborations, each partner comes to learn—firsthand—the mission, the policies and procedures, the decision-making mechanisms, and the key individuals. Frequent, honest, and professional communications are essential. All partners must fully understand each other's contribution to and expectations from any relationship. In any successful long-term relationship, some adjustments and compromises will be necessary. For instance, education institutions may need to place greater emphasis on marketing their capabilities to industries. Conversely, industries may need to convey their potential contributions to academic institutions. The tangible benefits of collaborations must be clearly articulated to all.

An exit strategy for the collaborative relationship should be planned as early as possible. This may simply be an agreed-upon termination date for a project, a well-defined licensing agreement, or an understanding of a continuing relationship from year to year with clearly defined milestones.

Companies typically have well-defined goals, and nonprofits usually have well-defined service interests. Attempting to force one organization to fit into the other in the absence of a natural match almost certainly will result in problems rather than desired solutions. Bottom line: force-fits won't work.

Collaboration Mechanisms

Regardless of the type of collaborative relationship established with a corporation—informal, consortia, interdisciplinary or center-based—corporations and nonprofits are both heterogeneous organizations. There may be as many differences within organizations as between them. In the quest for cooperative ventures, the mechanism of collaboration may include any of the following:

1. Unrestricted corporate financial support for nonprofits
2. Corporate financial support of key personnel
3. Cooperative education programs
4. Corporate associate and affiliate programs
5. Research agreements: bilateral and consortial
6. Training programs

7. Personnel exchanges: internships and sabbaticals
8. Conferences, colloquia, and symposia
9. Consultancies, lectureships, and personnel loans
10. Participation on advisory boards
11. Corporate access to physical facilities resources
12. Corporate recruiting of personnel

These are the major options for cooperation. Where you begin is not as important as the fact that you start to work together. Nothing overcomes prior stereotypes, misconceptions, and misunderstandings like attacking and successfully resolving a problem or an issue of mutual concern. Each industry nonprofit relationship must be carefully crafted so that whatever the relationship, both parties win. And that will happen when they start talking, for therein lie the vectors of innovation.

Corporate/Nonprofit Collaborations Gone Astray

Many factors can serve as barriers to collaborations or cause successful ones to go astray. Most breakdowns are a result of cultural insensitivities or poor communications rather than mission mismatches. For example, a university or hospital research administrator might grow impatient with the time it takes to sign a research contract, failing to recognize the "big picture" that the immediate contract is part of building a successful long-term collaboration. Alternatively, a corporate contract administrator may insist on all patent rights, not recognizing that most firms really seek a manufacturer's licensing agreement that will introduce a new product to the marketplace, thereby bringing new profits to stakeholders and a patent royalty revenue stream to its inventor. Universities and hospitals can temporarily delay publications until patent applications have been filed. Nondisclosure agreement can protect company "secrets." In essence, ways can be found to collaborate when the will exists. Innovation begins with people of vision and determination.

Corporate Internet References

Foundation Center. At present, few direct sources of corporate funding information reside on the Internet. The Foundation Center Web site, www.fdncenter.org, is the most comprehensive source available for corporate grant support. These references typically include such information as contacts, funding priorities and sample grant awards. Not all corporate giving programs are listed at this Web site—or any other. Listings are done on a volunteer basis; some corporations are more public with their giving intentions than others.

Thomas Register. Thomas Register, a 100-year-old company, has established an online presence for its well-known directory, free once you register. It lists 156,000 U.S. and Canadian companies that provide industrial products and services in 68,000 different categories. It also includes links to online catalogs and corporate Web sites. Search engines permit use of keywords and Boolean terms: AND, OR, NOT. Visit www3.thomasregister.com.

How can you use the Thomas Register to bolster your corporate grantseeking? First, determine what type of business might be interested in supporting your project; then use the Thomas Register to find those corporations with similar commercial interests. For instance, if your project deals with infant nutrition, the Thomas Register could identify for you those firms that manufacture baby food and infant formula. If you have a health or wellness project, consider insurance companies or HMO providers. At your next office staff meeting, identify five different types of corporations that might support your organization, and then seek them out in the Thomas Register.

Corporate Web Sites. Beyond the Foundation Center and Thomas Register sites, you can explore corporate commercial sites, most of which follow the standard address www.organizationname.com. Often, you will encounter corporate descriptions, not specific grant-related information, although there are some exceptions, as the IBM www.ibm.com/IBM/IBM Gives/ address (Exhibit 23) reveals.

Lycos Finance. One of the most comprehensive sources of timely, accurate information about a company and its presence in the marketplace is at www.finance.lycos.com. It provides at no user cost a wealth of information on companies traded on major U.S. stock exchanges, including NYSE and NASDAQ. Information on individual companies includes quotes updated every fifteen minutes during the trading day, charts of stock performance on an hourly, daily, weekly, or monthly basis, a snapshot view of the company's historical market and business performance, and an up-to-date news portfolio with links to recent news items from the Associated Press, Reuters, Dow Jones, and other sources.

Corporate Information. Use the Web to track down valuable prospect information on potential domestic and international corporate sponsors. At www.corporateinformation.com you will find more than 350,000 corporate profiles covering 30 major industries in 65 different countries. The company profiles by state will be particularly valuable to many nonprofit organizations.

SEC Information. If you are contemplating a corporate solicitation, study the Securities and Exchange

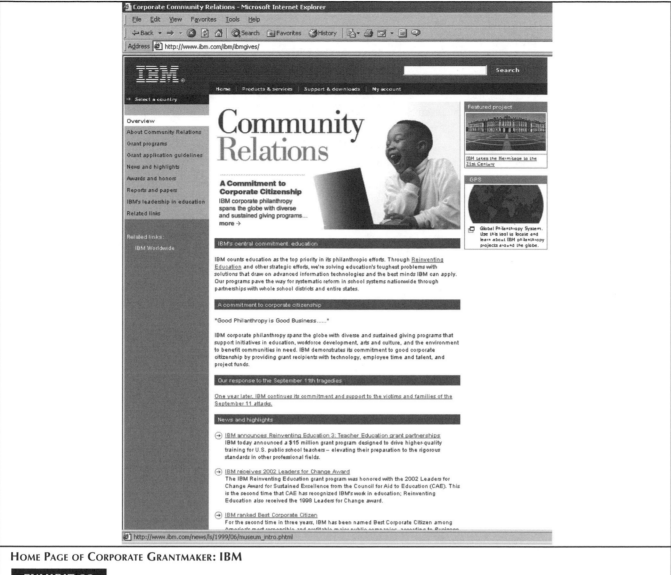

HOME PAGE OF CORPORATE GRANTMAKER: IBM

EXHIBIT 23

Commission Web site. It'll provide very useful information about the prospect's values and financial history. Go to www.sec.gov and click on the EDGAR database to search for actual company filings with the SEC. A friendly tutorial is available to help you interpret the SEC forms.

U.S. Patent and Trademark Office. The USPTO maintains an excellent Web site at www.uspto.gov of all patents and trademarks ever issued in this country. This database is very current, with patents typically listed in their entirety within a week of being issued. Patent applications and provisional patent applications are not yet listed, but some may become available in the future under the American Inventors Protection Act.

Patent information often gives another useful insight on a company's product development interests and needs. This database is obviously a good place to begin a search of a company's patent portfolio, to identify patents that the company might be asked to donate or otherwise make available at no cost to your organization. One caveat, however, is that it takes two to three years for a patent to issue after its original application. In some cases, by the time a patent issues, the company may have moved away from that technology. In such cases, a company might be willing to donate nonessential patents to your organization.

State Corporate Records Files. Most states require corporations—and in many cases, other business entities such as limited liability companies (LLCs)—to file brief annual reports that list the company's registered agent and registered address at a minimum, plus other information that varies from state to state. Such information may include names of officers, names of board members, and previous names and addresses the company has used. Most often, such records are kept by a state's Secretary of State office, but sometimes the records are more difficult to locate. Some states such as Wisconsin, California and Georgia provide this information at no cost over the Internet to residents and nonresidents alike. To find state corporate records, go to the state home page, www.state.xx.us (where *xx* is the two-letter postal abbreviation) and then look under the Secretary of State's entry.

Corporate Grant Print References

Information on government grants is quite accessible and is even backed legally by the Freedom of Information Act. Information about private foundation grants is somewhat less accessible than in the government arena, although many foundations go to considerable effort and expense to publish information about their interests. Additionally, the public accessibility of foundation tax records keeps philanthropic information flowing. Access to information becomes quite restricted in the case of corporations. As private, independent organizations, they have no obligation to disseminate information about their philanthropic activities. Corporations are responsible to their stockholders, not the general public. The stockholders have access to company finances, including philanthropic activities.

You can start gathering your corporate background information by requesting a copy of an annual report (for publicly held companies only) from the public relations office of your target corporation. It will provide you with a view of the world as seen through corporate eyes. It may or may not indicate the total dollar volume contributed for philanthropic purposes. Even if such information is disclosed, you may not find the level of detail you may wish, such as the names of grant recipients, their grant titles, and their grant amounts.

If you are having trouble getting corporate information through the usual channels, try getting the information from a stockholder—or buy one share of stock and become a stockholder yourself. As a stockholder, you will have privileged access to information about charitable corporate contributions.

If your organization doesn't have a history of attracting corporate donations, start small and request larger grants as you establish credibility. For your first approach, you may wish to request nonmonetary support, e.g., donation of a used computer or "borrow" an

executive. Corporations are very cost conscious; therefore, challenge grants have special appeal because corporations feel they are getting the most for their dollar. While there are nearly 2.5 million corporations, only about one-third of them make general contributions to nonprofit organizations.

Corporate Giving Directory. Unlike government and foundation grants, few reference books list corporate giving preferences. One basic reference document is the Taft publication *Corporate Giving Directory*. The 22nd edition provides detailed profiles of 1,082 of the top corporate charitable giving programs in the United States. Each listing includes biographical data on corporate officers and trustees, types of grants given, giving priorities and budgets, typical recipients, contact person, application procedures, and relevant data on the sponsoring company. Its multiple indexes cross-reference sponsors by headquarters state, operating location, type of grant, nonmonetary support, recipient type, application deadlines, and names of and background information on key personnel.

Corporate Giving Yellow Pages. Another Taft publication, Corporate Giving Yellow Pages, provides contact information on more than 2,000 corporate giving programs. It does not provide detailed information about giving priorities. Rather, it is a quick reference guide listing contact names, titles, addresses, and phone numbers to ensure that you approach the right person. Useful indexes categorize companies by type of industry, headquarters, state, operating location, and type of nonmonetary support. Finally, an appendix identifies companies that publish information and guidelines about themselves.

Directory of International Corporate Giving in America. A final Taft publication, *Directory of International Corporate Giving in America*, concentrates on the growing number of foreign-owned, U.S.-based companies with charitable giving programs. Each corporate profile lists giving summaries, information on geographic preferences, program descriptions, typical recipients, types of support, and recent grants. Indexes cross-reference information by headquarters' state, operation location, grant type, nonmonetary support type, recipient type, corporate offices by name, major products, parent company name, parent company country, and recent grants by state.

National Directory of Corporate Giving. The *National Directory of Corporate Giving*, published by the Foundation Center, gives you reliable, fact-filled, and up-to-date entries on approximately 3,000 corporate foundations and direct giving programs. It presents detailed portraits of close to 1,900 corporate foundations, and an additional thousand or more direct giving programs feature essential information: application procedures, names of key personnel, types of support generally awarded, giving limitations, financial data, and purpose and activities statements. Many entries include descriptions of recently awarded grants, an excellent indication of funding priorities. Many of the large corporate entries include program analyses to further illustrate their grantmaker's interests. In addition to details on corporate grantmaking activities, all entries include the company's name and address, a review of the types of business, financial data, and plant and subsidiary locations. Seven indexes help you target the best funding prospects for your program.

Corporate General Business References

Beyond the prospect research tools that provide direct information about corporate grant information sources, several large business directories might be useful for grantseeking purposes. None contain specific grant information. However, they contain contact and financial information that could point you along the right path. The following corporate business references are available in the business section of most public libraries. As you peruse these references, look for linkages, connections, and networks that can help establish a contact between your organization and the corporation.

1. *Fortune 500 Directory*. It lists the 500 largest industrial corporations and pertinent information about sales, profits, assets, market value, earnings per share, and total return to investors. Visit www.fortune.com to see the complete list.
2. *Fortune* Magazine. The late May or early June issues list the top 500 industrial and top 500 service corporations. Read the online version at www.fortune.com.
3. *Forbes Market 500*. Forbes ranks both industrial and nonindustrial corporations and includes information on market value, sales volume, assets, and profits.
4. *Dun and Bradstreet's Million Dollar Directory*. This reference tool lists information on corporations with a net worth of over $1 million. Electronic information is available at www.dnbmdd.com/mddi.
5. *Standard and Poor's Register of Corporations, Executives, and Industries*. A good beginning point in your search for corporate grants, the entries include corporate name, address, phone; a list of major corporate officers; sales volume; number of employees; primary bank; and description of products, including corporate trademarks.

6. *Directory of Corporate Affiliations*. This directory indicates "Who Owns Whom." More precisely, it lists the names of senior management officials and directors for the parent company and lists the names and products for subsidiary companies. Visit www.corporatelinkage.com/dca_print.htm.
7. **State Manufacturing Directories**. To research corporations within your state, locate your state manufacturing association directory in your public library. Most states have one that lists names of key personnel, company size and dollar volume, products manufactured, and locations of company plants. Check with the nearest business reference librarian for specifics.
8. **Business Journals**. The larger metropolitan areas publish a regular business journal, a business newspaper that reports regional business information. It is a valuable source of detail about the financial and philanthropic health of business firms in your areas. To read online versions of business journals, visit www.newspapers.com and click on "Business Publications."

Not all of the references cited above have online Web sites; some online references are free, while others do charge an access fee. After reviewing these basic business materials, start networking with your corporate contacts following the suggestions in Chapter 4, Preproposal Contacts.

Clip File Action Item #8
Finding Private Funds

As you expand your Finding Private Funds clip file, consider including items like the following.

- Copies of grant opportunities from the print and electronic reference sources cited above
- Names of past grant winners
- Model letters requesting application forms and guidelines
- Tax records from private foundations
- Annual reports from foundations and corporations
- Copies of successful proposals

Time Saver Tip #6
Procrastination

To stop procrastinating, adopt a more realistic sense of time. It will aid in getting things done. Break the project down into small, manageable parts. List each step necessary to complete the task. Modify your schedule to work on the larger task one step at a time.

CHAPTER 4
Preproposal Contacts

Personal relationships are the fertile soil from which all advancement, all success, all achievement in real life grows.
Ben Stein

OVERVIEW

You now have several ideas for seeking grants (Chapter 1). You've looked at public and private funding sources (Chapters 2 and 3) for your ideas. Next, you wonder which "suspects," among many, offer the best chance of getting funded; that is, which "suspects" are really the best "prospects?" It's now time to heed Ben Stein's advice and launch some new personal relationships.

This chapter details the many things you can do to increase your chances of getting funded by using preproposal contacts. At the moment, your list of "suspects" falls into a "maybe" category: "maybe" they will fund you, "maybe" they won't. You can move those "suspects" from the "maybe" category to either a "yes" or "no" category by following the four-step process described below. The outcome will identify your real "prospects," those sponsors with a higher probability of funding your proposals.

RATIONALE

Preproposal contact is a process that helps you see the grant world from the sponsor's perspective. You already know your viewpoint. Preproposal contact lets you judge how well your needs match those of the sponsor. In essence, you are evaluating them first, before they evaluate your proposal. Ask yourself questions like these:

- "Are these the kind of people I can and want to do business with?"
- "Can my services solve their problems?"

- "Should I send them a proposal?"
- "If so, what are they looking for?"

In order to produce a win-win situation, both you and the sponsor must be satisfied with each other.

You can make successful preproposal contacts by following these four steps that will validate the information obtained from your initial funding search to identify potential public and private grantseekers.

1. Write to the program officer requesting basic application information.
2. Call a past grant winner to learn success secrets.
3. Call a past grant reviewer to learn proposal evaluation policies and procedures.
4. Call the program officer to validate prospect information.

After making these contacts, detailed below, you can easily decide if you should submit a proposal to any given sponsor on your "suspect" list. If the answer is "yes," you substantially increase your likelihood of getting funded. If the answer is "no," then you have not wasted your time in writing a proposal for this sponsor; instead, you can move on to another one that is a better match for your situation. This chapter explains precisely how to conduct your preproposal contacts by specifying to whom you should talk, what questions you should ask, and how you can interpret their answers.

The initial tendency of beginning grantseekers is to just write, mail, and hope for the best. Frankly, we know of no better way to get turned down. In contrast, experienced grantseekers know the value of preproposal contact and typically report three benefits:

1. It is crucial in selecting a sponsor who is highly likely to fund your proposal.
2. It pinpoints what is required to put together a winning proposal.
3. It prepares for possible site visits, if you end up on the short list for funding.

Beginning grantseekers, on the other hand, are sometimes reluctant to contact people who can provide valuable grant information; they develop a bad case of the "jitters."

Overcoming Preproposal Contact Jitters

Making preproposal contacts, whether through calls, visits, letters, or e-mails with grant officers, is a key first step in grant writing. If you are stalled at this point, you may be suffering from Preproposal Contact Jitters (PCJ), a common malady that strikes all grantseekers.

The typical symptoms of PCJ include fear of failure, anxiety, vacillating between making the contact and postponing it, helplessness, and lack of focus. The basic cause of PCJ is lack of preparation.

Imagine that at four o'clock this afternoon you get a letter saying you have been funded. Ask yourself: "What's the first thing I will do in the morning?" You can't really answer this question unless you've first answered questions like these:

- "What do I specifically want to accomplish in this project?"
- "What have I done, up to now, to get the project started?"
- "How's it working out?"
- "What else could I do?"
- "What will happen to the project if it doesn't get funded?"
- "Exactly what are my resources (people, equipment, experience, money) for this project?"
- "Precisely what do I want from the grantor?"
- "Have I talked with everyone involved and clearly planned the project?"
- "Specifically, when, where and how will I make the preproposal contact?"

You will think of more questions that you must answer before you make your preproposal contact, and we will list many that you'll find helpful. Most grant officers welcome contacts from well-prepared potential applicants. Knowing that you are a likely fit saves both of you time and effort.

Another manifestation of PCJ arises when beginning grantseekers wonder, "Why would the program officer want to talk to me?" The answer: program officers would much rather formally review a strong than a weak proposal. The preproposal communications affords the program officer with opportunities to strengthen the quality of proposals officially received. Since not all worthy proposals can be funded, program officers sometimes use the high quality of rejected proposals as a basis for seeking increased funding for the next fiscal year.

When asked about the importance of preproposal contact before submitting an application, a federal program officer recently said it best: "It's THE most important thing to do." Moreover, it sometimes yields unexpected dividends. For example, experienced grantseekers have, because of preproposal contacts, done the following:

- Learned about new grant opportunities not yet announced
- Critiqued draft proposal application forms and guidelines
- Been asked to serve as beta test sites on new computerized grantseeking ventures

All of these outcomes provide you with early access to valuable grant information.

Beginning grantseekers sometimes feel that even though preproposal contacts have value, the program officers are much like salespeople for their agencies, only looking out for their interests and not yours. In other words agency staff members benefit when the number of proposals in their interest area increases. Encouragement from program officers to submit a proposal needs to be weighed carefully; their optimism and hope can sometimes mask very real barriers to funding, such as budget constraints, geographic award criteria, or changing funding priorities. Successful grantseekers gather information from multiple sources (program officers, past grant winners, prior grant reviewers) before deciding whether to submit a proposal. Triangulating your information and resources will maximize your likelihood of getting funded.

STEP ONE: INITIAL CONTACT WITH PROGRAM OFFICER

Why Do Step One?

Making initial contact with the program officer satisfies two objectives. First, you obtain the application forms and guidelines to follow should you decide to submit a proposal. When these materials arrive, study them to determine if you have the interest and capacity to respond. Second, it is an important beginning step in relationship building with the program officer.

Whom to Contact—and How

Contact the program officer who was identified from your initial prospect research. If you have no prior relationship with the program officer, send a letter, because it will help build the name recognition of your organization, in addition to securing basic grantseeking information. If you have dealt with this program officer in the past, a phone call or e-mail will suffice.

A federal program office recently offered this advice to grantseekers: "Consolidate your questions; too many e-mails can be annoying." E-mail has become too user friendly. It's too easy to fire off a question whenever you think of one. Moreover, because e-mail is so easy, we also expect realistic and immediate responses. This program officer added, "I e-mail back and forth twice, then I pick up the phone and call." Her rationale: Phone calls allow for verbal clues, e.g., pauses that alert her to and allow her to clear up potential misunderstandings.

What to Request—and Why

Contact the program officer when you are ready to evaluate your funding prospects. You are seeking three pieces of information.

1. A copy of the current application forms and guidelines
2. The names of several past grant winners
3. The names of several past grant reviewers

You do not need to explain your project in any detail. On the contrary, you want to know what the sponsor considers important in order to determine how you might cast your proposal. At this point, any detailed description of your proposal to the program officer is premature and should await the finding from your pre-proposal contacts.

Contacting the past grant reviewers will give you valuable insights into the review process. To submit a successful proposal, you need to know how your proposal will be reviewed, especially time frames and points awarded for proposal sections. Learning from the experiences of past grant reviewers and knowing what they were instructed to look for in their reviews will help you decide whether to submit your proposal.

Sample Letter to Program Officer

Your letter to a program officer should do the following:

1. Introduce yourself and your organization.
2. State a benefit that appeals to them, based on your initial prospect research.
3. Explain that to deliver your potential benefits, you need more information.

The following sample letter in Exhibit 24 was used by a social service agency to seek basic information from a local private foundation. It could easily be modified to other types of sponsors. Be sure to use your organization's letterhead; you want the sponsor to begin to recognize your agency's name and logo.

As you review this sample letter, note first that the administrative assistant opening the letter reads the phrase "Letter Requesting Grant Application Information." This header phrase helps the reader determine the purpose of the letter without having to read it in detail; that is, the header provides a quick basis for referral or response. Second, the header also signals that this letter is not a grant application and should not be treated as such. Finally, notice the enclosures. Some sponsors have response packets already assembled in sealed envelopes. If that is the case, they appreciate your thoughtfulness in providing a gummed address label. On the other hand, if they don't have information packets preassembled, they can gather pertinent materials and put them in your large manila, self-addressed envelope bearing plenty of postage in case they have large information packets. Either way, this courtesy makes it easier for them to respond; you'll get your information much sooner, and you'll be taking an important first step in establishing your organizational efficiency.

In sum, Step One represents a reconnaissance, information-gathering stage. You must gather information before deciding if you should submit, and these three individuals—program officers, past winners, and past reviewers—can furnish crucial information. Step One happens quickly. A generic letter, once on your word processor, can easily be adapted in two minutes—well worth the investment!

STEP TWO: CONTACT A PAST GRANT WINNER

Why Do Step Two?

You want to contact past grant winners to learn their secrets of success. Obviously, they did something right,

Today's Date

Ms. Program Officer Name
Agency Title
Agency Name
Mailing Address

Dear Ms. Program Officer:

Teen Pregnancy Services specializes in working with inner city teenage mothers in Atlanta, helping them ensure their infants receive good nutrition, while, at the same time, reducing developmental health problems. Recently, the Governor of Georgia cited our work as a "role model for social service agencies throughout the state."

We have some ideas that may be of value to you and the Healthy Baby Foundation. Accordingly, we request three specific items:

_____1. A copy of your current application forms and guidelines

_____2. A list of your recent grant winners

_____3. Names of three past grant reviewers

These three items will help us understand better your current priorities to see if our ideas would be worthwhile for you to look at.

Sincerely,

Your Name
Title

Enclosure
    Address Label
    Self-Addressed, Stamped Envelope

LETTER REQUESTING GRANT INFORMATION

EXHIBIT 24

because they were funded. Their success tips and experiences in dealing with the sponsor will help you decide whether to submit your proposal. You will not be asking their feedback on your proposal idea; rather, you will be idea-mining for those good information nuggets that might be useful as you develop your proposal. (You can profit from their experience because experience is a wonderful teacher.)

Whom to Contact—and How

With the information you received in Step One, you now want to contact someone who received a grant from your target sponsor—preferably an organization that is similar to yours or working on a project like yours, although this is not always possible.

Government organizations are very open about identifying their grant recipients; it is one means of encouraging other grant applicants. Besides, the names of government grant winners are in the public domain and available under the Freedom of Information Act.

The situation is a little different with private sponsors. Some private foundations volunteer the names of their grant recipients, for they like to be known for doing charitable good. About 15 percent of the private foundations publish annual reports that often include lists of recipient names. For those foundations that neither publish grant winner names nor include them in your Step One request, your fallback position is to examine the sponsor's tax records (Form 990, see Chapter 3) to learn the names of recipients; that information is public.

Corporate grant award information is less available than from private foundations. If your potential corporate sponsor does not include names of past grant winners in response to your Step One letter, then a shareholder or stockbroker may be able to secure this information for you. If not, your fallback position is to ask the corporate sponsor directly for a profile of a typical grant winner: type of organization, size, and geographic location. If your profile is substantially different from their typical grant winner, then you should discuss this fact with the sponsor to see if you should apply.

In sum, you should be able to identify the names of all past public grant winners and many (but not all) private grant winners. The preferred method of contact is by telephone: it's easier, cheaper, quicker, and most important, the informants will often say things verbally they would be reluctant to put in writing. Your telephone approach has two key parts: the opening statement and some follow-up questions. Both parts are described below.

The Opening Statement to Past Grant Winners

You want to use an attention-getting opening statement that will pique their curiosity and elicit further communications. Within the first few seconds, you'll either create interest or resistance. TV advertisers, for example, have known this for years: if you don't get viewers' attention immediately, they will go channel surfing or head for the refrigerator.

Here's a three-step formula for opening success on the telephone. Briefly, explain the following.

1. *Who* are you? Introduce yourself and organization.
2. *Why* are you calling? State an interest-stimulating, curiosity-creating benefit that appeals to their desire to gain, or avoid loss.
3. *What's* in it for them? Involve them in the conversation; you want to do more listening than talking. Tell them that in order to deliver potential benefits, you need to get information.

Beginning grantseekers often wonder, "Why should a past grant winner talk to me? Won't they see me as competition? Why should they share their success secrets with me?"

These are good questions that deserve a solid answer! People who worry that past grant winners won't talk freely can counter those concerns by offering something of value: information exchanges, collaboration possibilities, proposals swaps. Consider these opening statements to winners of government, private foundation, and corporate grants.

Call from a university history professor to the winner of a federal humanities grant:

Dr. Maki, Fred Johnson from the National Endowment for the Humanities suggested I give you a call [Why]. I'm Bob Iacopino with the Children's History Institute at Midwest University [Who]. Like you, we're investigating the role of children in the Civil War. Fred thought since our efforts seem to overlap, it might make sense to consider some type of mutually benefi-

cial collaboration [What]. If I've caught you at a good time, I'd like to learn more about your project, tell you what we're doing, and ask you some questions about your experiences with NEH. (95 words)

Call from a youth agency to the winner of a national foundation grant:

Hi, Mr. Rockefeller. I'm Shandel Lear with the Why Care Agency [Who]. I understand you recently got a grant from the Ford Foundation to teach geometry to middle school children. Congratulations. We are also doing something similar in this area. I'm calling today because depending on your situation, there's a possibility we might be able to informally collaborate in some fashion [Why]. If I've caught you at a good time, I'd like to exchange project information and discuss your experiences with Ford [What]. (81 words)

Call from a nonprofit dental clinic to the winner of a corporate grant:

Hello, Mr. Metal. I'm Dr. Mona Molar with Midwest Dental Associates [Who]. I understand you were recently selected as a winner of a Sullivan Community Oral Health Grant. The reason I'm call is this: depending on your priorities, there's a good chance our ideas might dovetail with your project [What]. If I've caught you at a good time, I'd like to get a brief update on your project, explore possible linkages, and learn more about your experiences with Sullivan Dental Products Company [Why]. (81 words)

These opening statements are designed to get consent to move on to the next phase—the investigating, questioning stage. These three examples can be uttered in 30–40 seconds. Write out your opening statement, verbatim—45 seconds, max! (The average adult speaks approximately 160 words per minute.)

Follow-up Questions to Past Grant Winners

Questioning is the foundation of preproposal contacts, getting essential background information to decide (1) if you should submit a proposal, and (2) if you submit, how best to frame the proposal so it matches the "values glasses" of the sponsor. The list of questions that one could pose to a past grant winner is theoretically endless. Nevertheless, if you want to write a successful grant, you must PREP first. *PREP* is an acronym by which to remember four basic types of questions you want to ask:

1. *Position.* What are the baseline situations, present circumstances, and basic facts?

2. *Rationale.* What are the problems, needs, and injustices that exist today?
3. *Expectation.* What are the implications for addressing these problems?
4. *Priority.* What approaches are most likely to lead to an improved situation now?

Collectively, PREP questions span a continuum of time, from past actions to future intentions. Beginning grantseekers often ask too many Position questions and too few Rationale-Expectation-Priority questions. Here are some "starter questions" in each category, to which you will undoubtedly add your own.

Position Questions: The Baseline Situation

Position questions explore baseline information and relationships with the sponsor from the perspective of past grant winners, and lay the foundation for more probing types of questions.

- "Did you call or go see the sponsor before writing the proposal?"
  Preproposal Contact. This question will reveal the extent to which the grantee engaged in preproposal contact.
- "What materials did you find most helpful in developing your proposals?"
  Proposal Development Materials. This answer will suggest those reference materials and tools that the grantee found valuable in writing the proposal, e.g., Web sites, government reports, primary and secondary text references.
- "Who did you find most helpful on the funding source staff?"
  Internal Advocate. This query will help identify an "in-house hero," an agency staff person who may be the best source of inside information for you.
- "Did you use any special advocates on your behalf?"
  Special Advocates. This question will indicate what role, if any, people outside of their organization (board officials, lobbyists, politicians) played in securing the grant.
- "Did the funding source review a preproposal or a proposal draft prior to final submission?"
  Review Drafts. This query identifies their receptivity to preproposal contact. Most agencies welcome this contact, given sufficient lead time. One federal program officer recently commented, "Less than 1 percent of our proposals are funded 'cold,' without any preproposal contact."
- "How close was your initial budget to the awarded amount?"

Budgets. The answer to this question identifies the extent to which budget negotiations took place. What was cut or increased? What level of documentation was required to justify budget items?
- "Did you have a site visit?"
  Site Visit. If one occurred, ask what took place; that is, who attended, how long did it last, were you able to supplement your proposal with additional materials, and to whom did they speak?

Rationale Questions: Problems Existing Today

Rationale questions go to the heart of sponsor-giving from the perspective of past grant winners: the problems, needs, and injustices that exist today. Problems may be either (1) in your topic area, if it's the same as past grant winners, or (2) in an area different from yours, in which case your interest is in learning about sponsor motivations in funding past grant winners' projects.

- "You got funded because the sponsor was convinced you could solve some big problems they were concerned about. What were those big problems?"
  Big Picture Problems. Look for big picture problems that really trouble the sponsor.
- "What are some of the biggest dissatisfactions with the current approaches to this problem?"
  Current Failures. Listen for sore spots and raw nerves.
- "Generally speaking, what are the disadvantages of the way these problems are being handled now?"
  Status Quo Shortcomings. Pay attention to what's wrong today and will be worse tomorrow.
- "Are there problems or difficulties in this area that are particularly challenging now?"
  Major Hurdles. Take note of priorities among complex problems: what are the top issues?
- "What kinds of problems are the biggest at the moment? Personnel problems? Financial problems? Management problems? Training problems? Reliability problems? Quality problems? Other?"
  Problem Categories. Help your informant focus on different dimensions of the problem.

Obviously, these questions are not discrete. The overlap is intentional; good interviewers know the importance of asking a question more than one way to get at the heart of an issue.

Expectation Questions: Basic Implications for Addressing Problems

Expectation questions look at the "so what" implications of the rationale questions from the vantage point of past grant winners. These questions also identify the sponsor's outlook for changing the problem situation.

- "Was there a hidden agenda to the program's guidelines?"
  Hidden Agenda. Priorities change and what was top priority at the time the grantee's proposal was funded may have changed again as you plan to submit now.
- "Given the problems you identified, what are the implications of those difficulties?"
  Implications. Get the informant talking about the consequences of existing problems.
- "What's the desired impact on these problems, balancing project breadth, depth, and financial resources available?"
  Project Balance. Proposals can be too broad or too narrow. The answer to this question helps you find a proper balance within budgetary constraints.
- "What are some other implications?"
  More Implications. One of the most revealing questions in interviewing: "What else?"
- "Among the many consequences of these problems, which ones are most significant? Reduced self-esteem, workplace bottlenecks, lost hopes, limited aspirations, impaired health status, financial drains, personnel turnover, high training costs, lost productivity, dependency on others, higher costs, slowed down expansion, reduced output, other?"
  Implication Priorities. One final pass at "What else?"
- "What would you do differently next time?"
  Things to Change. Invariably, people learn from the positive experience of getting a grant and have concrete suggestions about things they would change to strengthen their next grant proposal.

Priority Questions: Approaches for an Improved Situation

Priority questions concentrate on identifying the top activities that will effectively and efficiently improve the conditions surrounding the identified problems, needs, and injustices that exist today, as seen by past grant winners.

- "Why did the sponsor think it important to solve the problem you identified?"
  Significance. Look for the sponsor's motivation in solving the problem.
- "How does your project really help?"
  Solution Impact. Is this an area the sponsor wants to speed up?
- "What are the benefits you see of your approach?"

General Benefits. Look for the reasons that the sponsor found this solution so useful.
- "Would this approach be useful for cost reasons or something else?"
  Economic Benefits. Narrow the general benefits to that major motivator: money.
- "Will your approach reduce the frequency or severity of the problem?"
  Programmatic Benefits. Look for the things that will change, e.g., the incidence or magnitude of the problem.
- "Could you clarify how this would help?"
  Additional Benefits. One last call for "What else?"

Do you need to ask all of these questions? Absolutely not! Choose those from each category that you find most helpful, recognizing that other questions will arise in the natural course of the conversation. In the course of a 10-minute phone call, you will have a much better idea how your needs mesh with those of the sponsor.

STEP THREE: CALL TO PAST GRANT REVIEWERS

Why Do Step Three?

Past grant reviewers have firsthand experience in evaluating proposals like yours. They actually measured the psychological impact of the proposals they read. Your goal in contacting past grant reviewers is to learn about the actual process followed when your proposal is reviewed. For example, if a reviewer has only three minutes to review your proposal, you will write differently than if the reviewer has three hours to review it. As another benefit of talking with past grant reviewers, you will learn about the scoring system used to review proposals; some proposal sections may be more important than others.

Whom to Contact—and How

Step One should have identified the names of some past grant reviewers. They may be specialists in the field or internal staff members. Sometimes, one can find the names of federal program reviewers on agency Web sites. Private sponsors may not always provide the names of reviewers. If not, ask your program officer for information about a typical reviewer's profile, because your proposal should be written to the level of expertise of the reviewer. Just like your contact with past grant winners in Step Two, you need both an opening statement to pique interest and information-yielding follow-up questions.

The Opening Statement to Past Grant Reviewers

These opening statements follow the same model discussed for past grant winners, although the actual content is different, as the following examples illustrate.

Call from a researcher in a local environmental protection agency to a recent reviewer of a federal grant:

> Hi, Dr. Pro. I'm Gary Grant with the SandCrab Agency [Who]. I understand you recently served as a reviewer for the National Institute of Seashells. We are in the process of putting together a proposal to NIS [Why]. I'm calling today to request a friendly favor. If I've caught you at a good time, I'd like to discuss your experiences with NIS so we can see if our proposal would be of value to them [What]. (74 words)

Call from a health agency administrator to a reviewer of a health care foundation proposals:

> Hello, Ms. Lawson, I'm June Thompson with the Atlanta Lung Society [Who]. Dr. Barry Gimbel mentioned that you recently reviewed grant proposals for the National Breathright Association. We are completing a proposal to the NBA and I'm calling today wondering if we can exchange professional favors [Why]. If I've caught you at a good time, I'd like to discuss your experiences with the NBA so we can be sure that what we propose would be of value to them. In turn, I'd like to send you a copy of our proposal, if that would be of interest. [What]. We've done this successfully in the past and actually ended up collaborating with our new-found friends. May I send you a proposal copy? (119 words)

Call from a fire chief to a reviewer of corporate proposals:

> Hello, this is Chief John Hunkel from the Detroit Fire Department calling [Who]. The folks at Mitsubishi Communications said you recently served as a reviewer for their Emergency Communications Program. We're targeting a proposal to them for their next deadline. As you know, you won't be reviewing our proposal since they regularly rotate reviewers in each competition cycle. So I'm wondering if you can extend to us a professional courtesy [What]. If I've caught you at a good time, I'd like to get your perspectives on the proposals you reviewed [Why]. What were the typical shortcomings of the proposals you looked at? (99 words)

Follow-up Questions to Past Grant Reviewers

Again, many PREP questions could be asked; those that follow are suggestive, not prescriptive.

Position Questions: The Baseline Situation

Position questions explore baseline information and relationships with the sponsor, and lay the foundation for more probing types of questions from the viewpoint of past grant reviewers.

- "How did you get to be a reviewer?"
  Selection as Reviewer. Usually you just submit a resume and express an interest, showing how your background and expertise meshes with agency interests. Consider being a reviewer yourself. It's an easy way to get "inside information" and improve your success rate.
- "Did you review the proposals at the sponsor's office or at home?"
  Review Environment. The difference here is between a mail and a panel review. Mail reviews are done under more relaxed conditions but often require greater documentation, whereas a panel review is apt to be done more quickly, placing a higher premium on proposal readability and scannability.
- "Did you follow a particular scoring system?"
  Proposal Scoring System. Invariably some portions of a proposal carry greater weight than other portions. This information will enable you to concentrate your efforts on the highest scoring portions.
- "How much time did you have to read the proposals?"
  Review Time. If the reviewers have essentially unlimited time to read a proposal (as in a mail review), then you write one way, but if they are under severe time constraints, then you write another way. One reviewer recently noted that in a panel review situation he could allow approximately 20 seconds per page to finish the review process on time. While that is not the norm for proposal review, it does suggest that one uses different proposal-writing strategies under such conditions, e.g., simple and short sentences, creative use of headers and subheaders, lots of white space, bolding for emphasis, and bulleted lists.

Rationale Questions: Problems Existing Today

Rationale questions go to the heart of sponsor-giving from the vantage point of past grant reviewers: the problems, needs, and injustices that exist today. Whether the past grant reviewer evaluated proposals in your topic area or another area, your interest is in learning about what motivates sponsors to fund projects.

- "What were you told to look for?"
  Identification of Problems. Invariably the reviewers are told to look especially at the statement of the problem or need. Any special "red flags" raised by the reviewers should be addressed as you develop your proposal. Sometimes, reviewers are instructed to look for elements of proposals that are not requested in the application guidelines. Your proposal should respond to all items on the application guidelines and the reviewer's evaluation form.
- "How often did you notice this problem in proposals?"
  Frequency of Problems. This answer will help determine the more frequently occurring proposal problems. The problems may deal with proposal content or format. For instance, one reviewer lamented that proposals were written in 10-point type—like this. Although this was allowable according to the guidelines, the reviewer found it very tiring to read.
- "What were the disadvantages of the way this problem areas was being approached in the proposals you read?"
  General Barriers. This answer highlights the reviewers' insights into problems not being addressed in the proposals they reviewed, problems that you may able to incorporate into your proposals.
- "What are the biggest hurdles people face in reaching their grant objectives?"
  Specific Barriers. This answer prioritizes existing problems in meeting grant objectives.
- "What difficulties linger that still are not being addressed?"
  Unanswered Issues. This answer spotlights existing problems that are still being avoided.
- "How does the existing data support this problem?"
  Need Documentation. This answer indicates data sources for quantifying existing problems.

Expectation Questions: Basic Implications for Addressing Problems

Expectation questions look at the "so what" implications of the rationale questions, as seen by past grant reviewers. They also identify the sponsor's outlook for changing the problem situation.

- "What were the most common mistakes you saw?"
  Avoiding Common Errors. The resulting answers should clearly list those errors that you want to avoid, like failing to number the pages or to list the résumés of project directors or consultants, or math mistakes on the budget.
- "What are the implications of those mistakes?"

Implications of Mistakes. The answer indicates both the logical and psychological dimensions of proposal errors and suggests ways in which proposals could be improved.
- "What happens when those proposal problems occur?"
  Consequences. This answer implies a relationship between proposal problems and their impact on reviewers.
- "How does this problem relate to the bigger picture?"
  Impact on Bigger Picture. This response places the current problems in a larger context.
- "If there were no budget limits, what should have been proposed that wasn't?"
  Overcoming Financial Barriers. Playing "what if," this answer invites creative solutions that are not fiscally constrained.
- "Of the many probable causes, which one is most significant?"
  Causation. Although most problems have multiple causes, this question probes for the most significant factors.
- "Could a higher scoring proposal get bumped out in favor of a lower scoring proposal that meets other special criteria?"
  Special Criteria. This question recognizes that awards are made sometimes on a basis other than merit, e.g., geographic location of the applicant, type of organization, extensive collaborative relationships, or prior relationships with sponsor.
- "Was there a staff review following your peer review?"
  Staff vs. Peer Review. This answer suggests what happens after the review process is over. You especially want to find out how much discretionary authority the program officers have over the peer review results.
- "How would you write a proposal differently now that you have been a reviewer?"
  Avoiding Reviewer Aggravation. People invariably learn from the positive experience of seeing the inside process of awarding grants and have a number of suggestions about things they would do if they were asked to write a proposal again—something that is called "learning."

Priority Questions: Approaches for an Improved Situation

Priority questions concentrate on identifying the top activities that will effectively and efficiently improve the conditions surrounding the identified problems, needs, and injustices that exist today from the perspective of past grant reviewers.

- "What's not happening in this area that should?"

Intervention Failure. This answer highlights areas that need intervention.

- "How would that close the gap?"
  Needed Intervention. The response suggests how to intervene.
- "Which actions are most likely to solve the problem?"
  Intervention Options. This implies probable intervention options.
- "What would be the key features of an ideal solution?"
  Ideal Intervention. Among various options, this answer indicates the components of an ideal solution.
- "Why would this solution be useful?"
  Intervention Justification. This query probes why the ideal solution has value.
- "What might be the benefits from this approach?"
  Intervention Benefits. The response compiles the benefits list for the intervention strategy.
- "Are there other ways this might help?"
  Other Outcomes. This question explores for other anticipated outcomes.

Answers to such questions, resulting from a 10-minute phone conversation, will help you to shape your proposal format and content.

STEP FOUR: FOLLOW-UP CONTACT WITH PROGRAM OFFICER

Why Do Step Four?

The information you gain in Steps One through Three will leave you with some preliminary ideas about the final scope of your proposal, along with some unanswered questions. Your follow-up contact with the program officer enables you to draw the final parameters around your proposal: what to emphasize, include, and exclude. In completing Step four, you synthesize grant information from multiple sources to develop a highly competitive proposal, should you decide to proceed with a submission.

Whom to Contact—and How

You are now going back to contact the same individual you wrote to in Step One, this time with a phone call or e-mail to thank the program officer for the information you recently received. Indicate while you have studied the information carefully, you still have additional questions that were not covered in the material you received.

Early in your relationship with program officers, ask them if they prefer phone, fax, or e-mail communications. Before you pick up the phone or send off a quick e-mail, ask yourself:

- Do I need this answered immediately?
- What other questions will I need answered?
- Can I wait a day or two to see if I come up with any additional questions?

Consolidate as many of your questions as possible into one concise message. Include your e-mail address and phone number at the end of your e-mail message. It may be easier for the program officer to answer your questions with a two-minute phone call than type a two-page e-mail.

Once again, your phone call consists of two parts: an opening statement and follow-up questions.

The Opening Statement to a Program Officer

Note that each opening statement consists of 80–90 words and takes approximately 40 seconds to present.

Call from a university researcher to a federal government program officer regarding a biosensors program:

> Hello, Dr. Jones. I'm Mo Johnson with the Neuroscience Research Laboratory at Midwest Medical College [Who]. Thanks for sending the recent application materials. I'm calling today because, depending on your current interests in biosensors, there's a possibility we might be able to help cut down on the time biomedical researchers spend preparing liquid phase sensors, while also increasing their accuracy and speed [What]. If I've caught you at a good time, I'd like to discuss your situation to see if our approach is something you'd like more information on [Why]. (89 words)

Call from a school administrator to a private foundation youth violence program officer:

> Hello, Mr. Bancroft. I'm John Jones, principal of the West Division High School in Cleveland [Who]. Thanks for sending the recent application materials. I'm calling about your "Cops in Schools" program that was just announced [Why]. Depending on your main interests, there's a possibility our past experiences and existing networks might be of value. If your calendar permits, I'd like to ask some questions that were not addressed in the recent materials you sent me to see if our proposal ideas might be of value to you [What]. (85 words)

Call from a hospital administrator to a regional corporation:

> Hi, Mr. Goodwrench. I'm Larry Johnson with the Midwest Hospital [Who]. Thanks for send-

ing the recent application materials. I'm calling today because, depending on your current commitment to serving disabled adults, there's a possibility we might be able to reduce your difficulty in hiring physically challenged individuals while at the same time increasing your staff diversity [Why]. If I've caught you at a good time, I'd like to ask a few questions that were not addressed in your materials to see if this is something you'd like more information on [What]. (88 words)

Follow-up Questions to a Program Officer

When talking with program officers, explain that you analyzed their guidelines carefully, but you still have some unanswered question that you'd like to raise to ensure that your proposal would be of value to their agency. Briefly describe your project, stressing objectives and outcomes. As you formulate PREP questions, you should be asking many more "expectation" and "priority" questions than you did with the past grant reviewers and winners, which focused more on "position" and "rationale" questions.

Position Questions: The Baseline Situation

Position questions explore baseline information and relationships with the sponsor and lay the foundation for more probing types of questions from the viewpoint of the program officer.

- "What is your current budget?"
  Program Budget Amount. This answer will tell you how much money is allocated for your grant program, a starting point for the next more crucial question.
- "How much of that money will be available for new awards as opposed to noncompeting continuation awards?"
  Program Budget New Money. This answer will tell you how much money is actually available for new projects like the one you propose.
- "What is the anticipated application/award ratio?"
  Application Competitiveness. The funding odds will tell you your mathematical chances for success. Just remember that the grant business offers no guarantees. Funding odds are highly variable among grant programs and range from 5 to 50 percent.
- "Does the program provide one-time-only support, or will it permit other funding opportunities?"
  Continuation Funding. This answer will let you know if you can go back with future funding requests or if you are likely to receive only one award.
- "Would you review our preproposal (2-to 3-page concept paper)?"

Preproposal Review. If they will (and many do), then you will have an important opportunity to better match your proposal with their priorities.
- "Would you review our draft proposal if we got it to you early?"
  Draft Proposal Review. Again, a favorable response will help you better cast your proposal to their expectations. Do give them enough response time; don't expect them to do this three weeks before the program deadline.
- "Who officially reviews our final proposal?"
  Reviewer Expertise. Since proposals should be written to the expertise level of the reviewers, this answer will help determine the amount of technical detail you write.
- "How do you review proposals? Who does it? Outside experts? Board members? Staff?"
  Review Procedures. This information will help you analyze your reviewer audience and the conditions under which they read proposals. To illustrate, three individuals were assigned recently to review some federal grant proposals. Because of traffic delays, one reviewer was stuck at an airport, and a backup reviewer was called in and given one hour to read a 30-page proposal and write up 10 pages of evaluation. At best, this reviewer could skim-read a proposal, not read for elaborate details.
- "How are the proposals being evaluated? Against what yardstick are the proposals being measured?"
  Evaluation Criteria. The response suggests in general terms how your proposal will be evaluated. Is it scored independently against the guidelines? Is it ranked against the others? Is it prioritized within sponsor funding categories? Are proposals evaluated on a first-come, first-funded basis?
- "Do you plan to offer a workshop, teleconference, or preproposal conference to explain how to prepare an application?"
  Presubmission Training. Some sponsors conduct training sessions to help applicants prepare proposals, either through group meetings or conference calls. These sessions help you better understand how to prepare a competitive proposal, and provide insights into people who will be guiding your proposal review process.

Rationale Questions: Problems Existing Today

Rationale questions go to the heart of sponsor-giving from the vantagepoint of the program officer: the problems, needs, and injustices that exist today. Rationale questions explore sponsor motivations in funding projects.

- "Why does this problem persist?"
  Duration of Problem. This answer implies major barriers to problem resolution.
- "What are the major variables in this larger problem?"
  Dimensions of Problem. This answer suggests the different facets of the problem you seek to address.
- "What are the biggest hurdles in this area now?"
  Problematic Barriers. The response points out the biggest challenges people in the field now face.
- "Is the problem getting worse or better?"
  Changes Over Time. The reply draws a verbal trend line for the severity of the problem.
- "What are the biggest sources of dissatisfaction with current approaches?"
  Current Failures. This query probes to discover what hasn't worked to date.
- "Which dimensions of this problem need to be addressed next?"
  Problem Priorities. This answer points to the "big impact" needs.
- "Why have you targeted your program dollars to this problem?"
  Financial Priorities. This answer explains why money will solve the problem.

Expectation Questions Basic Implications for Addressing Problems

Expectation questions look at the "so what" implications of the rationale questions from the perspective of the program officer. Expectation questions also identify the sponsor's outlook for changing the problem situation.

- "Does my project fall within your current priorities?"
  Matching Your Project with Sponsor Priorities. If it does, begin writing. If it doesn't, explore different objectives that might yield a better fit or ask for suggestions of other grant programs that might be interested in your project.
- "Since your average award last year was $xx,xxx dollars, do you expect that to change?"
  Budget Request. This answer will help you determine the budget size you should request.
- "Will awards be made on the basis of any special criteria, e.g., geography or type of organization?"
  Special Award Criteria. This answer will help reveal legal or administrative considerations in the decision-making process. For instance, they may be especially interested in receiving proposals from small organizations in the Midwest or private hospitals in the Southeast.

- "Are there any unannounced programs or unsolicited funds in my area to support my project?"
  "Hip Pocket" Dollars. Sometimes you will discover unobligated or uncommitted funds in the "hip pocket" of the program officer by asking this question.
- "What are the most common mistakes in proposals you receive?"
  Typical Proposal Errors. Pay particular attention to the answer, for they are things you want to avoid.
- "What would you like to see addressed in a proposal that other applicants may have overlooked?"
  Pet Ideas. Many program officers like to feel a partner relationship in the proposal development process. This question provides them with an opportunity to articulate their pet ideas.
- "Would you recommend a previously funded proposal for us to read for format and style?"
  Getting Sample Proposals. Sometimes a model proposal is helpful to review. Either they will provide you with a copy or refer you to a source where you can get it, e.g., project director.
- "Should the proposal be written for reviewers with nontechnical backgrounds?"
  Proposal Technical Writing Style. The level of technicality in your proposal should be geared to the background of your reviewers.
- "What percentage of your awards is made in response to unsolicited proposals?"
  Competitiveness of Unsolicited Proposals. If they fund few unsolicited proposals, you may be wasting your time. Responses vary among program officers. One mission-oriented agency may award less than 5 percent of its funds in response to unsolicited proposals, whereas another may award 95 percent.
- "Can you provide me with a copy of the reviewer's evaluation form?"
  Reviewer's Evaluation Form. Use this form to organize your proposal, using the same headers and subheaders, even if they differ from those in the application guidelines. Sometimes discrepancies exist between the application guidelines and the reviewer's evaluation form, an agency oversight that often occurs when two different people are responsible for developing the documents. One person prepares the guidelines while another develops the evaluation criteria. In cases of conflict, follow the reviewer's evaluation criteria.

Priority Questions: Approaches for an Improved Situation

Priority questions concentrate on identifying the top activities that will effectively and efficiently improve the conditions surrounding the identified problems, needs, and injustices that exist today in the opinion of the program officer.

- "What's essential that isn't happening now?"
  Clarification of Need. The answer focuses on the key dimensions of today's problem.
- "Why solve this problem?"
  Magnitude of Need. This answer tells how big your problem is; the bigger, the better.
- "What's needed to close the gap?"
  Bridging the Gap. Another question that tells how to narrow the discrepancy between "what is" and "what should be."
- "Would this approach produce what is needed?"
  Solution Feasibility. This answer provides a "trial balloon" response to your proposed action plan.
- "How do you think this would work?"
  Implementation Strategies. This answer helps map out a successful action plan to solve the problem.
- "How would this really help?"
  Distinctive Features. This answer points out the distinctive benefits or payoff of your solution.
- "What are the long-term benefits of this solution?"
  Long-Range Payoffs. This answer describes the long-range implications of your solution.
- "What outcomes do you expect from grantees?"
  Program Officer Expectations. This answer clarifies what the program officer will expect from you.

Again, a 10-minute phone call will give you a substantial competitive edge. This four-step process is one that successful grantseekers follow. After looking at the information gleaned from following it, you can see the disadvantage you would face if you **didn't** follow it.

USING COMPUTERS TO TRACK PREPROPOSAL CONTACTS

Over time, successful grantseekers contact many individuals. Database programs like Paradox, Access, or Outlook, allow you to create and maintain files of facts, figures, names, mailing lists, grant ideas, sponsor contact histories, and the like. With database programs, you can define new databases, specifying the type and length of information allowed into each field. It is an easy matter to add, delete, edit, and display information from your files. All such programs let you generate customized reports, complete with subtotals, totals, counts, and simple arithmetic operations on numeric fields. Usually you can search or sort for specific information within a record, regardless of upper- and lowercase letters. Further, you can

search for certain records and replace any or all of the information contained in them. It is a simple matter to create new databases from existing ones, adding new fields within the record and discarding unneeded ones. Sometimes, you can export the information in databases to word processors, spreadsheets, or other database packages.

One of your first database applications should be to configure a file of preproposal contacts that includes information about program officers, past grant winners, and past grant reviewers. Each of the following could be a separate element in your database: name, title, address, phone, fax, e-mail, World Wide Web address, sponsor type (public or private), contact type (program officer, past grant winner, past grant reviewer), program name, deadline, last contact date, eligibility requirements, restrictions on funding, special linkages, average grant size, initial contact preferred, special comments, and whatever else might suit your particular needs. You may wish to create a special form for this purpose using a "Wizard" that accompanies most software programs, a self-instructional pathway to easily creating your own customized application.

Clip File Action Item #9 Preproposal Contacts

Develop your Preproposal Contacts clip file by taking the following actions:

- Write out sample opening statements that you could use on the telephone to past grant winners, past grant reviewers, and program officers; adapt the models in this chapter to your situation.
- Generate an electronic list of the four question categories (PREP) that can be used with past grant winners, past grant reviewers, and program officers. Have the list on your computer screen when you make the calls; type in answers during the telephone conversations.

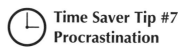

Time Saver Tip #7 Procrastination

To stop procrastinating, consider your "to do" list inviolate. If you write it down, it *shall* get done. Examples:

- Call program officer to get copy of reviewer's evaluation form.
- Talk with past grant winner.
- Review guidelines.
- Outline proposal.
- Draft three pages.

PART II
Writing Private Foundation and Corporate Proposals

Preview of Part II

Some private foundations and corporations have no particular format to follow when submitting proposals to them. Others have very specific guidelines to follow. Part II provides guidance in both situations.

When no particular format is specified, the letter proposal detailed in Chapter 5 will meet sponsor needs. It prescribes seven essential components to include for foundations and corporations. The letter proposal is perhaps the most commonly written type of private grant proposal.

The foundations and corporations that do require specific formats vary considerably in their proposal re-quirements; that is, there is no common application form among them, although some cities are trying to develop one form that can be used for foundations in their region.

Because those foundations and corporations that have published guidelines lack a standardized format, successful grantseekers must ensure that all essential information is included in the proposal, even if it is not necessarily requested. Chapter 5 concludes with a discussion of how to adapt the seven-step letter pro-posal format to fit the guidelines—when they exist—for private sponsors.

CHAPTER 5
The Letter Proposal

More than kisses, letters mingle souls.

John Donne

OVERVIEW

A letter proposal is a short grant proposal, usually two to five pages long. As the name implies, it is written in letter form and used in these instances when a foundation or corporation has no specific submission guidelines to follow, hopefully for some soul mingling, as poet John Donne suggests.

Often private sponsors will decide if you get funded simply on the basis of your brief letter proposal, regardless if you are asking for $100 or $1 million. A few private sponsors use the letter proposal as a screening device and request an expanded proposal if your idea captures their interest. In either case, as a final draft or a screening device, the letter must be clear and concise.

You can also use the letter proposal as a transmittal letter for the completed application form. Some foundations and corporations have rather restrictive application forms; that is, their forms do not always let you put your best foot forward or tell all the information you regard as critical. In these instances, you can use the letter proposal format to transmit such information. It allows you to present a stronger case for securing support. A complete example of how a letter proposal can be used to transmit an agency's proposal is shown in Exhibit 31, page 79.

LETTER PROPOSAL VERSUS LETTER OF INTENT

A letter of intent is not the same thing as a letter proposal. Sponsors sometimes request a letter of intent (also called a letter of inquiry) when they want to get an approximate idea of how many applications to anticipate. Armed with this estimate, they can more efficiently organize the review process, e.g., determine size of staff needed to administer the reviews and respond to applicant postsubmission inquiries.

To illustrate, a recent request for a letter of intent was published in the *Federal Register* by the Center for Disease Control and Prevention. It read as follows:

> A one-page non-binding letter of intent (LOI) is requested to enable CDC to determine the level of interest in this announcement. The LOI should provide a brief description of the proposed project and identify the principal investigator, organizations actively involved in the proposed project, and the address and telephone number for key contacts.

This CDC request is typical of most issued by private foundations and government agencies. Corporations seldom request an LOI. LOIs are submitted in response to a specific request for proposals; in contrast, letter proposals may be submitted in response to both solicited and unsolicited proposals. In essence, a letter of intent simply notifies the sponsor of your plan to submit a proposal, as Exhibit 25 indicates.

ELEMENTS OF A LETTER PROPOSAL

In certain respects, a short proposal is more challenging to write than a long proposal, because each sentence must carry a heavy information load. As a result, it is helpful to segment the writing process into seven components.

Part One: *Summary*—a one-sentence proposal overview.

Part Two: *Appeal*—the rationale for approaching the sponsor.

Today's Date

Ms. Jerri Kurri, President
Finnish Athletic Foundation
123 Maki Drive
Helsinki, California 90120

RE: Letter of Intent
Your Proposal Title
Your Organizational Name

Dear Ms. Kurri:

This letter conveys our intent to submit a formal proposal in response to your recent initiative on dental implant research with toothless hockey players. Our 10-year history of implant research enables us to bring unique value to your programmatic goals. The collaborators for this project include the California Sports Authority, three California dental schools, and the California Dental Association. You will receive the required original and six proposal copies in advance of your October 3rd deadline. In the meantime, feel free to contact me for further information.

Sincerely,

Your Name
Your Title

LETTER OF INTENT

EXHIBIT 25

Part Three: *Problem*—description of a need or gap.
Part Four: *Solution*—method for solving a problem.
Part Five: *Capabilities*—your credentials to solve the problem.
Part Six: *Budget*—your specific request for funds.
Part Seven: *Closing*—a check-writing nudge to the sponsor.

In seven brief sections, you anticipate and answer the major questions that private sponsors will be asking as they read your letter proposal. These seven proposal parts are suggestive, not prescriptive. Deviate without guilt from the letter proposal format when it makes sense to do so. In the samples that follow, each part identifies what you are trying to accomplish as you write that section and provides some paragraphs to help you start writing.

PART ONE: SUMMARY

Objective: To summarize the entire proposal in one or two sentences.

Preparing to Write: Study the critical elements of the model sentence, including

- *Self-Identification:* Who are you? What is your organizational name?
- *Organizational Uniqueness:* Cite a brief "claim to fame" from a mission statement that explains your reason for being.
- *Sponsor Expectation:* Explain what you want them to do.
- *Budget Request:* Identify how much money you are requesting.
- *Project Benefit:* State the major project outcome for the sponsor, not you.

The model summary sentence takes on the following structure:

[Identification], [uniqueness], [expectation] in a [request] that [benefits].

Examples

As you study the following five examples, note how they all include the five critical summary elements. These examples represent a range of funding requests and can be adapted easily to your situation. Additional examples can be found in the complete letter proposals at the end of this chapter.

1. The Basic Summary Sentence for a University Research Project:

> Midwest University [identification], as Wisconsin's largest independent educational institution [uniqueness], invites your investment [expectation] in a $250,000 research project [request] that builds the long-term infrastructure for scientific advancements in biomedical research [benefit].

or without prompts:

> Midwest University, as Wisconsin's largest independent educational institution, requests your investment in a $250,000 research project that builds the long-term infrastructure for scientific advancements in biomedical research. (28 words; one sentence)

2. Three examples show how the same basic summary sentence form can be adapted to three different private foundation proposals on similar topics: child, elderly and infant abuse:

> It is with pleasure that I present the following proposal requesting that the Big Bucks Foundation grant the Family Welfare Agency $30,000, payable over three years. This amount would be used in the Parenting Center, the only Center of its kind in the region, to teach parenting skills to urban teens. (52 words; two sentences)

> It is with pleasure that I present the following proposal requesting that the Big Bucks Corporation grant the Geriatric Care Center $30,000, payable over three years. This amount would be used in the Geriatric Care Center, the only Center of its kind in the region, to reduce abuse of the elderly. (52 words; two sentences)

> It is with pleasure that I present the following proposal requesting that the Big Bucks Foundation grant the Baptist Hospital System $30,000, payable over three years. This amount would be used in the hospital's Teen Parenting Center, the only Center of its kind in the region, to prevent infant abuse. (51 words; two sentences)

3. A public school seeking foundation funding for a cultural diversity project:

> Quinkleberry High School, recently described by the Governor of Wisconsin as "a benchmark of public school excellence that others should strive to follow," invites your participation in a $200,000 special project to increase the multicultural learning experiences of its students. (42 words; one sentence)

4. A hospital seeking corporate support to increase its service delivery:

> Top Flite Hospital, the most comprehensive health care facility within the eastern region of the state, invites you to increase your investment in the delivery of rural health care services with a $500,000 service project, payable over three years. (40 words; one sentence)

5. A faith-based organization seeking foundation funding for a food pantry program:

> Houston Unity Church, the most centrally located church in the inner city, invites you to share in a $15,000 service project to coordinate disjointed food programs for the poor. (30 words; one sentence)

As you now write your summary statement for your proposal, avoid the trap that beginning grantwriters often encounter: expressing the benefit to themselves instead of to the sponsors. Contrast these two pairs of examples.

Self-Oriented Benefit	Sponsor-Oriented Benefit
"Lincolnwood Fire Department, exclusively responsible for the fire safety of 85,000 residences and 12,000 businesses, invites your investment in a $750,000 grant to buy a new fire truck."	*"Lincolnwood Fire Department, exclusively responsible for the fire safety of 137,000 individuals and $42 million in property, invites your investment in a $750,000 grant to insure continued community welfare during a period of increased vulnerability."*
"The Family Welfare Agency, Atlanta's only urban family crisis intervention agency, respectfully requests a grant of $75,000 to meet its operating expenses."	*"The Family Welfare Agency, Atlanta's only urban family crisis intervention agency, respectfully requests a grant of $75,000 to sustain the delivery of crucial welfare services to victims of violence and abuse."*

In both pairs of examples, the message is clear and simple: sponsors usually give money to organizations that help other people; sponsors seldom give money to organizations that only help themselves. After you write your summary sentence, reread it and see if it presents a self- or sponsor-oriented benefit.

PART TWO: APPEAL

Objective: To explain why you are appealing to the sponsor for funding.

Preparing to Write

These tips will help to explain why you "knock on their door":

- Conduct prospect research on the sponsor as described in Chapters 3 and 4.
- From your prospect research, identify values that the sponsor seems to cherish, e.g., high-risk projects not normally funded by the government, cutting-edge research, demonstration projects with a national impact, or low-cost-high-benefit projects.
- Summarize key funding patterns that attract you to the sponsor, e.g., "80 percent of your award dollars in the last two years have gone to support projects like this," or "Last year, you awarded $2.5 million to private universities in support of projects on technology transfer." When you analyze a sponsor's giving history, you can usually find a pattern of giving that attracts you to them.

Examples

Six examples follow: three target foundations, and three target corporations. As you write your sponsor appeal paragraph in your next letter proposal, you may wish to "cherry pick" the sentences that best fit your situation. Each sample paragraph ends with a word count; although there is no "ideal" number of words, paragraphs may range from 80 to 150 words.

1. A research institute seeking foundation support for a biomedical project:

> We are encouraged that the R. U. Rich Foundation supports new frontiers in biomedical research; over 75 percent of your grant dollars during the last three years have been invested in cutting-edge genetics technology research. The Foundation has been an inspiration because you have supported biomedical projects over the years with absolute consistency. Clearly your support fills a valuable niche in light of the more conservative and traditional funding offered by the federal government. This strong commitment to innovative research is shared by researchers in our Biomedical Research Institute. (90 words)

2. A faith-based organization seeking foundation support for an international missionary project:

> The best ideas are ones that help people. For decades, you have directed your resources to promoting the religious and educational well-being of millions. More precisely, since 1969, you have systematically examined the increasing impact of missionary work on almost every aspect of our lives. For instance, your current list of grant awards shows over $400,000 in project support targeted for missionary service. Because of your unprecedented concern for the needs of the financially and spiritually impoverished in third-world countries as well as your position of leadership in the philanthropic community, we turn to the Big Bucks Foundation for its support of a $90,000 international missionary project. (109 words)

3. A private university seeking foundation support for student scholarships:

> We are encouraged that the George and Martha Washington Foundation has given $681,389, or 53 percent of all its awards, in the last two years to private colleges and universities. This type of recognition is essential for independent universities that are tuition-dependent and lack state financial support. Midwest University wants to attract the brightest students into our ranks: people with fresh perspectives on current issues who we can encourage to become tomorrow's top leaders. Midwest has a national reputation for providing a rock-solid, values-based, liberal arts education; this reputation, in turn, attracts many top-caliber applicants. Unfortunately, the number of academically talented students in all areas of study who deserve our help strains our limited scholarship funds. Your contribution will be especially important in providing vital student assistance to our nation's future leaders. (133 words)

4. A child welfare agency seeking corporate support for a social services project:

> In our shared commitment to making our community a better place to live and work, we look forward to finding avenues of mutual support. Such a partnership is particularly timely because public funding for human services and

civic needs continues to decline at a dramatic rate. Because of your demonstrated concern for children as well as your position of leadership in our city, we turn to the Big Bucks Corporation for its support in expanding community outreach services to at-risk youth. (82 words)

5. A health agency seeking corporate support for a community health program:

We recognize your commitment to being an outstanding corporate citizen, and we appreciate the fact that you are as concerned about the health of our community as you are with the health of your business. Indeed, it is sometimes difficult to determine where business interests end and community interests begin. Since you provide important work for the good of others, your investment in this project would contribute significantly to maintaining a community health program of the highest quality and national distinction, based here in San Antonio. Moreover, it would also serve as a standard of committed civic responsibility, inspiring others to support this important fund raising effort. As a result, your philanthropic generosity could be leveraged to attract additional support from the business community. (124 words)

6. A local police department seeking corporate matching funds for a juvenile justice project:

Like many communities, the Evergreen Police Department (EPD) must cope with the consequences of escalating juvenile crimes. The rise in crime rate comes at a time when local government budgets are retrenching as a result of our dwindling tax base. Accordingly, EPD must rely on support from external sources if it is to remain financially healthy and meet community service obligations. We have been fortunate in attracting partial funding from the Department of Justice through their Community Oriented Policing program. Their matching grant will provide three-year funding to hire one juvenile justice officer, if the community will fund a second officer. In response, the City Council has committed a one-half salary for a second officer, wishing that the budget allowed full matching funds. Since your support over the years has played a catalytic role in local efforts to help nurture and challenge ideas that are locally developed, we now seek your generous support to secure this co-funding opportunity—and secure the future of our troubled youth. We hope you are able to take advantage of this opportunity to leverage your support dollars in continued partnership with the City. (190 words)

PART THREE: PROBLEM

Objective: To briefly summarize the current problem and its long-term implications.

Preparing to Write

Focus the problem or need statement from their perspective, not yours. Funding your project is not their end goal. You must show how funding your project can be a means for them to reach their end goal—namely, their mission.

A "need" is really a gap between "what is" and "what ought to be." Document that gap with statistics, quotations, reasoning, or surveys, and express it in human terms. Limit your documentation to brief but clear statements. Beware of the excessive use of statistics, which may only confuse the reader.

Examples

1. A research institute seeking foundation equipment funding:

As you know, interdisciplinary research combined with genetic technology fuels the rapid advancements in the modern life sciences. To remain at the cutting edge of these discoveries, Institute researchers must consolidate and expand the analytical methods they now use to study the expression of gene regulation. Currently, our researchers lack the capability for genomic analysis at levels of detail now possible with new technology. This lack of powerful and productive equipment inhibits our ability to use state-of-the-art methodology, to perform critical experiments, and to develop more efficient, definitive, and versatile research programs.

There are two major consequences from this lack of modern equipment. First, it presents insurmountable barriers to scientific progress in understanding the mechanisms underlying such diseases as Alzheimer's and cancer. Neuroscience questions on the mechanisms that alter gene functions often require equipment support that extends beyond the financial boundaries of individual research projects. Maintaining state-of-the-art equipment has become prohibitive. Second, the Institute has a serious responsibility to train scientists who will contribute to an ever-changing technological society in the future. To meet this challenge, our laboratories must be equipped with modern, sophisticated instrumentation. (186 words; 10 sentences)

2. A social service agency counseling proposal to a community foundation:

The purpose of this proposal is to initiate a psychological support service for inner-city families with teenage parents. The results of a recent Community Life Survey revealed 68 percent of the households in the 53206 zip code region have single mothers with an average of 2.3 children. These families—mothers, grandmothers, and great-grandmothers alike—experience a growing strain in trying to balance family and work responsibilities. As a result, there is a significant and spiraling gap between the stress levels in urban and suburban households in our community.

The problem is further exacerbated by the collision between service providers in the two communities. More precisely, suburban households have more financial resources and coping mechanisms to deal with stressors than what exists in corresponding urban environments. Bottom line: very few service providers have the cultural expertise or multicultural staff to be seen as credible and affordable helping agencies. Clearly, this lag in inner-city family support services is a problem that needs to be creatively addressed. (167 words; eight sentences)

3. A medical school curriculum development proposal to a pharmaceutical corporation:

Genetics is one of the most rapidly developing areas of neuroscience.

While physicians must understand genes and their function in health and disease, today's medicals students receive little training in the human genetics: its basic science concepts or clinical applications.

A recent survey of American medical schools revealed that medical students receive an average of only 18 hours of genetics instruction. Now that the human genomic code has been cracked, demands for genetic testing are coming with growing demands from patients and insurance companies alike. Additionally, new issues in confidentiality, patient counseling, informed consent and societal perceptions have added new dimensions of complexity for medical students.

To close the gap between rapid advances in medical science and the training received by future physicians, there is need to develop a model course in medical genetics that could be integrated into medical school curricula nationwide. By reason of its multiplier effect, educa-

tion is one of the most constructive longer-term approaches to ameliorating troubling genetics questions. (164 words; seven sentences)

4. A geriatric health agency seeking corporate support for consolidation of services:

The rationale for this project is driven by the demographics of aging. The elderly population is growing older:

- By 2020, 40% of our population will be over age 65.
- One-half of the elderly will be 75-plus years old.
- Elderly women will outnumber elderly men three to two.
- At age 85, there will be 4 men for every 10 women.

As a result of these demographics, there will be a marked increase in consumer demands for specialized health care services. Presently, local health services for the elderly are fragmented. Geographically, they exist in many different locations. Their disparate locations result in reduced purchasing power, ineffective case management, and duplication of records. (115 words; nine sentences)

PART FOUR: SOLUTION

Objective: To describe your approach to the problem.

Preparing to Write

- Justify your selection of methodology.
- Summarize the outcomes that you will meet with your approach.
- Convey confidence that you can solve the problem.
- Use a one-page attached time-and-task chart to detail your methodology.

Examples

1. A child welfare agency proposal seeking foundation support to train parents of pre-school children:

This proposal addresses a crucial service to our community: counseling and support for parents of pre-school children. In recent months, we have witnessed a tragic series of cases of children who have been neglected and abused. The plight of these youngsters is dramatic evidence of the need for young parents to learn proper care and development of their children—one of the most important responsibilities of their lives. The Parenting Center was established to meet these needs. Its centerpiece is a theory-driven training program called STAR: Stop, Think, Assess, Respond. This four-step response to childlike behaviors is preferable to the more customary use of corporal punishment for our target population. STAR has an established track record across various culture groups and is ready for implementation here. (128 words; seven sentences)

2. A hospital seeking corporate funding for a teen smoking prevention project:

Our intervention strategy directly addresses the number-one teen health hazard: smoking. The project approach will close the health hazard gap by getting at the root causes that lead to addiction. We will avoid the two primary unsuccessful techniques used in the past: (1) Fear of death: too remote of a concern during the teen years; and (2) Health impairment: permanent lung damage has little stimulus value to change behavior. Instead, we will initiate a five-pronged approach that is targeted at the average age of the first-time smoker—13 years old. Our campaign, called Butt Out Now, will do the following:

- Develop in-house program to fight tobacco use in middle schools
- Create Web sites to discourage youth smoking
- Empower teen smokers to quit successfully
- Enact peer teaching programs to defend youth against advertising and peer pressure
- Remind physicians to take a proactive role

Our accompanying Time and Task Chart describes in detail how campaign phases interrelate. (14 words; 11 sentences)

3. A social service agency seeking foundation funding for research on families at-risk for domestic violence:

Our approach uses both qualitative and quantitative methods. We will use interviews and questionnaires to determine responses to aggression and its impact on the family. Two key questionnaires are the Ryder Aggression Scale and the Intent to Institutionalize Scale. Both instruments will be given to a random selection of the clients at the Family Wellness Center over the past two years. To aid in the interpretation of the resulting scale values, focus group interviews will be conducted with the clients to

better understand their perceptions of core family values. The outcome of this research has implications for the training of social welfare personnel and will be submitted for publication to the *Journal of Domestic Tranquility*. (115 words: six sentences)

4. A collaborative university/community agency proposal seeking foundation funding for adult literacy training:

The attached Time and Task Chart summarizes the project methodology, including major milestones, responsible personnel, and duration. The innovative aspects of the project include close supervision of tutors, emphasis on family approaches to literacy training for adults, and the inclusion of graduate students earning academic credit. Since methods of teaching reading to children are not directly transferable to adults, the method of choice is the Randolph Reading Review, which presents adult level stimulus material in a combined phonetic and sight vocabulary approach. A 2002 study by Chenitz documented the effectiveness of this technique with a similar population, when compared with other common intervention strategies. (105 words; four sentences)

PART FIVE: CAPABILITIES

Objective: To establish your credentials to do the project.

Preparing to Write

Your job is to establish three types of credibility: your organization, your project idea, and your key project staff.

Examples

1. A pediatric hospital seeking foundation funding to work with emotionally disturbed preschoolers:

The State Pediatric Hospital has been meeting the needs of emotionally disturbed preschoolers for 13 years. The trained staff represents over 300 years of experience in this specialized area. The hospital's geographic location is less than a two-hour drive for 80% of the state's population. The hospital is in a unique position to conduct this project for two reasons. First, veteran physicians and child psychiatrists with extensive national networks will conduct this project. Second, as a private institution not dependent upon public funding, it can provide a detached perspective without the constraints that publicly funded hospitals might experience. (99 words; six sentences)

2. A university biology department seeking corporate funding for genetics research:

Here are some things you should know about us. Our biology department is uniquely suited to conduct this crucial genetics research. Stemming from the department's solid past of 30 years of doctoral studies in biological science, its faculty includes Drs. Smith, Johnson, and O'Connor. This distinguished academic core cumulatively represents 224 years of productive research experience at our university. With special focus on the molecular basis of oncogenesis, our current research uses unique systems to analyze the genetic and hormonal factors responsible for gene regulation. While these systems are not widely studied in established programs of cell biology, they are most suitable for answering the cutting-edge questions of gene expression and regulation—and our department is endowed with the intellectual talent to succeed. (124 words; seven sentences)

3. A geriatrics institute seeking foundation funding to coordinate services for the elderly:

The Roxbury Elder Institute is uniquely positioned to develop an integrated system of geriatric medical and nonhealth services. Since 1980, the Institute has provided quality health, education, and research services. As a result, it serves a full range of seniors' needs. The Institute has a 20-plus-year history of positive networking with the business community. Accordingly, this project represents a systematic continuation of prior geriatric efforts in the area where we've transformed vision into success. It organically grows out of our past activities in the area of integration of essential services. We are solidly endowed with the intellectual resources, a skilled population, and healthy attitude to successfully implement our action plan. (113 words; seven sentences)

4. An environmentally conscious agency seeking corporate funding to train volunteers:

The Greenspace Society is similar to many other organizations that are dedicated, as our mission statement says, to environmental protection and preservation. During the past two years, we have successfully trained volunteers, as evidenced by the fact that annual volunteer hours now exceed 18,000 (up 46%) and donations total $25,000 (up 12%). As a result, we now request funding to systematically develop a formal training model, complete with a curriculum and instructional materials; since we are like other environmentally conscious volunteer organizations, a training model developed here can be replicated in many other equivalent institutions. (96 words; four sentences)

PART SIX: BUDGET

Objective: To request a specific dollar amount in the proposal.

Preparing to Write

- Ask for a precise amount.
- Base your request on your preproposal contact information.
- Express your request in meaningful units, e.g., hours of instruction, numbers of students, or healthy patients.
- If the per unit costs are too high, spread the figures out over several years.
- Advise the sponsor if you plan to submit this or a similar proposal to other sponsors as well.

Examples

1. A public high school requesting corporate support for new computers:

To meet our obligation of training computer-literate children, it is essential that they have access to today's technology. The cost of maintaining state-of-the-art computer technologies is quickly becoming prohibitive. Quite frankly, this project extends beyond the financial boundaries of our high school. Accordingly, we must now reach out for assistance in what surely is a vital service to our entire community. Although we are expanding our budget allocations for technology upgrades as rapidly as possible, we intend to build an endowment that will provide ongoing support for suitable technology and staff without relying on annual operating dollars. With the interest that you've shown in this area, we are requesting a grant in the amount of $150,000. This represents an investment of $1.25 in every student that will use these computers in the next five years, or a cost of $0.018 per hour of instruction. (146 words; seven sentences)

2. A social service agency seeking corporate funding for a conference on rural poverty:

> It is in the spirit of this beneficial synergism between business and the community it serves that I respectfully request the John Doe Tractor Corporation to grant $10,000 to provide funds for a conference on rural poverty. This project would not only flow logically from your great corporate interest in supporting communities in which your employees live and work, but it would also yield fresh perspectives on the plight faced by many of your rural customers. In making such a contribution, the John Doe Tractor Corporation will join the Rural Social Service Agency and the state Bureau of Agriculture in this effort to serve our community by finding contemporary solutions to nagging problems. Corporate marketing professionals, government policy makers, and social service agencies can use the conference findings to strength the vitality of rural communities throughout the nation. (139 words: four sentences)

3. A local library seeking foundation funding to digitize its holdings:

> With the commitment shown by the Brush Foundation to promote literary and educational efforts, we are seeking a $25,000 grant to digitize our entire library holding of more than 10,000 volumes. Over a 10-year period, your support will touch the lives of 50,000 library patrons. Such a gift will ensure that timely and quality services are provided, but also extend its outreach to turn every community household into a virtual library. Clearly, this project will enrich the lives of all whom it reaches. The average library checkout entails four books; this project has the attractive investment of five cents (5¢) per person. (104 words; five sentences)

PART SEVEN: CLOSING

Objective: To nudge the sponsor to a favorable funding decision.

Preparing to Write

- Avoid the hackneyed "We'd be happy to talk with you further about this. Please call if you want more information."
- Identify a contact person for more details, if requested.
- Have a "heavyweight" sign the letter.

Examples

1. A university seeking student financial aid from a foundation:

> We hope the Marcy Foundation will be able to support these Midwest scholars as they continue their tradition of the pursuit of knowledge. In making such a contribution, Marcy—and indeed, society—will benefit by investing in the ideas of the future. Quite simply, your investment will perpetuate excellent educational opportunities for future leaders throughout the nation. Dr. Robert Wheeler, Director of Student Financial Aid, can provide additional information or answer questions via telephone (414-234-5678) or e-mail (robert.wheeler@midwest.edu). (80 words; four sentences)

2. A research institute seeking corporate support for a pain management project:

> Your support really does make a difference. The impact of your contribution will last for years to come as a key player in the management of pain in patients with advanced disease. Your support will contribute to the only business worth pursuing, as Albert Schweitzer noted, "the business of doing purposeful good." Although this proposal follows the businesslike brevity your guidelines request, Dr. Smith can be reached at (890) 123-4567 to answer questions or give further information. (77 words; four sentences)

3. A Family Resource Center seeking foundation support for a parenting project:

> Strengthening family ties is clearly a priority in our country. This is evidenced by collaborations between myriad local agencies to achieve these goals and the increased demand for family support services. With your investment we will be able to foster healthy relationships between parents and their children. Please contact Cameron Bork directly to answer questions or provide additional information by phone at (202) 123-4567 or e-mail Cameron@frc.org. (69 words; four sentences)

COMPLETE LETTER PROPOSAL #1

An example of a complete 648-word letter proposal to a private foundation that seeks support for a project to improve police-community relations follows in Exhibit 26. It contains all seven sections described above and makes good use of subheaders. The two most common attachments for a letter proposal are (1) a copy of your IRS letter certifying that you are a nonprofit organization, and (2) a time-and-task chart.

Today's Date

Mr. Hubert Williams, President
Law Enforcement Foundation
1001 23rd Street, N.W., Suite 200
Washington, DC 20037

Dear Mr. Williams:

The Center for Urban Problems (CUP), as Washington's largest organization dealing with police-community relations, invites your investment in a $66,240 special project to improve community relations among minorities.

We are encouraged that the Law Enforcement Foundation supports innovative projects that improve the delivery of police services. Over 85 percent of your grant dollars during that past three years have been invested at the local community level. Clearly, your support fills valuable niche in light of the more conservative funding offered by the federal government. The researchers and evaluation specialists at CUP share your strong commitment to unique community based projects.

The Problem: Spiraling Tensions. Despite proactive community relations programs, an unchecked tension exists between municipal police and minority community members. Relationships between law enforcement officers and minorities – Hispanics and African-Americans – are at a critical stage. One out of every three arrests in Washington, DC currently involves a member of a minority community; the incidence is even higher in such cities as San Antonio, Kansas City, and Los Angeles.

Many factors contribute to the growing minority community – police tensions: unemployment, and inadequate housing, and the increasing complexity of urban life. Although the police did not create these nationwide social problems, they must cope with the consequences of these problems. This vast social dislocation spawns minority attitudes of prejudice and contempt. To counterbalance these problems, many police communities have adopted public relations programs to "sell" their departments to the minority communities without the concomitant need to be ready to work with those communities. As a result, there is an ever-widening split between present and potential minority community acceptance of police behavior. Long term, this spiraling gap further alienates citizens, limits cooperation, and erects barriers to community development.

The Solution: Evaluating Police/Community Relations Bureaus. The most effective approach to successful community-based mediation lies in forming citizen/government collaborations (often called "bureaus"), according to the latest community action research. However, success claims regarding the effectiveness of police-community relations bureaus remain undocumented. Police departments adopt a new fad without understanding the key components of a police/community relations program. Some features of the bureau approach appear to work; others don't. The goal of the project is to identify the successful features of existing bureaus so that success can be delivered more quickly to police departments serving substantial numbers of minority citizens. The CUP research staff will follow standard social science research techniques as detailed in our Time and Task Chart, Attachment A.

CUP Credentials: National Experience and Networks. CUP is uniquely suited to conduct this evaluation project on police/community relations bureaus. As a nonpolice-linked organization we can objectively and independently assess current practices. This project represents a systematic continuation of prior CUP efforts in this area with state and municipal organizations and private police-related associations. Our staff has a cumulative 127 years of experience in evaluating the outcomes of police-related projects. Finally, location and national networking with 28 regional offices makes CUP well postured to effectively conduct this assessment.

Budget Request: $66,240. With the demonstrated concern that you've shown in the delivery of police services to minorities, we are requesting a grant of $66,240. Quite frankly, this project extends beyond the financial boundaries of CUP. Accordingly, we must now reach out to the community for assistance in what surely is a vital service to the police community. The outcome of this project will touch the operations of over 6,000 law enforcement groups nationwide, results in an $13 investment in each existing municipal and state police organization, or a cost of seven cents (7¢) per police official.

SAMPLE LETTER PROPOSAL #1

EXHIBIT 26

In making this investment, the Law Enforcement Foundation will be supporting a cost-effective approach to the delivery of police services for the minority communities where major problems exist. Ms. Jane O'Connor, National Program Director for CUP, can be reached at (202) 123-4567 or oconnor@cup.org to answer questions or give further information.

Sincerely,

Organizational Heavyweight

P.S. Come visit us and see for yourself how this project helps people in need

Enclosure: Attachment A: Project Planner
Attachment B: IRS Nonprofit Certification

SAMPLE LETTER PROPOSAL #1

EXHIBIT 26 (continued from p. 72)

The project planner is a combination of a time-and-task chart (Chapter 9) and a budget (Chapter 12). For a complete copy of Attachment A, cited above, see Exhibit 36, page 110, for specifics.

COMPLETE LETTER PROPOSAL #2

Exhibit 27 shows a first draft of a letter proposal to a private foundation seeking support for developmentally disabled adults. Like all first drafts, it contains some good points and some rough spots. As you write your first draft, concentrate on getting it down, not on getting it good; your revisions will improve proposal content and format. Read the draft and the critique that follows. Finally, compare it to the improved version of the proposal that follows.

Critique of Letter Proposal #2

This 272-word proposal opens with a good summary statement, although the uniqueness phrase lacks punch. The greenhouse is abruptly introduced in the second paragraph without a meaningful context for mentioning it. Paragraph subheaders would enhance the skimming quality of the proposal. The statement of need focuses on the applicant's need for greenhouse facilities rather than the training needs of the developmentally disabled; the greenhouse is a means to help the trainees reach their full potential. The broad network base is important and well worth additional emphasis. The budget request of $10,000 is confusing in light of the introductory paragraph that mentions $250,000. In reality, the applicant is requesting the sponsor to contribute $10,000 toward a $250,000 total, but that is not clear from the proposal. To lower the $66 per adult figure, recalculate it in terms of instructional costs per hour. The benefit to the sponsor is unclear. Proposal readability is increased with the use of additional line spacing between paragraphs and subheaders in a different font. Overall, the proposal is too brief and should be expanded slightly. On the basis of these observations, the proposal was rewritten and expanded to 596 words, as shown in Exhibit 28.

LETTER PROPOSAL EXAMPLE #3

Exhibit 29 is a 648-word letter proposal to a private foundation seeking support for a geriatric project to centralize the delivery of services. It is organized, highly readable, and contains the essential information.

LETTER PROPOSAL EXAMPLE #4

As another example, Exhibit 30 is a 731-word letter proposal to a private foundation seeking support for a rural community-based health prevention and promotion project.

USE WITH PRIVATE SPONSOR GUIDELINES

So far, this chapter has focused on how to write a letter proposal to private foundations and corporations who **do not** have particular guidelines to follow. And this is the case for most—but not all—of them. This chapter now concludes with strategies for writing proposals to private sponsors when they **do** have submission guidelines to be followed.

Today's Date

Mr. Charles Nelson, President
Big Job Foundation
123 Any Street
Hometown, TX 08173

Dear Mr. Nelson:

St. Mary's School, the only private institution in the state providing training to developmentally disabled adults, invites your investment in a $250,000 job training project.

We are encouraged that the Big Job Foundation invests 33 percent of its contributions in social service and welfare projects within Texas. You will be interested in the St. Mary's Greenhouse because you care that young men and women with disabilities find meaningful employment.

St. Mary's School strives to supply mentally retarded individuals with the vocational skills and work habits required to find a prospective job. To meet this challenge, we must be equipped with a functional and realistic work setting in the form of a greenhouse.

Groups of 50 mentally retarded people will be challenged at the St. Mary's Greenhouse and prepared for possible employment within the greater community. Many will be placed in competitive work settings. Presently, St. Mary's clientele represent 35 states.

This project continues a systematic approach of St. Mary's prior efforts in "mainstreaming," where we have transformed vision into success since 1904.

With the proven concern that the Big Job Foundation has shown in this area, I request a grant in the amount of $10,000. This represents an investment of $66 in every adult that will receive training in the next five years.

I can assure you that your investment in St. Mary's School will greatly assist us in perpetuating excellent vocational training opportunities for future productive workers. Please come and visit us and see for yourself how important this project is.

Mrs. Cheryl Scott, St. Mary's Director of Development, can be reached at (915) 555-1212 to answer questions or give further information.

Sincerely,

Sr. Josephine
Administrator

FIRST DRAFT OF LETTER PROPOSAL #2

EXHIBIT 27

Today's Date

Mr. Charles Nelson, President
Big Job Foundation
123 Any Street
Hometown, TX 08173

Dear Mr. Nelson:

St. Mary's School, the only private faith-based center for adults with developmental disabilities in Texas, invites your investment in a $10,000 vocational education project.

The Big Job Foundation invests more than one-third of its contributions in social service projects for people with disabilities. Because of your unprecedented concern for the welfare of the developmentally disabled, we turn to the Big Job Foundation for its support to expand vocational training services for a special needs population.

The Problem: The Gap between Competence and Performance. One of people's great needs is the ability to achieve, and through achievement, experience psychological and financial growth. Developmentally disabled adults have limited aspirations and lost choices. Right now, only 15 percent of those capable of holding gainful employment have paying jobs. The challenge for this special needs population is to identify important work environments where they can develop and nourish job skills.

People with disabilities can work independently in only a handful of job environments. As a result, they can seldom put their limited talents to full use and rarely experience job satisfaction commensurate with their abilities. Since the number of developmentally disabled people is growing faster than the general population, the need for job training is escalating as more of them experience this competence—performance gap.

The Solution: Job Training in Plant Care. This project will close the competence—performance gap by training developmentally disabled adults in the care of plants and flowers. Two major factors justify this horticultural project. First, the results of our needs assessment documents that greenhouse owners are willing to hire such people if they can work reliably. Second, a 12-month pilot project with six developmentally disabled adults demonstrated that with proper training, these individuals can achieve functional independence.

St. Mary's has a greenhouse and a three-person groundskeeper crew to maintain the appearance of our 20-acre facility. The botanical expertise already resides at the School where the staff has a collective 79 years of greenhouse experience in such things as soil analysis, seeds, germination conditions, watering, fertilization, planting and pruning.

Credential: Botany Expertise and Job Networks. This project naturally grows out of our philosophy of maximizing existing resources. The current greenhouse also represents a botanical learning laboratory, where special people can be trained in a nonthreatening environment. The staff has developed specific learning objectives for each botany area. Administrators have secured agreements for tentative job placement sites as Attachment One shows. According, this project resents a systematic approach of St. Mary's prior efforts in "mainstreaming," by which we have transformed vision into success since 1904.

Budget Request: $10,000. With the demonstrated concern that the Big Job Foundation has shown in this area, we are requested a grant of $10,000. This represents an investment of $0.04 per hour in the 350 developmentally disabled adults who will use the greenhouse over the next five years. The funds will be used to purchase additional gardening tools (shovels, hoses, watering systems) in order to create 20 worksites. In making this investment the Foundation will be supporting a cost-effective approach to the delivery of vocation training for the developmentally disabled. Such a grant will assure the quality and regularity of the botany training program; more important, it will enrich many lives and, indirectly, create taxpayers, not tax takers.

REVISED LETTER PROPOSAL #2

EXHIBIT 28

Your support will make a critical difference, one that will last for years as job training services expand. Most of all, you will be investing in the ideas that will help exceptional people for decades. Please contact Mrs. Cheryl Scott, Director of Development, at 915-555-1212 or Scott@stmarys.org to answer questions or provide additional information.

Sincerely,

Organizational Heavyweight

P.S. Come visit us and let Randy tell you about his flower garden.

Enclosures
      Attachment One: Tentative Job Placement Sites
      Attachment Two: IRS Tax Exempt Certification

REVISED LETTER PROPOSAL #2

EXHIBIT 28 (continued from p. 75)

Today's Date

Mr. Gray American, President
Senior Foundation
123 Any Street
Somewhere, TN 40239

Dear Mr. American:

The Roxbury Elder Institute, the largest hospital-based senior service system in Memphis, invites your investment in a $100,000 special project to centralize 50 elderly services.

We are encouraged that the Senior Foundation supports innovative projects that improve the delivery of elderly services. Over 69 percent of your grant dollars the past three years have been invested at the local community level. Clearly, your support fills a valuable niche in light of the more conservative and traditional federal government funding. This strong commitment to unique projects is shared by our 35 professional staff members at Roxbury who have a cumulative 348 years of service to the elderly.

The Problem: Fragmented Services and Multiple Vendors. The elderly population is growing older. By the year 2000, half of this population is projected to be over age 75. Elderly women now outnumber elderly men three to two. This disparity is even higher at age 85 and older, where there are only 40 men for every 100 women.

According to the National Center for Health Statistics, 20 percent of the elderly use one or more community health services. The most commonly used services were those provided outside the home rather than in the home. The most widely used service was senior center, then congregate meals, followed by special transportation.

Their needs extend to information and referral, legal assistance, counseling, housing and employment services, outpatient rehabilitation and physical therapy, case management, and social and recreational activities. Gaining access to these specialists involves many trips to different locations.

The Solution: One-Stop Shopping and a Few Vendors. Current research verifies that seniors prefer "one-stop shopping" and dealing with only a few vendors. Specifically, about two-thirds prefer purchasing additional products or services from the same vendor rather than dealing with different ones. The goal of this project is to consolidate a broad range of deliverables designed to meet the needs of older adults and their caregivers. The delivery of these services will be characterized by consistency of quality, accessibility, and single-source reliability. The composition and utilization of these services will be determined by the needs of the individual. The consumer is advised on the best utilization of the services as a result of an intake evaluation and needs assessment. The program offers flexibility to select from a menu of services.

LETTER PROPOSAL #3

EXHIBIT 29

Roxbury Elder Institute Credentials: Senior Service Experiences. The Roxbury Elder Institute is uniquely positioned to develop an integrated system of medical and nonhealth services. The Institute was established six years ago with its goal to provide quality health, education, and research services. As a result, it has established a full range of services in response to the seniors' needs. During this time, positive working relationships have been established with all sectors of business.

These working relations will provide entrees to develop the nonmedical component. This project represents a systematic continuation of prior efforts to establish a diversified continuum of services and the vision to reallocate existing resources to meet the needs of the older clients.

Budget Request: $100,000 payable over three years. With the demonstrated concern that you have shown in the delivery of senior services, I am requesting a grant in the amount of $100,000, payable in thirds over three years. Quite frankly, this project extends beyond the financial boundaries of the Roxbury Elder Institute. Accordingly we must now reach out to the community for assistance in what surely is a vital service to seniors. In making this investment, The Senior Foundation will be supporting a cost-effective, client-sensitive service that will address major access problems. More precisely, our 10,000 senior citizens average 10 health-related visits per year; your support represents an investment of 20¢ per patient visit.

Please come visit us and see for yourself how important this project is – and how your support will truly make a difference. Ms. Beatrice J. Hiccock, Administrative Director of the Roxbury Elder Institute, can be reached at 615-456-7890 to answer questions or give further information.

Sincerely,

Shandel Lear
President

LETTER PROPOSAL #3

EXHIBIT 29 (continued from p. 76)

Today's Date

Mr. Wayne Curry
Executive Director
Nebraska Children's Charities
Omaha, NE 85031

Dear Mr. Curry:

Nebraska Hospital System (NHS), the only statewide hospital system delivering community health services to rural Nebraska, invites your investment in a $25,000 dissemination project to improve community health status and enhance the quality of life among rural poor and vulnerable families.

We are encouraged that the Nebraska Children's Charities has demonstrated a deep concern for children and their families. Your support will play a catalytic role in efforts to help nurture and challenge ideas that are locally developed, but have gained regional prominence. We share your commitment to making rural communities a better place to live.

The 1990s: Rural Community Health Problems and Solutions. In the early 1990s, rural Nebraska faced some serious community health problems: underweight births, birth defects, infant mortality, illegitimate births, adolescent pregnancy, abortions, and physician under representation. In this health provider shortage area, underweight births and adolescent pregnancy were 33% higher than the statewide average. The psychological ramifications of these community health problems were lost aspirations and limited choices.

To address these problems directly, the NHS marshaled concerned community citizens in support of a plan of responsible community volunteer action. The result was a community task force known as Children and Families Support Network. The Support Network program has been very successful over the last three years, as evidenced by Attachment One.

LETTER PROPOSAL #4

EXHIBIT 30

The 2000s: The Growing Need for Replication. The program's success has, quite frankly, caused another problem. We are receiving many requests (over 2000 in the past year) from other communities seeking information on how to establish their own Support Network program. These requests have accelerated since the Nebraska Legislative Task Force cited us as a model program in May 2000. Since the program operates without paid employees or funding, we must rely on support from external sources to prepare an information tool that will share our "secrets of success." Currently, a growing gap exists between our requests for information and our ability to provide that information to those who also face serious rural community health problems.

The Solution: Videotaped Information Dissemination. To close the growing information gap, we propose to create a videotape that will tell the Support Network story: how we got started, how to generate community support, what works and what doesn't, and how to start a similar program in other communities. By reason of its Network story: how we got started, how to generate community support, what works and what doesn't, and how to start a similar program in other communities. By reason of its multiplier effect, education is one of the most constructive longer-term approaches to ameliorating community health problems.

Technical expertise and production will be provided by the Instruction Media Center at Creighton University. The instructional content and overall production will be administered by Mr. Harold Bates, Director, Cook County Office, Nebraska Department of Human Services. He will be assisted by Robert Bannon, Instructor, Cook County High School. (See resumes in Attachment Two.) A Leadership Training Manual will accompany the videotape. It will serve as a follow-up resource guide for leaders in other communities wishing to implement a similar Support Network program. The target dissemination audiences will include Nebraska school administrators and public health professionals in the state s rural communities. The enclosed Time and Task Chart (Attachment Three) describes in detail how the needs will be solved.

NHS has played a catalytic role in launching the Support Network Program. It has a track record of success as evidenced by Attachment Four, which compares a three-year average before and after the onset of the Support Network activities. Note in particular that the most alarming county public health facts clustered around adolescent pregnancy issues. It seemed as if babies were producing babies instead of completing their education and joining the work force, especially in the service-oriented industries. The proposed information dissemination project represents a systematic continuation of our prior efforts in the public health area where we've transformed vision into success.

Budget Request: $25,000. Based on your expressed interest in rural health, we are requesting a grant in the amount of $25,000. If 50 schools with estimated enrollments of 500 students start similar programs next year, this would represent an investment of 20 cents in every student who will be exposed to the Support Network program in the next five years. Such a gift from the Nebraska Children's Charities will assure the quality and regularity of the Support Network program and enrich the lives of all whom the program reaches.

I can assure you that this project has the highest level of support throughout the community because it will assist us in perpetuating a unique community-based program. Please contact Mr. Bates at 308-111-7777 to answer any questions or give further information.

Sincerely,

Dwayne Buck
NHS Administrator

Enclosures:
    Attachment One: Support Network Brochure
    Attachment Two: Harold Bates and Robert Bannon Resumes
    Attachment Three: Time and Task Chart
    Attachment Four: Before/After Comparison Graph
    Attachment Five: NHS Tax Exempt Certification

LETTER PROPOSAL #4

EXHIBIT 30 (continued from page 77)

Today's Date

Federal Emergency Management Agency
USFA Grant Program Technical Assistance Center
16825 South Seton Avenue
Emmitsburg, MD 21727-8898

RE: FIRE Grant Proposal
Northshore (WI) Fire District

Dear Colleague:

Northshore Fire District (NFD), Milwaukee's suburban community with the greatest population density, invites your investment of $50,000 in a fire prevention project for the frail minority elderly.

Enclosed you will find the required original and two copies of our proposal, entitled PROJECT FIRE. As you review specific details in the accompanying proposal, you will note in particular the following:

- The frail minority elderly represents the most rapidly growing – and most at-risk – segment of our community population.
- The existing firefighting staff have had limited experience in interacting with the target population and their special needs.
- There is a growing need for a culturally sensitive fire prevention program that will decrease exposure of the minority elderly to fire hazards while, at the same time, increase their fire safety.

Accordingly, this proposal offers dual benefits to: (1) firefighters, through customized training and access to essential resources; and, (2) citizens, through installing and training in fire detection devices.

The proposed program is decidedly cost beneficial to firefighters and the community alike. All direct firefighters will participate in PROJECT FIRE at a nominal opportunity cost, while 1000 citizens will benefit at a one-penny per hour cost, amortized over a five-year product life.

NFD is uniquely postured to conduct this project, which is similar to an early project targeting at-risk youth, a project recognized by the Governor of Wisconsin as a "model youth fire safety project." However, given the population size at risk among the frail minority elder, this proposed project simply extends beyond the financial boundaries of the community. For this reason, we reach out to FEMA in providing essential services to a worthy, deserving, and needy population.

Sincerely,

Organization Heavyweight

LETTER PROPOSAL ADAPTATION AS TRANSMITTAL LETTER

EXHIBIT 31

A growing number of foundations use what is called a "common application form," a phrase that can be used in your favorite search engine to find current examples used in larger cities. Some states have also developed one form that many foundations use statewide; a similar movement exists at the national level. More precisely the National Network of Grantmakers, an organization of grantmakers committed to social justice and philanthropic reform, has developed a common application form, which is available at www.nng.org. It consists of five pages: a cover letter, participating funders list, cover sheet, narrative instructions, and budget page.

Whether the sponsor requires use of a common application form or has a unique one, you can adapt the letter proposal format described above to serve as a transmittal letter. Sometimes, a sponsor's guidelines may be constraining, not letting you advance all of the information you think will present your strongest proposal. Accordingly, the transmittal letter approach enables you to supplement the sponsor's guidelines with additional important information. An example of a letter proposal adapted as a transmittal letter appears in Exhibit 31.

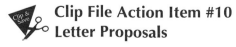

Clip File Action Item #10
Letter Proposals

Start your Letter Proposals clip file by doing the following:

- Select two letter proposals from this chapter and create electronic copies as models.

- Add an electronic copy of a letter proposal used as a transmittal letter (see Exhibit 31).
- Choose sample electronic paragraphs for all seven sections of a letter proposal that can be edited and adapted as you write your next one.

Time Saver Tip #8
Procrastination

No time available? To stop procrastinating, carve out 30 minutes from your existing time. If you want to do it, you'll find the time.

- Arrive early tomorrow.
- Close the door during lunch.
- Schedule an appointment with yourself.

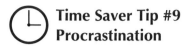

Time Saver Tip #9
Procrastination

To stop procrastinating, look at your work space. Perhaps it's simply not convenient. Rearrange it. Clear your work area of everything but your proposal documents so your eyes don't wander.

- Clear your desktop.
- File papers.
- Color-code project folders.

PART III
Writing Government Proposals
Preview of Part III

A complete government proposal usually requires substantial detail; most include nine basic sections. The following table lists those sections in the sequence in which proposal reviewers typically read them as well as the sequence in which proposal writers usually write them; these are not the same.

Proposal Reviewer Sequence	Proposal Writer Sequence
Abstract or Summary (Chapter 14)	Need or Problem (Chapter 7)
Introduction (Chapter 6)	Goals, Objectives and Outcomes (Chapter 8)
Need or Problem (Chapter 7)	Methods (Chapter 9)
Goals, Objectives and Outcomes (Chapter 8)	Evaluation (Chapter 10)
Methods (Chapter 9)	Dissemination (Chapter 11)
Evaluation (Chapter 10)	Budget (Chapter 12)
Dissemination (Chapter 11)	Appendixes (Chapter 13)
Budget (Chapter 12)	Introduction (Chapter 6)
Appendixes (Chapter 13)	Abstract or Summary (Chapter 14)

The reviewer column shows the way in which most proposals are assembled for mailing; the writer column shows the progression followed when authoring a government proposal. For example, to begin writing your proposal, start with the need section first.

In contrast to proposals to private sponsors, which typically involve two to five pages, a complete government proposal to a local, state, or federal agency may range from 10 double-spaced pages to 100+ single-spaced pages. Some government agencies use a two-tier application process; that is, they initially require a short proposal of all applicants, and those writing proposals of greatest interest are invited to submit longer and more detailed proposals. The U.S. Department of Education Fund for the Improvement of Post-Secondary Education (FIPSE) is one example of an agency that uses the two-tier application process.

Part III discusses each proposal section and its following elements:

- Purpose
- Key questions to answer as you begin writing
- Examples from successful grant proposals
- Writing tips
- Rejection reasons from actual proposals that were declined

Not all public proposals require all of these sections, so you should follow your grant guidelines. Finally, successful grantwriters sometimes include valuable information, even if it in not requested. For example, if no dissemination discussion is requested, include it in your methods section. If no needs statement is called for, include it when you introduce your agency's mission.

CHAPTER 6
The Proposal Introduction

The beginning is the most important part of the work.

Plato

PURPOSE OF THE INTRODUCTION STATEMENT

Since grantseekers seldom receive grants without applying, it's important to get started now on your next proposal, as Plato implies.

The introductory section establishes the context of your proposal. More precisely, the introduction establishes the credibility of your project personnel, your organization and your idea. Your qualifications, or credibility, may contribute more to you being funded than anything else. Sponsors will not award you money if they believe you will not be a good steward of their funds. If the application guidelines do not ask for an introductory section, you should include your credibility statements in your methodology section, indicating that you have prior experience and expertise that will transfer to this project.

In essence, the introductory section should communicate your uniqueness. Your uniqueness should be reflected in your mission statement because it explains how you are different from other organizations.

KEY QUESTIONS TO ANSWER

As you write the introduction section, answer these questions. Does it

1. Establish clearly who you are?
2. Describe your organizational goals?
3. Establish your credibility in the project topic area?
4. Lead logically to the problem statement?

When writing an introductory section, many beginning grantwriters err by writing too much text that focuses on their own organization: its history, mission, organizational structure, accomplishments, and so forth. In contrast, experienced grantwriters focus on the sponsor's priorities and emphasize how their own mission matches up with the values of the sponsor.

TYPES OF INTRODUCTION STATEMENTS

Four different types of introductions are used in writing to a sponsor: a summary statement, a philosophy statement, an historical statement, and crisis statement.

Summary Statement

The summary statement tells who, what, where, when, and why. In newspaper fashion, it presents the basic facts of the proposal in a succinct manner. It is perhaps the most common approach in writing introductory statements. More precisely, a lead paragraph or two outlines the high points of the proposal and is followed by one or two "so what" sections that explain the proposal background and significance. Finally, elaboration follows, either chronologically or in descending order of importance.

The following paragraphs are from a summary introduction in a drug rehabilitation proposal submitted to a vocational rehabilitation agency:

> This proposal requests $50,000 to refurbish the Drug Abuse Treatment Center at St. Michael's Hospital, Knoxville, Tennessee. Refurbishment of the physical environment is vital to reflect the positive self-esteem so needed by recovering drug abusers and to comply with the environmental standards of the Joint Commission on

Accreditation of Hospital Organizations Standards for Drug Abuse Programs.

As a long-term supporter of alcohol and drug rehabilitation, you know, better than many, the complexities and challenges that recovering addicts face. Since 1960, our Treatment Center has dedicated itself to serving those individuals with lost hopes and limited aspirations. While we have an established track record of providing successful treatment—over 500 in the past decade—our patient dismissal interviews repeatedly point to our decaying physical facilities as a treatment barrier. Accordingly, we seek a joint partnership with the Division of Vocational Rehabilitation to improve and expand our outreach services.

Philosophy Statement

The statement of philosophy is used to convince sponsors that you and they think alike, an especially useful approach with innovative projects. If your organizational philosophy has changed or is misunderstood, this strategy is a good approach. On the other hand, if your philosophical statement doesn't match with the sponsor's or you have misread the sponsor's values, you risk creating troublesome psychological noise and proposal rejection. Consider this philosophical introductory statement from a children's social service agency to a government-based family welfare program.

All children have the right to physical, emotional, and education support and care in order to realize their full potential.
The Kent County Children's Counsel has adopted this statement as its goal for all children throughout the county. We are concerned about the spiraling gap between the competence and performance levels of today's youth, as evidenced by rising juvenile delinquency rates, increased school absenteeism, and the growing numbers of battered youth.
Since the philosophy underpinning the Counsel's activities corresponds with the mission of the Agency for Family and Children's Services, we seek an opportunity to pool mutual fiscal and personnel resources to help local youth realize—as our mission statement says—"their full potential."

Historical Statement

The historical statement is used to indicate that you are uniquely able to carry out a proposed project be-

cause you have special ability or an established track record to solve problems like the one you are proposing. You can also use this approach if you are making a "comeback" from a "rocky road." A brief example follows.

The Wayne County Museum of Detroit, Michigan, was founded in 1879 to preserve the history of the area from the time of the Native Americans to the present. Numerous Native American artifacts are displayed along with the Native American history of the area. These exhibits are followed by the pioneer displays with history and articles that are from or duplicate those used by the early pioneer settlers in the area. Many of the original land deeds and early written documents are preserved and are on display. In 1940, another wing was added to the original museum building to store and display more of the historical documents and artifacts that were donated by the county when the old county building was razed and a new building built. In 1960, the entire museum was renovated with revenue-sharing funds from the city and federal government. This revenue stream served the Museum well through the mid-1980s.
The last 15 years have produced a systematic decline in Museum revenues, to the point that its future is uncertain. The nationwide fluctuations in the economy have been particularly exacerbated in a community so heavily dependent on the automotive industry, which has had to counterattack rising labor costs, restrictive trade barriers, diminishing consumer demand, escalating steel prices, and shrinking distribution channels.
While the Museum's rocky road has been well publicized in the mass media, the untold story today is our dramatic turnaround. Subscriptions are up by 25%. A new marketing plan is reaching out to a wider audience. Attendance has systematically increased by more than 10% in each of the last two years. In essence, we have "bottomed out" and started on the upswing. Unfortunately, we lack the resources to sustain our recovery and now reach out to the Institute of Museum Services for valuable and timely assistance.

Crisis Statement

The crisis statement is intended to immediately involve the sponsor in the need to fund your program. It is a "shotgun" approach, taken with direct aim and risking an all-or-nothing approach. It must communicate a sense of urgency while avoiding overkill. The following example was submitted by an urban housing welfare organization to a county Department of Housing.

Rising utility costs are causing a major crisis in Lake County due to a 25 percent increase over the past six months. From last October to May, a total of 483 families—including 600 adults and 900 children, one-half under age three—received shut-off notices, according to the local gas and electric company. Utility experts predict this number will increase during the coming winter.

The utility company predictions are based upon comprehensive meteorological analyses. While long-term weather forecasts are not always reliable, specialists do agree the weather will be severe; they only differ on the severity of the inclement weather. At a minimum, they conclude that 483 families will be adversely affected—again.

Unfortunately, the utility company prediction models do not reflect the 17% increase in Hispanic population in the community over the past year, due mostly to the opening of two large manufacturing firms. With the increased community population, many of whom are in the lower socioeconomic status, the actual number of families to receive shut-off notices is likely to climb to 575. With the first frost just around the corner, the time to act is now, and for this reason, the Safe Places Agency turns to the Department of Housing for what is—without exaggeration—life-saving assistance to worthy and needy families.

EXAMPLES FROM GRANT PROPOSALS

Environmental Engineering Proposal Introduction

The following introductory section is from a proposal written by a group of environmental engineers in a research institute that was concerned about preventing zebra mussels from clogging public water systems. Their proposal was submitted to a federal environmental protection agency.

The introduction of the zebra mussel, *Dreissena polymorpha,* in North American inland waters will have a significant impact on both municipal and industrial water intake and distribution systems. The greatest impact will be due to fouling of surfaces by adult mussels. These fouling

problems can also create conditions that will stimulate corrosion of the underlying substratum. Methods used to control fouling by zebra mussels have largely involved chemical and/or physical measures, many of which are expensive or not environmentally acceptable.

The use of electrical methods to control the distribution of mussels has included electric currents and pulse fields. One type of electrical method that has not been explored in the control of zebra mussels is the use of continuous high-voltage electrostatic fields with strengths of several kilovolts per centimeter and no electric current except for the extremely low leakage (stray) currents in the nanoampere range. These types of fields have been shown to adversely affect a number of different microorganisms. This method of control of zebra mussels will have uses in protecting municipal and industrial water intake structures and conduits.

This proposal will cover the effects of these high-voltage electrostatic fields on zebra mussel larvae and adults and on nontarget plankton organisms. Experiments will be conducted in the laboratory under both static and flowing conditions, and in the field situation in the Great Lakes. These investigations will provide important information on a new safe and cost-effective method for the control of zebra mussel attachment on municipal and industrial structures. If settling stage veligers do not attach while under the influence of high voltage electrostatic fields, the flow of water will carry the veligers past the protected structure.

Humanities Proposal Introduction

The next example comes from a curriculum development proposal submitted by a university history department to the National Endowment for the Humanities. The first paragraph describes the university. The second paragraph describes the academic housing for the humanities at Midwest University, including introductory perspectives on the History Department.

This request for a $1 million challenge grant arises from an academic environment deeply rooted in the humanities. Founded in 1881, Midwest University is a private institution of higher learning located in Chicago. It is committed to undergraduate, professional, and graduate education, as well as scholarly research. The University now consists of 13 colleges, schools, and programs. The Midwest campus encompasses 37 buildings on 64 acres. The enrollment of 13,900 students represents all 50 states and 37 foreign countries. Their academic achievement is guided by 535 full-time and 366 part-time faculty scholars.

Midwest's College of Liberal Arts, the largest of the university's thirteen colleges, houses all humanities curricula as well as the Departments of Biology, Chemistry, Mathematics, and Physics. Within this fold is the Department of History, which confers Bachelor of Arts, Master of Arts, and Doctor of Philosophy degrees. The department boasts the university's strongest reputation for scholarship and teaching excellence. The 19-member history faculty includes such people as Drs. Smith, Jones, and Prucha. Seven members of the current history faculty have received the coveted Outstanding Teacher Award bestowed annually by the university president. Student evaluations regularly place the department in the top five campuswide for teaching excellence. The History Department has ranked first in this category for the last two academic years. It frequently collaborates with colleagues in theology, philosophy, English, and foreign languages regarding interdisciplinary degrees and scholarly research.

Bioethics Proposal Introduction

This biomedical ethics proposal involving collaboration between two health care organizations was submitted to a federal health care agency. The introductory paragraphs draw the parameters around the ethical dimensions of health care. Note how the last paragraph foreshadows the next proposal section namely the statement of the problem. The proposal reader can anticipate the reasoning that is forthcoming.

The study of ethics becomes increasingly vital as the nation struggles to reorient deeply held beliefs in the health sciences. Ethics are critical to all professional activities, to all situations of human responsibility, and to all disciplines leading to health and wellness.

Despite its centrality to health care, only about 20 percent of health professionals study the principles and applications of ethical decision-making. The ethical dilemmas that students and practitioners face are becoming more complex in all areas of life. Much of this complexity stems from the sheer volume of ethics information within disciplines, the lack of information exchange across disciplines, and the proliferation of new medical technologies. The impact of new medical technology on social values still awaits study. Although the social significance of medical management is far-reaching, clinicians have yet to devote themselves to the ethical dimensions of health care as they have to the mastery of new health care technologies.

Medical technology advances pose enormous ethical dilemmas surrounding the treatment of patients in a range of circumstances and ages. Examples include issues of nontreatment, withdrawal of life support, rights of individuals to decline treatment, and genetic therapy. Concerns about rising costs raise questions about the "rationing" of health care. Who will receive medical care and of what type? Who will make these choices? How will they be made? The evolution of technology in our society, and the evolution of society itself, demand that these issues become an integral part of the clinical decision-making process.

Ethics are central to medical education and patient management programs. With the trend toward compartmentalized education, specialization, and technological expertise, the crucial and oftentimes neglected role of ethics in medical education is becoming ever more troublesome. Colleges and universities produce students who are proficient in technical skills but deficient in a sound knowledge of the ethical dimensions of the human condition. The lack of a shared ethical perspective undermines both the collectivity of humanity and the opportunity to build future achievements on the accomplishments of the past.

Clinicians face difficult ethical decisions whenever they attempt to balance the cost and quality of health care delivery. The social evolution of medicine has involved an ever-increasing participation by patients and their families. The rapid expansion of diagnostic and therapeutic possibilities has created circumstances that provide new challenges to the value systems within our society.

The field of clinical ethics includes an ever-expanding base of information derived from research studies, case examples, legal decisions, and legislative acts. The issues addressed are of concern to physicians and other health care workers, to patients and their families, and to both the professional and lay members of hospital ethics committees. A need exists to collate available information and to provide access to it for the many groups who require it. This necessity poses another challenge for information technology. It also demands that communication networks be established that allow ethics specialists and ethics committees to share experiences regionally and nationally.

This introductory section lays the groundwork for presenting a needs argument to establish a clearinghouse for information on ethical decision making.

WRITING TIPS FOR INTRODUCTION

1. Consider this section as a credibility statement about you and your environment.
2. Your resumé is an important credibility statement, particularly in government proposals. However, it may not communicate the fact that you work in an environment conductive to your project. Weave this point into your introduction.
3. Tell the reviewer about your track record in similar projects.
4. If you don't have a strong track record in your proposed project area, borrow credibility from other field experts through the use of project consultants, letters of endorsement, and supporting statistics.
5. Explain how this project fits into your overall organizational goals.
6. In many proposals, the introductory section contains some "boilerplate" language; that is, it contains standard descriptive language about your organization and its mission. Experienced proposal writers have several versions of boilerplate that can be quickly retrieved from a computer clip file and inserted into proposals—edited, of course, for the values of the sponsor. Your boilerplate is based upon your mission statement, annual reports, endorsements from experts, bibliographies, resumés, organizational self-assessment tools, and other documents that help establish your credibility.

REJECTION REASONS

The language used below is taken directly from rejection notices on federal grants. These rejection reasons imply flaws in writing the introductory section.

1. The applicants propose to enter a research area for which they are not adequately trained.
2. The reviewers do not have sufficient confidence in the applicants to approve the present applica-

tion, which is largely based on the past efforts of the applicants.
3. The investigators will be required to devote too much time to teaching or other nonresearch duties.
4. Better liaison is needed with colleagues in collateral disciplines.
5. The proposal narrative does not describe how the applicant was selected to be the lead agency in this collaborative effort.
6. Although individual agencies have experience serving the target population, this is a relatively new collaborative venture without an established track record of success. Their admission on page three does little to inspire confidence: "This proposal represents the first time that the service providers in the target area have collaborated to create a holistic and efficient referral system."
7. It is doubtful that new or useful information will result from the project.
8. The basic hypothesis is unsound.

All these comments suggest credibility problems for the applicants. Specifically, four dimensions of credibility are cited as insufficient: training, track record, effort, and interdisciplinary coordination. Establish your organization's uniqueness and credibility in the introduction.

Clip File Action Item #11 Establishing Your Uniqueness

Follow these uniqueness clip file ideas to identify your organizational niche.

- Use the Web to find out how to write a mission statement. Using the key words "mission statement" in your favorite search engine may produce links to the following Web site, which will help you get started writing your mission statement: http://management.about.com/smallbusiness/management/library/howto/ht_stmt.htm.
- Collect mission statements from other organizations to help you carve out your unique organizational position. This address will turn up some mission statements from other organizations: http://www.nonprofits.org/npofaq/keywords/1/in.html.
- Your endorsements from experts and self-assessment tools will help you identify uniqueness ideas to add to your clip file.

Clip File Action Item #12
Developing Proposal Introductions

These additions to your clip file will simplify writing introductory statements in proposals. Specifically, gather the following:

- Current organizational mission statement
- Latest copy of annual report
- One-page fact sheet describing your organization
- List of significant organizational milestones
- Copies of favorable publicity

 **Time Saver Tip #10**
Procrastination

To stop procrastinating, tell others what your deadline is. You'll be more motivated to meet it. "John, I'm determined to finish this proposal by Friday noon and I'm wearing my tunnel vision glasses."

CHAPTER 7
Statement of the Problem

A problem is a chance for you to do your best.
Duke Ellington

PURPOSE OF THE PROBLEM STATEMENT

For Duke Ellington, a problem was music to his ears. To grantseekers, your problem or need represents a gap between what exists presently and what could exist in the future—and your chance to orchestrate closing the gap. The problem section of your proposal describes the gap as it is now and indicates that your project outcomes will produce desirable changes. It should be

- Supported by evidence drawn from your experience, from statistics provided by authoritative sources and from appropriate literature reviews.
- Of reasonable dimensions, something that could be realistically done in the course of a grant.

In essence, a persuasive problem statement indicates the extent of the current problem, its frequency and severity, and the shortcomings of the present situation.

Beginning grantwriters often make the mistake of writing or describing the gap from *their* perspective.

- "We lack sufficient resources to serve our needy population: the frail elderly."
- "We need to strengthen our ability to instill core liberal arts skills in our graduates."
- "Our agency needs sufficient operating support to meet our growing client demands."

Unfortunately, these sentences all share one common problem: they are written from the perspective of the applicant, not the sponsor. Notice the use of pronouns like "we" and "our."

Experienced grantwriters avoid the self-focus and instead concentrate on the sponsor's needs when writing a statement of the problem. Seasoned grantwriters recognize that sponsors won't fund you because *you* have a need; rather, they will fund you because *they* have a need that you can fill as a change agent to solve a problem.

Another mistake of beginning grantwriters is to describe an opportunity instead of a problem. They reason, "Our organization doesn't really have a problem. We see grants as an opportunity to expand our outreach into the community."

In response, consider why sponsors might want to fund you. They award grants to solve problems. Indeed, it's their mission to solve societal problems. Opportunities focus on you, your wants, and your needs. Sponsors don't necessarily perceive your wants or needs to be their needs. Problems, on the other hand, represent the reasons behind your proposal. Sponsors fund you because they believe that your project will help them fill their need to close gaps in society. Funding you helps them to fill their mission. In other words, there are no solutions to opportunities, only to problems. When you write your next proposal, be sure you present the sponsor with a problem, not an opportunity.

Let's take a closer look at the difference between your needs and the sponsors'. If you ask a group of grant applicants why they are seeking funding, they provide you with commonly self-serving answers. In contrast, if you ask sponsors why they award grants, they offer quite different answers, as shown in Exhibit 32.

The two columns are quite different. Proposal writers who base their problem statement on the first column of needs severely limit their likelihood of getting funded, as the above examples did. A more successful approach would be to frame your need statement from the perspective of the sponsor. When sponsors see you

Applicant Needs	Sponsor Needs
• Ensure operating support	• Solve a societal need
• Expand services	• Fulfill existing mission
• Acquire new training materials	• Acquire new knowledge
• Make capital improvements	• Apply existing knowledge
• Purchase new technology	• Improve the community
• Obtain endowment funding	• Benefit from tax write-offs
• Support existing programs	• Increase name recognition
• Meet payroll costs	• Ensure a big bang for the buck
• Market services	• Help people
• Acquire new physical space	• Fill a gap in community services
• Run a conference	• Improve public image
• Conduct research	• Avoid loss
• Sustain operations	• Develop new products or systems

COMPARISON OF APPLICANT AND SPONSOR NEEDS

EXHIBIT 32

share their "values glasses," you increase your likelihood of getting funded.

In essence, this section of your proposal should quickly summarize the problem from the vantage point of the sponsor as revealed through your preproposal contacts (Chapter 4), show your familiarity with prior research or work on the problem, reinforce your credibility for investigating the problem, and justify why this problem should be investigated. Do not assume that everyone sees the problem as clearly as you do. Even if the problem is obvious, your reviewers want to know how clearly you can state it.

IMPORTANCE OF THE PROBLEM STATEMENT

The statement of the problem is the single most important section of your proposal that influences funding success.

The importance of the problem section in your proposal cannot be overestimated. It provides the rationale or motivation for conducting your project. It explains why your project is necessary. If you cannot provide a convincing statement of need, then there is no justification for proceeding.

The statement of the problem is so important in proposals that it should be stressed regardless of the point value assigned to it in the reviewer's evaluation form. That is, even when the reviewer's evaluation form allocates only a small percentage of the total allowable points to the problem section, you should consider this to be the most important proposal section because it will weigh most heavily in the minds of reviewers.

DEFINITION OF A PROBLEM

A problem or need is a gap, a discrepancy between the way things are and the way things ought to be. This gap provides the justification for how you address the problem. In general terms, you are painting a verbal portrait of the unacceptable conditions that exist today. Further, these conditions will worsen in the long term. Fortunately, you have a solution to reverse the problem and reduce or fill the need.

In specific terms, there are many dimensions to a need or problem: financial, personnel, technological, physical, service, training, policy, and so forth. Chapter 4 detailed four types of questions:

1. *Position*: What are the baseline situations, present circumstances, and basic facts?
2. *Rationale*: What are the problems, needs, and injustices that exist today?
3. *Expectation*: What are the implications for addressing these problems?
4. *Priority*: What approaches are most likely to lead to an improved situation now?

All four categories of questions try to do one thing: pinpoint the multiple dimensions of the need. Experienced grantwriters often use these questions as a guide to writing their problem section in proposals. For instance, consider the following preproposal question: What are some of the biggest dissatisfactions with the current approaches to this problem?

From the answers gleaned during preproposal contacts, a university-based grantseeker writing a proposal to secure funding for minority scholarships might write the following introductory sentence in a problem statement:

> There are three major dissatisfactions with the current approaches to recruiting minority students. First, the lack of financial aid is a major recruitment barrier; most minority students cannot attend college without financial support. Second, few institutions have a cultural infrastructure conducive to minority students; all minority students need peer relationships and social interactions with other minorities. Third, at most institutions, a multicultural student body is instructed by a monocultural professoriate. All three sources of dissatisfaction—financial aid, peer group, professorial ethnicity—present formidable barriers to recruiting minority students. The following sections of this proposal explain these barriers in greater detail and present a unique solution to existing problems.

KEY QUESTIONS TO ANSWER

As you write your statement of problem or need, answer these questions. Does your proposal do the following:

1. Contain citations to ongoing studies as well as earlier project findings?
2. Convey the focus of your project early in the narrative?
3. Create the theoretical or conceptual base for your project?
4. Demonstrate a precise understanding of the need you propose to solve?
5. Encourage the reviewer to read further?
6. Establish the importance and significance of the problem from the sponsor's perspective?
7. Explain why your problem should be of special interest to the sponsor?
8. Include appropriate statistical data?
9. Indicate how the problem relates to your organizational goals?
10. Justify why your particular focus has been chosen?
11. Make it obvious that your problem is solvable?
12. Point out the relationship of your project to a larger set of problems or issues?
13. Provide a rationale for your project's objectives and methods?
14. Show how your project will build on prior efforts?
15. Signify the potential generalizability and contribution of your project?
16. Specify clearly what is not addressed by your project?
17. Spell out the conditions you wish to change?
18. State the problem and outcomes in terms of human needs and societal benefits?
19. Supply an appropriate and compelling introduction to the rest of the application?
20. Define the gaps in existing programs and service?
21. Explain what is lacking or missing in the present shortcomings in delivery of services?
22. Identify barriers to services and programs?
23. Clarify what will happen if nothing is done about this problem?
24. Pinpoint the primary and secondary target populations?
25. Define the geographical area of the target population?
26. Discuss the types of data needed to outline the problem? Look at Clip File Action Item # 2 in Chapter 1 for ideas on how to redefine your project; each redefinition category suggests another type of data with which to document your problem.

Use this list both as a guide to develop your statement of the need and as a checklist to critique your draft, making sure you have included all essential elements.

EXAMPLES OF PROBLEM STATEMENTS

As you read the following examples, note the repeated emphasis on two points:

1. The frequency and severity of the current problem or need
2. The failure of the status quo to address the need

Example 1

This example is taken from an application for a research proposal submitted to a social and rehabilitation service agency to evaluate the comparative effectiveness of different types of service and income maintenance programs. This short excerpt is included to show you an approach for tying the statement of need at the local level to an interest of the funding agency itself.

> The national investment in social welfare demonstration projects continues to expand, yet the local consequences of these projects on client and family functioning have been only partially evaluated. Without careful assessment, the relative merits of any given project will be lost or incorrectly estimated while errors may be repeated if the project serves as a prototype.
>
> A favorable set of conditions allowing a careful assessment has arisen in a demonstration project jointly sponsored by the Bureau of Health and Family Services and the Department of Public Welfare. The State Department of Public Welfare has created four groups of AFDC clients who will receive various combinations of increased services assistance.

The gap in this example is the information void between national activities and local impact.

Example 2

This research proposal establishes the need for a new type of automotive engine. During preproposal contact, the sponsor requested heavy use of statistics to document the need.

> Energy, that nebulous term describing what few understand and rarely see, is universally agreed upon as wasted. Diminishing fossil fuel supplies and increasing production costs have prompted energy-conscious designs in the area of automotive transportation. Transportation consumes 55 percent of all petroleum used in the United States, with automotive travel consuming 85 percent of the fuel used by the transportation mode.
>
> Statistics indicate that the 150 million automobiles registered in the United States in 2000 consumed 78 billion gallons of fuel, an average of only 15.72 miles per gallon (MPG), due in large part to the popularity of sports utility vehicles. This low MPG figure reflects the fact that of the 1 trillion miles traveled, approximately 60% were driven on urban streets. It is in this urban stop-and-go driving environment where the engine is least efficient. For example, an au-

tomobile that weighs 3,000 pounds dissipates 90,186 foot-pounds of energy every time it decelerates from 30 miles per hour to a dead stop. In accelerating from this dead stop up to 30 miles per hour, not only are 90,186 foot-pounds of energy required, but because of the demand on the engine, the torque is increased dramatically, thereby decreasing the engine efficiency and increasing fuel consumption.

The gap here is the discrepancy between the national need for energy conservation and high automotive fuel consumption. Additionally, this excerpt shows how (1) a proposal can quickly summarize the problem and orient the reader to a more elaborate discussion, and (2) statistical data can be included without breaking up the flow of the narrative.

Example 3

This research proposal suggests a new way to produce a substance thought to cure certain types of cancer.

> Convincing evidence exists that interferon is a powerful antiviral and antitumor substance. Wide medical application of interferon therapy will depend upon production of large quantities at a price the public can afford. It is doubtful whether the current technology of cell culture will be economical enough to allow mass production of this material. Other alternatives include organic syntheses or productive insertion of the interferon gene into microorganisms. The proposed research offers a lead to both procedures, thereby opening the door to application of interferon therapy beyond a few clinical trials. Success in any one of the steps outlined in this proposal would be a major breakthrough in achieving progress toward eventual use of interferon in the treatment of human disease.
>
> Human interferon has only recently been obtained in preparations approaching homogeneity. The amounts of such highly purified preparations, available only in the laboratories where they have been produced, are exceedingly small. Partially purified preparations of human interferon, on the other hand, are commercially available.

The gap here is that current technologies cannot produce sufficient quantities of crucial medication. This proposal need section went on to delimit the specific topic and show its possible contribution. The sentences are short and use simple syntactic structures, making it easy for a reviewer to follow a technical topic.

Example 4

In the following a social service agency seeks foundation funding to expand its outreach to underserved people:

> Although the Family Crisis Center is currently operating at near capacity, the Center intends to reach more fully those families who are underserved. This group includes minority citizens, senior citizens, and individuals with disabilities. While approximately 5 percent of the general population in our catchment area uses the service of the Center, minorities and others do not traditionally use our services. In addition, the newly appointed Coordinator for Community Outreach Services has identified for the first time the community's population with disabilities—a potential new target group for specialized services.

The gap is the Center's disparity between its heavy service demands and its need to serve other clients. This problem statement is unpersuasive because it focuses on the needs of the Center: the need to add more staffing so it can do a better job of serving underserved families. A more persuasive approach would concentrate on the needs of the underserved, as the following rewritten example indicates.

> Inner city, urban living—what some would call ghetto survival—is stressful. As evidence, all social service agencies report heavy demands for social services, and many have lengthy waiting lists. The primary users of social services are families with more than high school educations and above average socioeconomic status.
>
> Unfortunately, three major community groups are notably underrepresented among social service agencies: minorities, seniors, and the handicapped. Each group faces special stressors that are further exacerbated by their urban environment. Most social service agencies have a monocultural staff and need to serve a multicultural clientele. Seniors face transportation barriers in traveling through what they perceive to be risky neighborhoods to receive various medical services. The handicapped face substantial architectural barriers in moving through urban neighborhoods.
>
> Since the Faith and Justice Foundation and the Family Crisis Center share the same mission of serving the needs of all community residents, we invite your investment in the following project.

This revised problem statement refocuses the gap on the inconsistency between the service needs of special populations and their ability to obtain those services.

Example 5

In the following a health care agency seeks funding for a Sudden Infant Death syndrome proposal to a private foundation. Note how the needs data addresses (1) quantifiable incidences of the problem and (2) the inadequacy of the current system to address the need.

> From 1995 through 2000 three hundred infants in California have died of Sudden Infant Death Syndrome. Another 227 died suddenly and unexpectedly. Our Sudden Infant Death Center has noted that there is more reluctance on the part of coroners and medical examiners to use the SIDS diagnosis as a cause of death if there is co-sleeping, stomach sleeping, or a child under one month of age or over six months of age. Designation of the cause of death by overlying, asphyxia, or the designation *sudden infant death* compounds the families' fears, adds to the complexity of these cases, and has challenged the nurses' ability to deal effectively with the families. A critical component of the services offered to families includes home visits by a local public health nurse. Input from public health nurses indicates that many feel the need for more training in order to work effectively with bereaved families.
>
> The home visits include a grief assessment, referral to community resources, and an opportunity to clarify any questions or concerns they have regarding the death of their baby. Families are invited to participate in an epidemiological questionnaire that seeks information about the mother's history of pregnancies, family health history, and information regarding the infant's health and the circumstances of the death. The questions are asked to gain information about the current practices of families regarding the health of their infant and the practices utilized by the family in the care of their infant, especially related to risk factors for SIDS. The information is helpful in understanding the factors that may have contributed to the death of the infants, and it is necessary information for the program and the state to utilize in determining programming needs and the distribution of limited resources.
>
> A recent family satisfaction survey indicates that 22% of bereaved families rated the public health nurse visits as bothersome or not helpful and indicated their belief that there is a need for more extensive public health nurse training. Only 25% found the public health nurse visit to be very helpful. In comparison 59% rated the counselors' calls as very helpful. One of the performance benchmarks of the program is data re-

ceived from public health nurse interviews. The number of interviews has been steadily decreasing, thereby inhibiting the nurses' capacity to improve their ability to complete the interview in an effective and compassionate manner. Finally, feedback from evaluations received from public health nurses in previous training reinforces the need and request for further training. This grant would allow the Center to provide the training at no charge to the local health departments and at a location close to their service area, which will encourage attendance.

Example 6

A hospital-based bioethics proposal submitted to a federal health care agency uses subheaders to help organize the various dimensions of the overall problem statement:

Overview of Need for Bioethical Sensitivity. While the relevance and rectitude of ethics in medicine are indisputable, their extent and form produce far less agreement. Ethics often has a second-class status in medical school training and subsequent patient management; both situations add to the ethical insensitivity prevalent in the contemporary world. Moreover, the complexities of the human condition require specialized and applied knowledge. The following paragraphs elaborate on the multiple dimensions of the need for this project.

Growing Insensitivity to Ethical Issues. The world has been described as becoming increasingly amoral. The prevalence of major ethical problems in the popular press, such as gambling among athletes, swindles in the ministry, or political sex scandals, underscore a lack of ethical sensitivity. Although the mass media has made the public well aware of the ethical problems of these celebrities, the scope of the problems in bioethics is less popularized but more prevalent.

- Use of an artificial heart as a bridge to transplant
- Economic dilemmas in ethical decision making
- Involuntary medical detention
- Withdrawal of feeding tube
- Forgoing CPR in elderly patients

In reality, many clinicians encounter these ethical decisions, and others, on a daily basis. Relegating ethics to a second-class status in medical training programs and practice, in effect, contributes to our society's lack of ethical awareness. Certainly, colleges and universities need a more salient and explicit focus on the le-

gitimacy of ethics to nurture the moral sensitivity of its students and of its local community.

Conflicting Trends in Biomedical Ethics. The study of ethics has become increasingly compartmentalized and applied, with specialists in such areas as nursing ethics, physician ethics, and patient ethics. These targeted emphases are notably deficient in the study of the theoretical principles of ethical decision making. Ironically, the 'technologizing' of ethics education has developed at the same time as a renewed national emphasis on holistic medicine.

In an analysis of trends in ethics, Marcus Singer noted, "The first thing to be said about ethics in this day and place is that it is different—different from what it was and has been and in the process of becoming what it is going to be. Philosophers automatically think of ethics as identical with moral philosophy. But there is a sense of ethics gaining currency in which it is not a branch of philosophy, in which ethics is regarded as a new, independent (yet interdisciplinary) subject, exercising the skills of physicians, psychologists, lawyers, economists, sociologists, scientists, and others who would not normally think of themselves as doing philosophy."

Distortion of Ethics Studies by Specialization. Ethics has a sweeping interdisciplinary nature with a multifaceted relevance to theoretical, characterological, professional, and theological domains. Consequently, the clinical application of ethical principles cannot be limited to a single discipline without producing a restricted and distorted sense of ethics. This constrained focus divorces ethics from its true richness as a central facet of the human experience and from the history of human intellectual and spiritual achievement. As one ethicist recently argued, "Is there one unitary discipline, ethics, somehow involved in these otherwise apparently diverse areas of environment—ecology, science, medicine, biology, engineering, technology, law, government, and business? This is not a question that can be answered merely a priori and in advance; it must wait for reasonable settlement until each of these areas has been explored further and until a better grasp than we have now is achieved of the underlying structure of ethical or moral problems in each of these areas of human endeavors."

AVOID CIRCULAR PROPOSAL LOGIC

Proposal writers often seek funding for new equipment, e.g., computers or highly technical research instruments. The proposal logic often argues as follows:

> The problem is that our institution lacks (and therefore needs) some new computer equipment. The objective of our proposal is to acquire the computer equipment. Our implementation strategy is to plan to acquire the equipment and put it to good use. Our evaluation plan will be to find out if we acquired and used the equipment.

This example used circular logic to form its problem statement; no real need was established first, the starting point for proposals. A much stronger approach would have been as follows:

> The problem is that our students' failure rate is too high in five key courses. Our activity objective is to decrease the failure rate from 40% to 30% in the next three years. Our implementation strategy, chosen from among many, is to acquire some new computer equipment. Our evaluation plan will focus on our implementation plan execution and will see if the failure rate decreases.

The lack of something does not justify acquisition: that's circular logic. Note that the revised example quantifies a problem, thereby creating a need that can be addressed in other proposal portions.

WRITING TIPS FOR THE PROBLEM SECTION

1. Describe the problem, its causes, and the consequences if it is not addressed.
2. Describe the need in human terms. For example, if you want to buy computers for your school, talk about the need to train computer-literate students. If you want to buy a van for your health clinic, talk about the transportation barriers that patients encounter when getting access to the health care to which they are entitled.
3. Review the preproposal contact questions in Chapter 4. They are all focused on pinpointing the need. They follow a logical progression from the baseline position to the existing rationale, future expectations, and the priorities that lead to the needs.
4. In your literature review, check on currently funded but unpublished research-in-progress. Contact the National Technical Information Service. This is a clearinghouse for recently initiated projects that will provide you with information at a nominal charge and indicate who might be doing something similar to what you propose. Its Web site address is www.ntis.gov.

5. Beyond discussing the importance of the project's topic, you should also demonstrate the need for your methodology; that is, the reviewers should be able to anticipate your solution based upon your analysis of the problem. The ability to foreshadow a solution from the problem statement represents a very logical, fluent writing technique.
6. Don't say "little is known about . . . ," "there is a lack of information about . . . ," or "no research dealt with . . . " Arguing for something that *isn't* is a weak need statement. Go one step further: Explain the consequences of the information void. So you don't know something about this problem So what?
7. Your problem section is the "sad" section of the proposal. Use appropriate "sad" words: *almost, barrier, below, bleak, bottom, decreased, deficit, dependent, depressed, desperate, destitute, disadvantaged, discouraged, disheartened, hurdle, disregarded, disruption, distressed, failed, gloomy, grim, harsh, highest, high-risk, hopeless, ignore, impaired, inadequate, increased, infested, lacking, less than, lowest, minimum, miserable, needy, neglect, obstacle, outbreak, overlooked, pathetic, pitiful, plagued, poorest, poverty, severe, sparse, substandard, trapped, unacceptable, violent, widespread, worst.*
8. Five major federal agencies collect, analyze, and disseminate data on virtually all aspects of society and its individuals. Web addresses are provided in Exhibit 33.

The national "fact finders" in Exhibit 33 are rich with data that are useful in most proposals. Beyond these federal agencies, consider approaching local and regional health planning councils; city, county, or regional planning departments; vocational rehabilitation agencies; crisis centers in your field; law enforcement and judicial departments; chambers of commerce; universities (libraries, academic departments, computer centers, and research offices); national associations; other grantees; United Way (community resource file); and development departments in state and local governments. Don't overlook your state and federal legislators. They survive in large part by providing constituency services. They can help you find government reports on your project topics.

REJECTION REASONS

Reviewers have rejected some proposals for the following reasons:

Agency	Web Address
Bureau of the Census -- general	www.census.gov
Bureau of the Census – data sets	factfinder.census.gov
Bureau of Justice Statistics	www.ojp.usdoj.gov/bjs
Bureau of Labor Statistics	stats.bls.gov
National Center on Education Statistics	nces.ed.gov
National Center for Health Statistics	www.cdc.gov/nchs/Default.htm

FEDERAL DATA COLLECTION AGENCIES

EXHIBIT 33

1. The problems to be investigated are more complex than the applicants realize.
2. The applicants need to acquire greater familiarity with the pertinent literature.
3. It is doubtful that new or useful information will result from the project.
4. The basic hypothesis is unsound.
5. The proposed research is scientifically premature; the supporting knowledge is inadequate.
6. The relationship of rationale to regional needs is not clearly delineated.
7. Some significant efforts in the state are not mentioned in the rationale.
8. The rationale is heavily based on local needs rather than regional impact.
9. The demographic analysis is not developed; implications are not explored.
10. Overall rationale is inadequate. Evidence to support training and patient care needs specific to this state is lacking.
11. The project director appears to lack knowledge of published relevant work in this area.
12. The project co-directors fail to present an acceptable scientific rationale for conducting this project.
13. The proposal narrative often relies on state-level data to justify local needs.
14. The problem statement should be twofold: identify and quantify the health care needs of the community, and discuss the inadequacies of the current system to address these needs.
15. Although the proposal targets expansion in year 2 to address mental health services and transportation issues, there is no discussion of the quantifiable need for such services.

16. This proposal offers no evidence of a formal needs assessment to identify and prioritize community needs. What sources were used to determine and prioritize the most important needs? Did this assessment solicit community input in identifying, defining, and assessing their needs?
17. The proposal does not quantify or support its claim that "The need for mental health services is great within the community."
18. This project doesn't explain why the needs of this subpopulation are greater than the needs of other community residents.
19. The applicants have great theories unsubstantiated by data.

In each case, the reviewers have serious reservations about the credibility of the investigators and/or the chosen topic area. After you write your problem statement in your next proposal, reread these rejection reasons and see if any of them cause you to say "ouch."

 **Clip File Action Item #13
Statement of Problem or Need**

Fill your clip file with data documenting the frequency and severity of the problem you propose to solve in ways that meet your sponsor's needs, not yours. Follow this tip: Sources of data include surveys, statistical analyses, key informants, community forums, case studies, legislative bureaus and officials, universities, community agencies, professional associations, crisis centers, chambers of commerce, planning commissions, and clearinghouses.

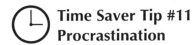

Time Saver Tip #11
Procrastination

To stop procrastinating, set small deadlines for yourself. Break big projects into small, manageable units. Example: to build a needs argument,

- Web surf for primary literature review.
- Use search engines (Chapter 17) to find documenting statistics.
- Check Bureau of Labor Statistics Web site.

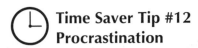

Time Saver Tip #12
Procrastination

To stop procrastinating, reward yourself after meeting each small deadline. What's your favorite treat? A five-minute power nap? Visit to a favorite joke Web site? A walk around the building?

CHAPTER 8
Goals, Objectives, and Outcomes

*Those who cannot tell what they desire or expect, still sigh
and struggle with indefinite thoughts and vast wishes.*
Ralph Waldo Emerson

OVERVIEW

Once your problem statement is clearly described (Chapter 7), your next step is to identify how you intend to solve the problem. You express your solution in terms of goals, objectives, methods, and outcomes. Goals—your Emersonian desires and expectations—represent long-range benefits, usually painted in broad-brush strokes; objectives are specific, measurable activities that will help you achieve your goals; methods (Chapter 9) are the detailed steps that you will follow to achieve your objectives; outcomes are the humanistic results of your project (Chapter 10). Clearly, an intimate relationship exists among goals, objectives, methods, and outcomes; completing your methods helps you to meet your objectives, which, in turn, allows you to achieve your goals and outcomes in order to solve an identified problem.

PURPOSE OF GOALS

Your project goals represent the idealized dream of what you want to accomplish. They are usually presented in terms of hopes, wishes, or desires. Goals project the "big picture" vision of what you wish to accomplish. They communicate global purposes. Typical goal-oriented words include *appreciate, understand, advocate, analyze, illustrate, participate, integrate,* or *recommend.* For instance, a recent health education proposal included four goal statements:

- To analyze the special needs of underserved populations and to develop new programs to meet those needs
- To extend services to underserved target populations
- To improve the quality of services while experiencing an increased demand for those services
- To integrate new educational materials for special focus programs

Although these are valuable goals, they cannot stand by themselves. They need to be followed by concrete, measurable objectives.

PURPOSE OF OBJECTIVES

Your objectives specify the end products of your project. When sponsors fund your project, they are literally "buying" your objectives. That's why it is extremely important to state your objectives in clear and measurable terms.

When you write your objectives, follow the acronymic advice: "Keep them S-I-M-P-L-E."—Specific, Immediate, Measurable, Practical, Logical, and Evaluable. Your objectives should be:

- *Specific.* Show precisely what you intend to change through your project. What will be different when your project is finished? What will people be able to do once the project is completed that they couldn't do before?

- *Immediate*. Indicate the time frame during which a current problem will be addressed. Why should the project be acted on right now? How long will it take to achieve your goals and objectives?
- *Measurable*. Specify what you would accept as proof of project success. What qualitative and quantitative data will you gather? What tools will you use to measure project success?
- *Practical*. Point out how each objective is a real solution to a real problem. Are your objectives realistic and feasible? Does your organization have the skill, experience, qualifications, resources, and personnel to carry out each objective?
- *Logical*. Describe how each objective systematically contributes to achieving your overall goal(s). Are you really doing what you think you're doing? Do your objectives relate to your goal and the sponsor's priorities?
- *Evaluable*. Define how much change has to occur for the project to be effective. What are your criteria for success? What impact will your project make? What is the value of your project?

Although these categories are not mutually exclusive, each of your objectives should meet at least several of these criteria.

For instance, given the goal of "improving the quality of life for homeless individuals in our city," a proposal objective might be stated as follows:

> Midwest Home Shelter Agency will reduce the number of homeless [Specific] [Practical] [Logical] during the next 24 months [Immediate] by 15 percent [Evaluable] as noted in the Department of Social Welfare Homeless Survey Report [Measurable].

The following example of a goal and its objectives is taken from a demonstration project submitted to the U.S. Department of Education. The objective has several parts that meet each of the six criteria, with some overlap.

> Goal. This program is designed to prepare parents to function independently and effectively in helping their children develop to their own potentials.
>
> Objectives. During the next 18 months [Immediate] the parents who participate in the program will be able to [Specific] do the following:

- identify the education content in the events that occur in the home [Logical]

- structure sequential and cumulative instructional tasks in the home for the child [Logical]
- observe the child and use checklists to monitor progress [Measurable]
- use available equipment and processes in the home to teach children specific skills [Evaluable]
- use packaged materials prepared by the project or other agencies in teaching specific skills [Practical]

Your objectives section is the intellectual heart of the proposal because you indicate precisely what you intend to change through your project and what you would accept as proof of project success for your target population. Your objectives represent the yardstick with which to evaluate your proposal results; that is, if you write your objectives in precise, measurable terms, it is easy to write your proposal evaluation section because you know exactly what will be evaluated.

PURPOSE OF OUTCOMES

Outcomes are the benefits, changes, or effects that occur to the target population as a result of participation in your project. Outcomes express project results in humanistic terms; they are the desired changes in people's knowledge, skills, attitudes, or behaviors. Identifying outcomes means going beyond outlining how the project will operate to describing how participants will be able to think, do, act, or behave differently by the conclusion of your project.

In the increasingly competitive world of grantseeking, accountability is key. Sponsors want to know that their funds are being spent wisely and that your project is really making a difference in the lives of people—hence, outcomes. Your proposal must balance process and outcome statements. Process statements answer "What?" What are you going to do? Outcome statements answer the question "So what?" What are the benefits of this project to the target population?

Consider the following pairs of statements. The first of each describes a process, and the second describes an outcome.

Process: Provide firefighters with new communications and personal protective equipment.

Outcome: Firefighters will increase coordinated service delivery to the community and decrease average response times.

Process: Conduct 10 cultural sensitivity training courses.

Outcome: Employees will respect and value diversity.

Process: Enroll 6,000 at-risk youth in summer school classes.

Outcome: Students' academic performance will improve.

Process: Provide 10,000 free meals to low-income senior citizens.

Outcome: Senior citizens are able to remain in independent living.

Process: Have 60 undergraduate university students contribute a total of 3,600 hours to service learning projects at the Hispanic Community Center.

Outcome #1: Students will make real world connections to the local community through service, educational outreach, and employment.

Outcome #2: Continuing education adults at the Hispanic Community Center will earn their General Educational Development (GED) diplomas.

Process: Distribute 25,000 "So You're Having A Baby" educational packets to pediatric physicians' offices.

Outcome #1: Teen mothers will immunize their babies by age 2.

Outcome #2: Teen mothers will understand the value of breastfeeding their babies during the first year of life.

Outcome #3: Teen mothers will not have a repeat pregnancy until after age 18.

The final two examples illustrate that even when projects appear on the surface to be similar, they may in fact target very different outcomes. That's why before you develop intervention strategies, you must identify outcomes that will be meaningful to your project. Outcomes borrowed from or imposed by individuals external to your organization are unlikely to be valuable to your efforts. Chapter 10 takes a closer look at evaluation and outcomes, including outcome indicators—specific characteristics selected for measurement to demonstrate success in achieving project outcomes.

KEY QUESTIONS TO ANSWER

Answer these key questions as you write your proposal objectives. Does your proposal do the following:

1. Clearly describe your project's objectives, hypotheses, and/or research questions?
2. Signal project objectives without burying them in a morass of narrative?
3. Demonstrate that your objectives are important, significant, and timely?
4. Include objectives that comprehensively describe the intended outcomes of the project?
5. Include objectives that are well-written, concise, and clear?
6. Demonstrate that your objectives flow logically from the statement of need?
7. Directly address the chosen problem?
8. State your objectives in a way that they can later be evaluated or tested?
9. Demonstrate why your project outcomes are appropriate and important to the sponsor?
10. Detail your project's hypotheses with conceptual clarity and sufficient documentation?
11. Justify that the project's outcomes are manageable and feasible?
12. Reflect the need for the project and show clearly its purpose and direction?
13. Include one or more objectives for each need discussed in the problem statement?
14. Propose objectives that are realistic and appropriate?
15. State objectives in terms of outcomes and not methods or activities?
16. Describe the population that will benefit?
17. State the time by which the objectives will be accomplished?

EXAMPLES OF OBJECTIVES

Example 1

The following example of a goal and four objectives is taken from a demonstration project submitted to the U.S. Department of Education:

> **Goal.** This program is designed to attract qualified minority students to graduate education programs.
>
> **Objectives.** By October 31, 2004, the students who participate in the program will be able to
>
> - identify graduate education pathways commensurate with their interests and aptitudes
> - locate five appropriate sources of financial aid to support their educational program
> - establish a supportive relationship with a faculty mentor
> - seek and gain meaningful employment

Example 2

A counseling center proposal to the National Institutes of Mental Health cites both goals and objectives:

Goal #1: To identify the special needs of underserved populations (minorities, commuter students, women, returning adult students, and people with disabilities) and to develop new programs to meet those needs.

Objective #1: By March 15, 2004, the paraprofessionals will assess the needs of the target group through the Environmental Assessment Survey program and develop new programs based on these needs.

Goal #2: To extend Counseling Center services to underserved target populations (minorities, commuter students, women, returning adult students, and people with disabilities).

Objective #2: By June 1, 2004, the paraprofessionals will develop a 30-minute slide/tape orientation to their counseling services and conduct six special orientation sessions for target populations.

Goal #3: To maintain the quality of Counseling Center services while experiencing an increased demand for those services.

Objective #3: By September 15, 2004, the 12 new paraprofessionals will be trained to serve as technicians in the area of biofeedback and stress management.

Goal #4: To develop new educational materials for special focus programs.

Objective #4: By October 31, 2004, the paraprofessional staff will develop six psychosocial dramas to be used to facilitate awareness in problem areas such as racial awareness and alcohol.

Example 3

A chemistry research proposal to the National Institutes of Health. The application form uses the language "Specific Aims," which means the same as "Objectives."

Specific Aims: Considerable attention has recently been focused on the use of phospholipid bilayer vesicles as a means for encapsulating and delivering antitumor agents to neoplastic cells. Although there have been some encouraging signs, the ultimate therapeutic value of this technique remains unclear. The basic premise underlying this proposal is that carriers of the type currently being examined have limited potential and that new ones need to be developed which are more stable and offer better control over drug delivery. Our immediate chemical objective is to synthesize and characterize four new classes of phospholipid carriers within the next two years. One carrier is based on vesicles whose lipids contain two polar head groups, each of which is covalently attached to the terminal positions of a rigid hydrocarbon chain.

Based on close analogy with surfactant analogs recently described in the literature, these molecules should yield monolayer phospholipid vesicles. A second type of carrier is based on vesicles comprised of phospholipid dimers covalently coupled at the polar head group. The third and fourth classes of carriers we propose are polymerized forms of micelles and vesicles, and are termed, ultrastable micelles and ultrastable vesicles. Each of the above has been specifically designed to equip the drug delivery vehicle with (1) greater intrinsic stability, (2) slower and more controllable time-release action, (3) preferred endocytotic and adsorption modes of interaction with cells, and (4) greater targeting potential.

Example 4

A chemistry research proposal to the National Science Foundation uses questions as a technique for stating proposal objectives:

The chemistry of molecular oxygen compounds has been studied extensively. Yet a number of basic questions remain unanswered. This reality is particularly true for the electronic and vibrational spectra of these compounds. The questions we propose to address are

1. What is the range of $v(02)$ and its relationship with the M-02 (M: a metal) bond strength?
2. Does $v(02)$ reflect the effect of the axial and equatorial legends?
3. Where are the M-02 CT bonds responsible for the embracement of $v(02)$ and $v(MO)$ in resonance Raman spectroscopy?
4. Is it possible to prepare novel symmetrical, side-on adducts with large legends such as metalloporphyins?

The objectives of our systematic spectroscopic study are to examine the effects of molecular oxygen adducts on a number of $CO(11)$ chelates. The techniques employed include UV-visible, enforced, resonance Raman, and C-13 NMR spectroscopy.

Beyond the use of questions, note that the last two sentences serve as a transitional bridge to the methodology section. This approach provides continuity in a proposal that flows smoothly between sections.

Example 5

Health objectives from a cholesterol education program to a health-oriented private foundation. Notice how three different objectives are included for each of three different target populations:

> For the next twelve months, the objectives of the programs are as follows.

Health Professionals

> • To increase awareness among health professionals that elevated blood cholesterol is a cause of coronary heart disease, and that reducing elevated blood cholesterol levels will contribute to the reduction of coronary heart disease risk, as measured by the Healthy Heart Inventory.
> • To identify five techniques proven to reduce elevated blood cholesterol.

Public/Patient

> • To increase by three percent the number of Americans who have reduced their dietary intake of total fat, saturated fat, and cholesterol as part of a nutritionally adequate diet.
> • To increase the proportion of Americans who have their blood cholesterol measured by five percent.

Community

> • To increase by thirty percent the knowledge level among secondary school students with respect to blood cholesterol and cardiovascular risk factors as measured on pre- and post-tests.
> • To introduce ten worksite activities that will reduce elevated blood cholesterol levels.

Example 6

The National Hemophilia Foundation has published a series of goals and objectives. An example follows that establishes seven target objectives for a broad goal:

> **Goal:** Modern care for all persons affected by hemophilia, related bleeding disorders, and complications of those disorders or their treatment, including HIV infection. By the target date of July 1, 2004, seven objectives will be met.
>
> **Objective #1:** 90 percent of the identified persons with hemophilia at risk of HIV infection enrolled in comprehensive care programs will be tested for HIV status with appropriate pre- and post-test counseling, with maximum consideration to confidentiality.

> **Objective #2:** 80 percent of persons with hemophilia, all their identified sexual partners, and their families will be provided with comprehensive risk-reduction information and psychosocial counseling and support.
>
> **Objective #3:** hemophilia treatment centers will provide or facilitate all hemophilia and HIV-related medical and psychosocial care to sexual partners and offspring of persons with hemophilia, with consideration given to their independent needs.
>
> **Objective #4:** 90 percent of persons identified with severe hemophilia will have access to medically supervised home therapy.
>
> **Objective #5:** the evaluation and full development of a virus-free, nonthrombogenic factor IX product will be complete and available.
>
> **Objective #6:** FDA-approved virus-free vWD products will be available.
>
> **Objective #7:** FDA-approved recombinant factor VIII products will be available.

Example 7

A community health asthma management project to a private foundation:

> The goal of this project is to develop a sustainable strategy for asthma management in the community. By October 31, 2004, we will accomplish the following key objectives:
>
> • Significantly improve asthma-related qualify of life among children participating in coalition intervention activities
> • Reduce missed school and childcare days by 25% among children participating in coalition intervention activities
> • Reduce the number of children admitted for acute asthma at the Midwest Pediatric Hospital by 15%
> • Reduce the number of children making emergency visits for asthma to five area hospitals by 15%
> • Institutionalize the coalition and develop a financially sustainable strategy for childhood asthma control
>
> We recognize that measuring outcomes for some objectives will be more challenging than others—for example, asthma-related quality of life among children under age five. Thus, survey tools selected will balance statistical reliability, validity, and responsiveness; cultural relevance

and sensitivity; and be minimally burdensome for community members. Collectively, these objectives contribute to achieving our ultimate outcome goal: to control asthma in the county's high-risk pediatric population.

Example 8

A child safety proposal to a local corporation expresses objectives in terms of process activities. A subsequent paragraph defines humanistic outcomes for parents participating in the project.

Misuse of child safety seats is widespread. Although 95% of parents believe they install their child seat correctly, 80% of children are improperly restrained. The goal of this project is to enhance existing collaborative partnerships to prevent injuries to motor vehicle occupants. By December 31, 2003, we will accomplish the following objectives:

Objective #1: Offer car seat education to 500 parents attending birthing/prenatal classes at County Community Hospital.

Objective #2: Train 50 staff members at 10 pediatric offices in our county on the importance of using car seats properly and motor vehicle safety resources available within our county.

Objective #3: Create 10,000 educational packets to be distributed at birthing/prenatal classes and pediatric offices, promoting car seat safety checks and other community resources.

We will measure the intended effects that this program is trying to produce on parents' knowledge, attitudes, and behaviors. Specifically, the outcomes of this project are to enable parents to better identify, access, and use community resources that will help to prevent unintentional childhood injuries. Increasing parents' knowledge of community resources will motivate them to participate in car seat checks at local fitting stations, i.e., police stations, fire departments, and hospitals. Education provided at fitting stations, in turn, will prompt behavior changes so parents continue to install and use car seats correctly.

WRITING TIPS FOR OBJECTIVES

1. List your specific objectives in no more than one or two sentences each in approximate order of importance.

2. List your specific objectives in expected chronological order of achievement if you are submitting a phased proposal.
3. Avoid confusing your objectives (ends) with your methods (means). A good objective emphasizes what will be done and when it will be done, whereas a method explains how it will be done.
4. Include goal (ultimate) and objectives (immediate) statements.
5. Limit this proposal section to less than one page.
6. Use action verbs. The following table provides a few action verbs to get you started. Usually, the action verbs are written in the infinitive verb form, e.g., to advocate, to analyze, to anticipate.

• Advocate	• Coordinate	• Explain
• Analyze	• Decrease	• Illustrate
• Anticipate	• Demonstrate	• Increase
• Arrange	• Describe	• Integrate
• Assemble	• Design	• Investigate
• Assess	• Detect	• Measure
• Build	• Discover	• Motivate
• Categorize	• Discriminate	• Organize
• Classify	• Display	• Participate
• Compare	• Distinguish	• Quantify
• Conduct	• Establish	• Solve
• Construct	• Estimate	• Stimulate
• Contrast	• Evaluate	• Summarize

7. Still stuck? Take a computer-based tutorial on writing objectives: www.csus.edu/uccs/training/online/design/d_clear.htm

REJECTION REASONS

These common rejection reasons were noted in actual reviewers' critiques of rejected proposals.

1. The objectives are more like global purposes than specific, measurable, achievable activities.
2. The realism of some objectives is questionable.
3. Some of the objectives are confusing, nonspecific, not measurable, and clearly not appropriate to the purpose of the grant.
4. Objectives are general and stated as "activities"— thus nonmeasurable. It is unclear how activities will relate to the professions involved.
5. The project objectives are more comprehensive than covered by the methods.
6. Project objectives are vague, nonspecific, and difficult to measure. No targets are set in terms of faculty reached, trainees enrolled, disciplines involved.

7. The project outcomes are of limited significance.
8. The project outcomes are nebulous, diffuse, or unclear.

Clip File Action Item #14
Goals, Objectives, and Outcomes

These suggestions will get you started on building your Goals, Objectives, and Outcomes clip file:

- To build your Goals, Objectives, and Outcomes clip file, collect lists of well-written statements from other proposals, whether or not they are in your interest area. Often, clear statements of goals, objectives, and outcomes can be adapted to other proposal circumstances.

- Beyond successful proposals, many program announcements have carefully worded goal, objective, and outcome statements that can be added to your clip file.

CHAPTER 9
Methods

Vision without action is merely a dream. Action without vision just passes the time.

Vision with action can change the world.

Joel Arthur Barker

PURPOSE OF THE METHODS SECTION

Your methods are your action plan to reach your eventual dream. Your methods section tells how your project activities will accomplish your objectives, including your project sequence, flow, and interrelationships. In essence, your methods section—sometimes called "methodology," "plan," "statement of work," "approach," or "procedures"—tells **who** is going to do **what** and **when** it will be done. Each of these three components is discussed below, followed by an example, tips for getting started, and common proposal rejection reasons due to methodological errors.

KEY QUESTIONS TO ANSWER

Here are some key questions to answer. Does your proposal

1. Explain why you chose one methodological approach and not another?
2. Describe the major activities for reaching each objective?
3. Indicate the key project personnel who will carry out each activity?
4. Show the interrelationship among project activities?
5. Identify all project data that will be collected for use in evaluating proposal outcomes?

The Who: Key Personnel

There are three categories of key personnel in most projects:

- The **staff** who will be conducting the project
- The **subjects** participating in the project
- The **collaborators** outside of your organization who will join you in conducting the project

Each should be described in sufficient detail to establish credibility.

Project Staff

Name all key project staff, including consultants and subcontractors, in your proposal. If this is not possible, include job descriptions for the people you propose to hire. At a minimum, describe the major roles each will play, whether, they are already onboard or proposed to hire, e.g., responsible for overall project management, liaison with project collaborators, office manager, project fiscal officer, recruiter of project participants, volunteer coordinator, or evaluation specialist. Your appendixes should contain brief resumés (or job descriptions) that stress prior relevant training and experience that will transfer to the proposed project (see Chapter 13, Appendixes, for preparing resumés). Add the number of years your project staff has worked in this area and mention the total in your proposal:

> "Our project staff of six has a cumulative 119 years of experience in dealing with this nagging problem."

Project Subjects

Most—but not all—grant projects involve interaction with some target audience, usually called "subjects," "clients," "patients," or "participants" who are your ultimate focal point. Often these projects involve some research, training, or service delivery that interface with people. Your methods section should answer these basic questions, as suggested in the examples that follow.

1. How will you recruit and retain your subjects?

- "All patients seen in the emergency room during the past 12 months between the ages of six and 16 will be contacted to solicit their participation in this project."
- "All children with Iowa Reading Test Scores one standard deviation below their grade level will constitute the initial project subject pool."
- "Each project collaborator will refer 10 subjects for participation in this study."
- "To select the participants for this project, volunteers will be sought from local community welfare agencies. Additionally, a newspaper advertisement will invite interested participants to call our office, where screening questions will determine subject eligibility."

2. What are their basic geographic and socioeconomic characteristics?

- "All subjects must live within the four-county area and have access to transportation, to be compensated by the project."
- "All participants must have an income level of at least 150% below the federal poverty level."
- "To be eligible for participation in this study, the children must have received a grade of "D" or below in eighth grade algebra within the past 12 months and parental approval for participation in our "Math Rules and You're the Ruler" Project."
- "All volunteers must be members of a community Senior Citizens Center and hold a valid driver's license."

3. How long will they be involved in the project?

- "The subjects will participate in three two-hour focus group sessions."
- "The participants will participate in a 30 minute check-up once a month for 12 months in the Emergency Room at no cost to them."
- "To measure attitudes, the clients will take a 45 minute pencil and paper test asking questions about their opinions regarding spirituality: The Grace Hope Scale."
- "Both the experimental and control groups will participate in pre- and post-tests of motor coordination. In addition, the experimental group will receive six one-hour training sessions of eye-hand coordination training."

4. To what extent do special client issues need to be addressed, e.g., compromised health status, transportation barriers, restrictive home environments, unsafe neighborhoods, unfavorable publicity, controversial policies, or limited educational opportunities?

- "To ensure the clients physical health status is not compromised during the period of intense physical exertion, an emergency room physician will oversee all stress testing."
- "Since the After-School Project ends after sunset, our mobile vans will transport the students directly to their homes, rather than risk them walking home in unsafe neighborhoods."
- "Our physical facilities comply wholly with the American Disabilities Act; accordingly, our wheelchair clients will face no physical barriers entering the building or negotiating its interior."
- "Since our HIV clients could risk unfavorable publicity if they were identified by name, all records will use fictitious first names only, and only the project director will have the master list of record identifier numbers in order to ensure confidentiality and respect individual privacy."

Project Collaborators

Increasingly, sponsors encourage—and indeed expect—collaboration. Collaborations show a large "buy-in" to projects and increase the likelihood of sustainability beyond the granting period as project components are institutionalized.

There are many different models of collaboration. Four common collaboration models were described in Chapter 3: informal collaborations, consortia, interdisciplinary teams, and centers or institutes. They exist along a continuum from casual to formal relationships. Regardless of the level of formality, good business practices warrant reducing the understanding and agreements to writing. Picking collaborators is like picking a mate: you want to do it carefully, for it has long-term relationship and financial consequences. In essence, project collaborations are valuable for informing people, solving problems, and creating support.

Successful collaborations often entail many hours of meetings. Experienced grantseekers have learned through trial and error these tips for conducting effective grant collaborations:

- Limit the meeting to no more than 1.5 hours.
- Invite no more than nine people.
- Include the key players in the meeting; if they can't come, reschedule.

- Provide a two-week advance notice of the meeting.
- Distribute a detailed written agenda one week in advance of the meeting.
- Take thorough minutes.

The What: Project Activities

Justification of Methods

Each project will have its own unique set of methods, activities, tasks to accomplish the stated objectives. Whatever methods you deem appropriate for your project, justify their selection. You had choices and reviewers will want to know why you chose this approach and not another alternative. A few sentences of methodological justification prior to describing specific project activities will anticipate and answer an important question in the minds of the reviewers: "Of the universe of possible methodologies, why did you pick this one?"

- "The method of choice is to use a double-blind study; it is the only experimental design available that can isolate the effects of the independent variable on the project outcomes."
- "This project is using the Grace Hope Scale to measure spirituality since it is, according to the Buros's *Yearbook of Mental Measurements,* the only instrument with acceptable reliability, validity, and normative data for our target population."
- "Since no psychometric instrument exists to measure teenage attitudes toward learning a foreign language, according to the Buros's *Yearbook of Mental Measurements,* it is necessary for us to develop our own measurement instrument; Dr. Don Sprengel from the Department of Research Methodology at the local university has agreed to serve as a project consultant in this regard."
- "Since it is imperative that we have the broadest possible community input in the most cost-effective manner, our approach relies on the time-proven benefits of using focus groups, a survey procedure that the project director has used successfully in similar past situations."
- "Since research over the past 15 years documents that mentoring is the most cost-effective approach to integrating individuals with severe physical disabilities into the workplace, it is our preferred method to solve the existing needs."

Data Collection

You will probably need to collect some data as a part of your project. Common types and sources of data collection include those listed in Exhibit 34.

You can either construct your own data-gathering instruments or use existing ones. To find out if an appropriate instrument already exists (and avoid reinventing the wheel), consider looking through Buros's *Yearbook of Mental Measurements,* a two-volume listing of available tests in many different fields. More specifically, the Buros's volumes review the various attitude, behavior, and motor tests that are commercially available. Each review includes a description by the test author(s) and critiques by several experts in the field. The descriptions include the purpose, statistical characteristics, and, when available, the test norms. For example, if you are studying the relationship between spirituality and wellness, you could look in Buros's to see if any attitudinal measures of spirituality exist. The Buros's reference can be found in most libraries or on the Internet at www.unl.edu/buros.

Relationship of Objectives and Methods

Your objectives tell your reviewers **what** you propose to do. Your methods tell your reviewers **how** you will accomplish each objective. Put differently, you should include one or more methods for each objective. Use transitional language in your proposal to signal to the reviewers the relationship between your objectives and your methods, as this example does.

> To address the first objective, developing an Internet-based geriatric dentistry program, the following action items will occur:
>
> a. An Internet service provider will be selected, one with prior experience in mounting distance learning programs.
> b. The instructional modules will be storyboarded to flesh out content.
> c. The instructional designer will take our content and develop visually literate formats.
> d. The first draft will be checked for content accuracy and user friendliness.
> e. The revised draft will be tested out with 10 geriatric dentists around the country.
> f. Appropriate revisions will be made.
> g. The service provider will market the resulting distance learning program.

The When: Project Timelines

Time and Task Charts

The use of a time and task chart represents one common and successful means of clearly communicating the methods section in your proposal. This visual device segments your total project into manageable steps

• Achievement tests	• Government records	• Referral forms
• Archival information	• Historical program records	• Reviews of literature
• Attendance records	• Interviews	• Role-playing exercises
• Case histories	• Personal diaries or logs	• Searches of news media
• Clinical examinations	• Physical tests	• Surveys
• Controlled observations	• Psychological tests	• Telephone logs
• Daily program records	• Questionnaires	• Tracking slips
• Focus groups	• Ratings by program staff	• University Research Offices

COMMON DATA COLLECTION TOOLS

EXHIBIT 34

and lets your reviewers know exactly who will be doing what and when. It tells reviewers that you are organized and have thought out the major steps of your project. This way, your reviewers know you have done significant planning and are not just proposing a wild whim. With a time and task chart, they can look at a road map of the territory you plan to cover. Finally, the time and task chart represents a clear, one-page, visual summary of the entire methodology section. It would, for example, be a logical addition to the end of the bioethics methodology section described in the example below.

Many different types of time and task charts can be used. Which type you use is not as important as the fact that you do include one that the reviewers can easily grasp. Some grantwriters like to include it at the beginning of the methods section to provide the reviewers with an orientation to the narrative that follows. Others like to put it at the end of the methods section as a visually summary of the preceding verbal narrative. The choice is yours. Successful grantseekers often include their favorite time and task chart, even if it is not requested in the application guidelines.

As you study the time and task chart in Exhibit 35, notice that it includes goals and objectives with pertinent activities, including beginning and ending dates as well as the responsible individual. In essence, it is a comprehensive work plan seeking funding for a preschool curriculum development project.

The second example of a time and task chart, Exhibit 36, is sometimes called a project planner. It outlines the major activities of the project and the key individuals responsible for conducting the activities. In addition, it lists the duration of each activity; rather than name specific calendar months, it identifies project months. The final column contains a budget for each activity. While it requires extra effort to determine costs for each activity, this information is useful in those instances when agencies ask you to reduce your budget. If you must reduce your budget by, for example, $10,000, which project activities will you eliminate? The program survey? The final publication? Neither makes sense for this project, which is the Project Planner for Exhibit 26, Sample Letter Proposal #1 in Chapter Five, Letter Proposals. Once sponsors realize how thoroughly you have planned your project, they may show more flexibility in funding your full budget request.

Getting Started

Begin with your objectives. Describe the precise steps you will follow to carry out each objective, including what will be done, who will do it, and when it will be done. If you have trouble writing this section, assume the sponsor's check just arrived in the mail. What is the first thing you would do? Hire additional staff? Order equipment? What would you do next? Keep asking and answering the "What's next?" question and you will lead yourself through the methodology section.

EXAMPLES OF METHODS

Example 1

A hospital seeking federal funding to establish a bioethics center:

Work Plan for June 1, 2000 through December 31, 2002

Goal: To enable 200 children between the ages of six weeks and four years the opportunity to maximize their cognitive, social and emotional potential through participation in a state-of-the-art early childhood learning experience.

Bioethics Center Approach and Methods

Overview. For each of the three major Center goals described above, this proposal section details precisely what will be accomplished, methods of choice, task sequences, responsible individuals, time frames, and expected outcomes.

Organization. From the objectives, it is apparent that the Center has a tripartite focus: clinical, educational, and administrative. The Center organization chart (see table 1, following page) reflects this service aim. The Center Project Director, Dr. David Schwartz, is a full-time staff member at the Jones Memorial Hospital. Additionally, Associate Directors in each service area will be appointed: Dr. Marvin Todd, Associate Director for Clinical Affairs, Jones Memorial Hospital; Dr. William Ashmore, Associate Director for Administrative Affairs, Medical Run University; and Dr.

Activity	Begin Date	End Date	Responsibility
Objective #1: Train 200 children on Houston's northwest side in a culturally competent early childhood program.	Jun 2000	Dec 2001	Executive Director, White's/Multicultural
• Activity 1.1. Develop and field test a modular early childhood enrichment curriculum based on early brain development research.	Jun 2000	Nov 2000	Curriculum Consultant, Health Education Center
• Activity 1.2. Train 10 trainers in the curriculum modules.	Aug 2001	Aug 2000	Curriculum Consultant
• Activity 1.3. Establish formal collaborations between White's Child Development Center, Multicultural Family Services, Silver Lake Neighborhood Center and affiliate family care.	Jul 2000	Dec 2002	Project Manager
• Activity 1.4. Disseminate project findings through regular monthly meetings with collaborators and quarterly newsletters.	Sep 2000	Dec 2002	Project Manager
Objective #2: Coordinate education, training and supportive services for parents of at least 200 young children.	Dec 2000	Dec 2002	Executive Director, White's/Multicultural
• Activity 2.1. Explain curriculum to 50 parents.	Aug 2001	Dec 2002	HEC, Project Manager
• Activity 2.2. Show 25 parents $\frac{1}{2}$-hour training video.	Sep 2001	Dec 2002	Project Manager
• Activity 2.3. Train 10 parents of special needs infants and toddlers, and link them with support services.	Dec 2001	Dec 2002	Curriculum Consultant
• Activity 2.4. Stimulate parental involvement in education sessions, parent-teacher meetings, and class volunteers.	Jan 2002	Dec 2002	HEC, Project Manager

TIME AND TASK CHART

EXHIBIT 35

Activities	Responsibility	Duration	Budget
• Identify Target Urban Areas	• Jane O'Connor, Project Director	• Month One	• $3,345
• Design Evaluation Tools	• Jane O'Connor	• Month One	• 2,845
• Survey Program Practices	• Audra Hill, Assistant Director	• Months One and Two	• 8,976
• Analyze Survey Data	• J. O'Connor, A. Hill	• Months Three and Four	• 5,190
• Draft Preliminary Report	• Tera Maki, Technical Writer	• Months Five and Six	• 4,690
• Publish Preliminary Report	• Wise Publishing Company	• Months Seven and Eight	• 7,345
• Disseminate Report	• T. Maki	• Month Nine	• 3,238
• Seek Report Feedback	• J. O'Connor	• Months Nine and Ten	• 4,345
• Revise Preliminary Report	• T. Maki	• Months Eleven and Twelve	• 5,805
• Publish Final Report	• Wise Publishing Company	• Months Thirteen and Fourteen	• 11,690
• Distribute Final Report	• T. Maki	• Month Fifteen	• 3,476
Total Direct Cost			• $57,600
+Administrative Cost			• 11,520
=Total Project Cost			• $69,120
−Cost Sharing			• 2,888
=Amount Requested			• $66,240

PROJECT PLANNER

EXHIBIT 36

Robert Starr, Associate Director for Educational Affairs, Midwest University. Brief personnel descriptions are provided in the institutional overview statements beginning on page 13. Complete curricula vitae are appended.

Mechanisms of Commitment and Cooperation. The three core institutions will sign the Consortium Agreement specified in Appendix 1. The agreement describes the programmatic, fiscal, and administrative protocols that form the foundation of the Center. Additionally, the Center will want to quickly expand its affiliation with other medical centers and universities who share a mutual interest and concern in clinical ethics. Those institutions will be ac-

tively encouraged to quickly sign the Affiliation Agreement listed in Appendix 2. This formal affiliation will give them early access to the Center and quickly build a national base of operation. Finally, some institutions may not be prepared to make a full affiliation commitment, but they may want to be formally identified with and participate in Center activities. Those institutions will be urged to sign the Participant Institution Agreement listed in Appendix 3.

The lengthy methodology section in this proposal went on to restate each specific objective and describe what specific actions would be taken to carry out each objective. Because the central focus of this proposal was to establish an ethics education program for health and allied health professionals, the methodology section then concluded with the following discussion of a Clinical Ethics Education Program.

Clinical Ethics Education Program. To promote ethics education programs, the Center proposes to establish a program in Clinical Ethics Education (CEE). The CEE program assumes that (1) ethics is appropriate for all health care providers and (2) instruction in clinical ethics demands a novel curricular implementation. Central to the program are two clinical institutes that will provide the groundwork for developing a strengthened interdisciplinary, hospital-wide curriculum in clinical ethics education and for training health care professionals to teach clinical ethics within the hospital. The CEE program also will include ethics seminars, speaker programs, and guest lecturing clinicians and ethicists.

The guiding vision of the CEE program will be to focus the attention of health care professionals upon the principles of ethical theory and their practical application to a broad range of health care matters in other disciplines. Each participating hospital will gain newly energized clinicians, an increase in ethical sensitivity, and relevantly revised training programs in clinical ethics. Moreover, health care providers will gain a new interdisciplinary perspective on ethics and will receive varied supports for collegiate collaboration.

In essence, the major Center outcome will be to provide this cadre of health professionals with focused training in ethics theory and cross-walks that foster interdisciplinary communication. This focus will allow the Center to more fully centralize its clinical ethics curriculum around fundamental philosophical and theological ethical models. Clinicians who are versed in the basic principles of the theoretical study of ethics are better able to see how these principles converge with applied practices.

Rather than allowing ethics to be learned in isolated fragments from different disciplines, the CEE program would coordinate the resources of different disciplines under one umbrella to provide clinicians with a more organized and integrated exploration of ethics. Ethics will achieve a first-class status within the participating hospital as a result of the CEE program. All clinicians will benefit from the increased excellence in the study of ethics.

CEE Program Administration. The Associate Director for Educational Affairs will administer the CEE program with extensive consultation from the Advisory Board of the Center for Ethics Studies at Midwest University, and a broad network of hospital affiliates. Specifically, Professor Starr, of Midwest's theology department, will serve as Program Coordinator. Professor Johnson, of the philosophy department, will function as Associate Coordinator. As shown in Appendix 5, both the Program Coordinator and Associate Coordinator have strong professional records in the field of ethics and are oriented to interdisciplinary ethics education. In general, the program administrators will be responsible for directing the functions of the program and for assessing the success of these activities.

CEE Program Functions. The CEE program will include the following three major functions:

- *A Series of Two Summer Clinical Institutes*
  These institutes will bring together clinicians from different specialties interested in ethics (a) to provide an organized seminar in basic ethical theory, (b) to explore the application of this theoretical framework to the various specialties, (c) to plan curricular changes in medical education at each affiliated hospital, and (d) to provide training for implementing the revised curriculum. Specifically, the first summer institute will concentrate upon the key elements of the theory of ethics. The following summer institute will explore curricular changes that incorporate the theory into practical situations.
- *Development of the Interdisciplinary Curriculum in Ethics*
  As previously described, the ultimate objective of the CEE program is to develop an explicitly highlighted interdisciplinary curriculum in clinical ethics. In light of the natural enrichment generated by interaction of ethicists and clinicians in diverse health care disciplines, proposals will be developed and implemented for incorporating clinical ethics components throughout the hospital system.
- *A Series of Sponsored Programmed Meetings*
  Interested clinicians and medical students will attend a regularly scheduled forum on clinical ethics to share their respective insights and efforts in the study of ethics. These seminars, administered jointly by the Associate Director for Clinical Affairs and the Associate Director for Educational Affairs, will address issues in ethical theory and the application of that theory to problems in the applied fields.

Example 2

A health education center seeking funding from a local private foundation to develop a video on early brain development for childcare providers:

> This program will be made available to communities throughout the Center's current service area. This includes 13 counties in southeastern Wyoming and two in northern Arizona. The intended audience for this program would be the parents, grandparents, guardians, public health nurses, parish nurses, home visitors, and child care providers. It is anticipated that approximately 30 people will participate in each session of the program. Twelve presentations will be made during the project period, thereby directly targeting 360 people.
>
> The content of the program will address the healthy growth and development of a child socially, physically, emotionally, and cognitively. A variety of learning formats will be employed, including lecture, small-group discussions, role-playing, interactive videos and models, and group participation. Among these training techniques, the research literature shows that interactive videos are particularly effective in producing long-term behavioral changes. This program will provide participants with the ability to model healthy adult-child interactions for each other. Most important, adults will learn skills that promote healthy brain development and relationship building from 0–3 years of age.

WRITING TIPS FOR THE METHODS SECTION

1. Justify your selection of methodology.
2. Tell what is unique about your approach. Have others used your procedures? Is there solid reason to believe they will work? If you use experimental methods, indicate why you chose them over others.
3. Segment your design into activity areas such as planning or testing; this organization makes the project design easier to understand.
4. If you use a consultant, explain the role the consultant will play.
5. Discuss the risks with your methods and why your success is probable.
6. Include a time and task chart. Including the names or titles of personnel who will carry out each activity foreshadows for the reader the role each person plays in your project budget.

REJECTION REASONS

This chapter concludes with 22 statements from rejected proposals; these methodological shortcomings are clustered into three categories: Project Personnel, Project Methods, and Project Timelines.

Project Personnel

1. The project appears to incorporate little faculty expertise in the disciplines involved.
2. Expertise appears to be primarily in subcontractors.
3. This proposal seems premature. Not until an interdisciplinary group is in place can this project be expected to operate effectively.
4. Project staff is not specified in the narrative, i.e., job descriptions are not included and prior relevant work experience is not explained.
5. The project director lacks experience in the essential methodology.
6. The number of current and projected training positions was unclear.
7. The applicant does not provide any indication of the number of clients to be served.
8. This proposal doesn't identify what resources collaborating partners are bringing to the table to sustain the project once grant funds run out.

Project Methods

1. There is insufficient experimental detail to approve the project.
2. The methodology is diffuse, superficial, and unfocused.
3. The proposal narrative does not describe why the target population of the homeless was selected over other needy populations. Are the homeless disproportionately represented compared to other groups, e.g., frail elderly, battered women, or drug abusers?
4. There is gap between the "problem" identified in the opening section of the proposal and the "solution" presented here. The "problem" focuses on the needs of uninsured patients. The "solution" focuses on meeting the needs of the providers.
5. The proposal narrative needs to describe in more detail the structure that will keep lines of communication open and flowing across partner agencies, especially since each objective has a different lead agent.

6. The proposal narrative describes how to ensure linguistic access to services, but what methods will be used to ensure that services are culturally appropriate? Will there be ongoing cultural competency training and education for staff and providers?
7. The project activities are disproportionately service delivery oriented rather than infrastructure building oriented.
8. The proposal narrative articulates "Recognition that the model works best when it is community driven, not just community focused" (p. 19), yet interestingly, the governance structure does not include much representation from the target consumer population. How does the governance structure secure ongoing involvement and input from members of the target population?
9. It would have been helpful if the applicant had delineated the existing activities versus the proposed program activities as directed in the application instructions.
10. The research plan is nebulous, diffuse, and not presented in concrete detail to adequately control for statistically accurate results, especially since no power analysis will be performed.

Project Timelines

1. Greater care in planning is needed. It is highly unlikely that the methods can be accomplished within the specified time frame.
2. No timelines are provided for the major tasks; this represents a serious planning gap on the part of the applicants.

3. While major time frames are provided for each milestone, the applicants do not indicate who is responsible for carrying out each activity.
4. The timelines are extraordinarily ambitious.

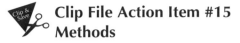

Clip File Action Item #15
Methods

The following action items will help build your Methods clip file:

- Gather examples of time and task charts from other proposals.
- Collect details on data collection instruments of interest in Buros's *Yearbook of Mental Measurements*.
- Compile names and resumés of consultants who might serve on future projects.
- List your resources that might support upcoming projects: computers, instruments, personnel, financial.

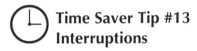

Time Saver Tip #13
Interruptions

To manage interruptions, teach colleagues that a closed door or a "Do Not Disturb" sign means business.

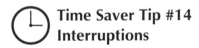

Time Saver Tip #14
Interruptions

To manage interruptions, don't check your e-mail and voicemail frequently. Schedule communications checks several times a day. Set your mail utility software to check e-mail once every two or three hours, not every five minutes.

CHAPTER 10
Evaluation

True genius resides in the capacity for evaluation of uncertain, hazardous and conflicting information.
Winston Churchill

PURPOSE OF EVALUATION

Evaluations pinpoint what is really happening in your project so you can improve its efficiency, effectiveness, and equity. That is, you can ensure project funds are being spent wisely, the project is making a difference, and project benefits are being distributed across the target population or community. Based on evaluation information, you can better allocate resources, improve your services, and strengthen your overall project performance. Beyond these immediate benefits, a good project evaluation can discover needs to be served in your next proposal as well as make it easier to get and sustain funding. As Churchill notes, grantseekers conduct their evaluation to resolve ambiguous or conflicting information.

In essence, evaluations are conducted for a combination of internal and external reasons. Externally, sponsors may require it to make sure that their project funds are having the desired impact, or as a prerequisite for renewed funding. Conceivably, sponsors may use evaluation information to deal with radical funding cutbacks; applicants without a strong evaluation component are particularly vulnerable to funding cuts.

Beyond these external reasons, many internal reasons exist for conducting an evaluation. You may not have a firm grasp of your project strengths and weaknesses or socioeconomic implications. You may wonder if you need to improve your project effectiveness or to eliminate some duplication of effort. Perhaps, your project is getting little publicity or, worse yet, negative publicity. Maybe your staff feels ineffective, frustrated, or in need of guidance. A comprehensive evaluation can provide answers to these important project questions.

If you want to include an evaluation component in your proposal but know nothing about the subject, consider borrowing ideas from the evaluation plans developed for other similar programs, or ask a colleague or consultant to review your proposal and develop an appropriate evaluation strategy. Too frequently, proposal writers don't explain how they will evaluate their projects. At best, they may mention some vague process such as a discussion meeting or assigning the evaluation to an expert, with no specifics on how the evaluation will be conducted or what will be learned from it.

TYPES OF EVALUATION

You may engage in different types of evaluations to assess the effectiveness of your proposed project during, at the conclusion of, and beyond the granting period. Three types of evaluations include, process, outcome, and impact. Public and private sponsors sometimes use different terminology to describe the same types of evaluations. For instance, the U.S. Department of Education uses the terms *formative* and *summative* evaluations, whereas the W. K. Kellogg Foundation uses the terms *process* and *outcome* evaluations. They are synonyms.

A few sponsors have refined distinctions in the types of evaluations they expect. For example, one program in the Health Resources and Services Administration requires you to distinguish between outputs (products) and outcomes (humanistic benefits) that will accrue by the conclusion of the grant period. Preproposal contacts (Chapter 4) will help you to identify the types, levels, and degrees of evaluation strategies you will need to include in your proposal. The sponsor may well require different types of evaluations during different time periods in the grant. Exhibit 37 lists some of the common evaluation terms used during different grant periods.

Note that some evaluation terms overlap; that is, one term can have more than one meaning. For instance, "process" is the umbrella name given to evaluations conducted during a grant; it is also the name of one facet of that evaluation, along with "structure." The semantics of evaluation terminology are not consistently clear; the following discussion attempts to "defuzzify" the different evaluation terms.

Process Evaluation

Process evaluations generate information that will improve the effectiveness of the project during the grant period. They systematically examine internal and external characteristics associated with the delivery and receipt of services. This may include evaluating structure, the environment and settings in which services occur. Understanding the strengths and weaknesses of the structure of your organization, the target population and their community environment, and the procedures your organization is using to interact with the community will provide immediate feedback to help you in the process of meeting project objectives. When writing a process evaluation, you'll need to consider the following types of questions.

- **Your Organization**. Are sufficient numbers of key personnel adequately trained to carry out the project? Do staff members reflect the ethnic, cultural, and linguistic makeup of the community? Are suitable facilities and equipment available? Do current services respond to the needs of the target population and community? What is your relation to other organizations that provide similar types of services?
- **Target Population & Community Environment**. Have individual and community needs been identified through a formal needs assessment or an informal survey of perceived needs? Has the community's knowledge, attitude, and behavior toward the problem been assessed? What is the prevalence and distribution of physical, social, and economic risks in the community? Does the community face any geographic, cultural, or linguistic barriers to overcoming the problem? Does the target population have access to additional personal, family, or community resources that will help your project succeed?
- **Organization & Community Interaction**. What types of services are being provided to whom and how often? Who from your organization is collect-

ing what type of evidence to document the quality and quantity of interactions? Is the target population satisfied with services? Are your staff members satisfied with their experiences? What barriers still need to be overcome in order to improve participant satisfaction?

Evaluation indicators are specific characteristics that you will track and measure to gauge project success. Process-level indicators may examine features such as the intensity of the intervention, the quality of service provided, and the cultural competence of the intervention. Structure-level indicators may assess elements such as who provided the intervention, what type of intervention was used, where the intervention occurred, when and how long the intervention took place, and the length of participant involvement.

Outcome Evaluation

Outcome evaluations, simply put, examine the end result of an intervention. The goal here is to document the extent to which the project did what it was designed to do. Outcomes are the benefits, changes, or effects that occur to the target population due to participation in your project. Outcomes are generally expressed in humanistic terms, e.g., improved health status, increased knowledge of parenting skills, decreased youth violence. Some sponsors may also ask you to identify outputs, products generated as a result of program activities, e.g., a curriculum to teach oral health to middle school students, the number of conflict resolution classes taught, the number of volunteers recruited. Keep in mind that "ideal" outcomes can vary with perspective: your organization, the target population, and potential sponsors may value different outcomes. Your project might need to evaluate several types of outcomes simultaneously.

The core of outcome evaluations is measurement: data collected to document the extent to which project objectives were accomplished. Outcome indicators—specific characteristics selected for measurement—must best describe an associated end result. For instance, a program whose desired outcome is to improve asthma-related quality of life could measure "improvement" through participants having a written asthma action plan; using anti-inflammatory inhalers, spacers, and peak flow meters; reducing the amount of sleep, exercise, and school days lost due to asthma; and reducing the number of hospital admissions and emergency room visits for asthma. Participants who demonstrate these behaviors are the indicators of the project's success in achieving this outcome.

During the grant period	*Conclusion* of grant period	*Beyond* the grant period
Process ♣ Structure ♣ Process	**Outcome** ♣ Outputs ♣ Outcomes	**Impact**
Formative	Summative	Impact
Immediate Outcomes	Short-term Outcomes	Long-term Outcomes
Initial Outcomes	Intermediate Outcomes	End Outcomes

EVALUATION TERMINOLOGY AT DIFFERENT GRANT TIME PERIODS

EXHIBIT 37

Three common types of outcome indicators include, functional status, humanistic, and economic. Collecting data to evaluate all aspects of each type of outcome indicator would be extremely difficult and prohibitively expensive. Instead, do as successful grantseekers do: identify a few outcome indicators that will demonstrate meaningful end results to your organization, the target population, and the sponsor.

Functional Status. Performance measures such as physical, mental, social, and spiritual well-being can be used to demonstrate individuals' functional status. Performance measures are generally evaluated at set intervals—for example, prior to intervention and six and twelve months after intervention. Functional status indicators demonstrate that, as a result of the intervention, the client's quality of life improved in a meaningful way.

Humanistic. Humanistic indicators tell you how clients feel about the intervention and reflect how well the project is working. Measures tend to be subjective in nature, for instance: awareness of program services, access to services, convenience of services, quality of services, satisfaction with services, and individual perceptions of well-being. Client satisfaction is a key outcome measure because those who are satisfied with their experiences are more likely to continue participating in an intervention.

Economic. Five measures typically used to calculate the costs and consequences of project interventions include cost-benefit analysis, cost-effectiveness analysis, cost-minimization analysis, cost-utility analysis, and return on investment analysis. Each type of analysis values costs in dollars but differs in the outcome measures used. Sponsors value project outcomes that demonstrate the greatest benefit at the lowest cost.

- *Cost-benefit analyses* identify the most favorable cost-to-benefit ratio of two or more alternatives that have similar or different outcomes for the target population; that is, given finite resources, which project intervention gives the best return for the dollars invested?
- *Cost-effectiveness analyses* compare two or more approaches to a specified outcome, assuming that members of the target population value the outcome equally and that adequate financial resources are available to pursue the most beneficial strategy.
- *Cost-minimization analyses* identify the least expensive of two or more alternatives that have identical outcomes for the target population.
- *Cost-utility analyses* compare the costs of two or more approaches to an outcome, adjusting for preferences of the target population. That is, a child with mild asthma may not value an additional year of life as much as an adult with an advanced stage of the AIDS virus.
- *Return on investment analyses* look at projected benefits or revenue generated by the intervention over a period of time compared to the initial investment and operating costs.

In the public arena, the fundamental method for formal economic assessment is cost-benefit analysis. Cost-benefit analyses attempt to identify the most economically efficient way of meeting a public objective, particularly when measurable benefits or costs extend three or more years into the future. You can get federal guidance for this analysis from the U.S. Office of Management and Budget's "Circular A-94 Guidelines and Discount Rates for Benefit Cost Analysis of Federal Programs," available at www.whitehouse.gov/omb/circulars/a094/a094.html.

Impact Evaluation

Impact evaluations generate information to measure the overall worth and utility of the project beyond the grant period. An impact evaluation goes beyond assessing whether goals and objectives were achieved and focuses on the project's larger value—long-term, fundamental changes in participants' knowledge, attitudes, or behaviors. That is, improving outcomes at the program level may impact change over time at the community level. By their nature, many outcomes are delayed, occurring beyond the granting period. Impact evaluations attempt to attribute outcomes exclusively to an intervention, although data may be difficult to obtain over the long term.

You can demonstrate impact at several levels: the target population, the community at large, and beyond. Lasting changes in the target population demonstrate the project's overall value. Inclusive participation by the community may contribute to long-term project sustainability. Regional and national buy-in for targeted interventions and outcomes can promote large-scale project replication. Consider the following types of questions when writing an impact evaluation:

- **Overall Value.** What enduring changes will occur in participants' knowledge, attitudes, or behaviors as a result of this project? Over the long term, will you be able to demonstrate that the project's impact extended beyond the target population to the entire community, area, or region? Will this project serve as a catalyst for other related community actions, services, and programs?
- **Sustainability.** Will project activities continue beyond the grant period? Will you be able to mobilize continued support for the project internally and/or externally? Will your organization institutionalize strategies deemed effective? Will key champions for the project be able to increase levels of community involvement and fiscal support? Will your project influence changes at provider, policy, or system levels?
- **Replicability.** Will key findings be disseminated to local, regional, and national stakeholders so that the project can be replicated? Does the project's design have flexibility to be adapted to other populations or topics? Could your organization serve as a national clearinghouse to educate and train other communities about implementing your program? Does your project have the potential to serve as a public policy model?

Collectively, conducting process, outcome, and impact evaluations is a strategy to achieve a competitive grantseeking advantage by increasing project accountability. These assessments also provide essential information about the direction that the project should take in the future and if additional public and private funding will be needed. As evaluation data are generated, be sure to disseminate relevant findings to key constituents.

CHOOSING AN EVALUATOR

Evaluations can be done using someone within or outside of your organization. An individual within your organization who conducts an internal evaluation has great intuitive knowledge of your program and is less likely to be seen as an intruder. Evaluation costs are usually less expensive when the evaluations are conducted in-house. The ability to communicate useful information is high. On the other hand, the internal evaluation may be biased because of involvement with certain program aspects. Evaluation findings may be ignored or not seen as professional enough; that is, the evaluation may not be taken seriously.

Using external evaluators offers considerable objectivity. They often have a fresh perspective and can see things previously unnoticed. They have a high autonomy and specialized training. Outside evaluators usually have high professional and scholarly competence. They can mediate and facilitate activities with staff and management while ensuring public confidence in evaluation results. On the other hand, they may be perceived as a threat by the staff and may require extra time to understand the program rationale. Outside evaluation costs may be high. The findings may be ignored because the evaluator doesn't really know the program and can miss essential issues or because the staff perceives this to be the case. Evaluation energies may distract from program activities.

USING EVALUATORS EFFECTIVELY

Whether you use an internal or an external evaluator—or both—be sure to include an evaluation section in your proposal. A common proposal-writing mistake is to budget an amount for evaluation costs and worry later about the evaluation procedure. Instead, involve the evaluators in the proposal writing. Be sure to give them a copy of your project objectives. Recall that pointed objectives will simplify the evaluation process.

Evaluators should provide you with important information to strengthen your proposal. Specifically, ask your evaluators to identify the following:

- What will be evaluated?
- What information will they need to conduct the evaluation?
- Where will that information be obtained?
- What data collection instruments will be used to get that information?
- What evaluation design will be used?
- What analyses will be completed?
- What questions will you be able to answer as a result of the evaluation?

If you are looking for a good evaluation consultant, contact the grants office at a nearby university. That office is familiar with its faculty expertise and often finds an appropriate evaluator for area organizations and agencies.

KEY QUESTIONS TO ANSWER

As you write this section of the proposal, ask yourself if it does the following:

1. Describe why evaluation of the project is needed?
2. Define what is meant by evaluation?
3. Identify the type and purpose of your evaluation and the audiences to be served by its results?
4. Demonstrate that an appropriate evaluation procedure is included for every project objective?
5. Provide a general organizational plan or model for your evaluation?
6. Demonstrate that the scope of the evaluation is appropriate to the project? To what extent is the project practical, relevant, and generalizable?
7. Describe the information that will be needed to complete the evaluation, the potential sources for this information, and the instruments that will be used for its collection?
8. Provide sufficient detail to demonstrate the technical soundness of all data collection instruments and procedures?
9. Identify and justify procedures for analysis, reporting, and utilization?
10. Define standards that will be used in judging the results of the evaluation?
11. Summarize any reports to be provided to the funding source based on the evaluation, and generally describe their content and timing?
12. Identify any anticipated constraints on the evaluation?
13. Discuss who will be responsible for the evaluation?
14. Establish the credentials of your evaluator, including pertinent prior experience and academic background?

15. Describe mechanisms to disseminate the results of your evaluation?

EXAMPLES OF EVALUATIONS

The three examples below show how definitions of evaluation can actually be used in proposals.

Example 1

A geriatrics education proposal submitted to a federal agency that trains health care personnel:

Process. Evaluation is a multifaceted term. In a general sense, the term "evaluation" means to gather information to judge the effectiveness of the project. However, more precise types of evaluation are warranted for this proposal. Specifically, we envision the following evaluation categories:

Formative Evaluation: Generating information to improve the educational effectiveness of the Center during the grant period. This evaluation will help determine whether the processes and procedures are working, whether the participants are satisfied with their instruction. This approach represents a good management tool for making "mid-course corrections," providing the center director and governance council with immediate feedback to make constructive revisions in the training, resource development, and technology transfer activities of the Center.

Summative Evaluation: Collecting data necessary to judge the ultimate success of the completed project. The goal is to document the extent to which the project objectives were achieved; that is, to what extent did the proposal do what it was designed to do? Evaluation feedback will be used for formulating or modifying the sponsor's policy and organization structure, which will improve the likelihood of successfully accomplishing program goals.

Impact Evaluation: Judging the overall worth and utility of the project results. The concern here is to assess the significance of the project achievements, especially to the Health Resources and Services Administration.

The Midwest Geriatric Education Center is not only a structure developed to provide multidisciplinary training, resources, and technology for staffing and service delivery objectives, but it is also a structure that serves as an administrative mechanism to achieve such objectives in the Urban Corridor, which is its geographical focus. This administrative mechanism is designed to be a catalyst and facilitator for change among the educational institutions, the elements of the service delivery system, and the organized professions that also serve the geographic region of the Urban Corridor. Therefore, particular attention will be paid in the evaluation plan to the effectiveness of the Center as an administrative mechanism for achieving professional and institutional change.

To achieve the evaluation goals of this project, the Assistant Directors of Geriatric Education Services will collaborate on the development of data-gathering instruments. This collaboration will express itself in the creation of an Evaluation Steering Committee that the assistant directors will chair. To this committee, the MGEC program director will name seven additional individuals representing the affiliate institutions, agencies, and professions.

The Evaluation Steering Committee shall be charged to agree upon specific measures and data-gathering strategies for each of the variables in the program evaluation protocol. The Evaluation Steering Committee will also review and recommend approval to the Program Director for requests to use data, programs, and products of the Midwest Geriatric Education Center for research, and will ensure that the evaluation of the Center is not compromised or contaminated. Finally, the Evaluation Steering Committee will review evaluation activities in progress to identify suggestions that should be made to the Program Director concerning program, structure, or policy that seem warranted on the basis of interim or final results obtained in either the process or outcome evaluation activities. Members of the Evaluation Steering Committee must be appointed in such a way that they are representative of the affiliates and target constituencies, but external to the operations of the MGEC. Thus, the Evaluation Steering Committee will ensure objectivity to the evaluation while permitting maximum feedback to the Center's operations.

The three types of evaluation (formative, summative, and impact) will be used to assess both the educational and programmatic aspects of this proposal. Orienting comments on each aspect are described below.

Educational Evaluation. Each of the four MGEC goals and the associated objectives are expressed in measurable terms. While the Evaluation Steering Committee bears the responsibility for specific evaluation methodology, their approach will seek, as a minimum, answers to the following questions for each MGEC goal:

1. *To increase the number of highly trained geriatrics educators*

Determine the number of health professional training institutions in the Urban Corridor. What percentage are consortium members? What are the characteristics of the decision makers within the institutions that joined the consortium? What reasons are given for not joining the consortium? How many geriatrics health care providers exist in the Urban Corridor? How many have links with the consortium academic faculty?

2. *To practice a multidisciplinary approach to geriatric health care*

To what extent was each faculty lecturer able to make an effective and pedagogically sound presentation as evidenced by trainee evaluations? To what extent will trainees be able to utilize multidisciplinary approaches to identify the need for effective patient training packages?

3. *To develop geriatrics education materials*

To what extent will trainees be able to effectively evaluate educational materials in concurrence with peer evaluations? To what extent will the faculty be able to produce and evaluate effective educational packages?

4. *To establish a geriatrics education resource center*

During the grant period, how many requests were received for information, technical assistance, instructional materials, and consultations?

Example 2

A proposal to a federal science agency seeking support for minority students:

The program evaluation process serves two purposes: (1) to provide feedback during program operation, and (2) to provide quantifiable data regarding the short- and long-term effectiveness of the program.

Near the end of the first and second semesters of each program year, each minority fellow and faculty mentor will complete a questionnaire, ending with a section of free commentary. The questionnaires will be prepared and evaluated by the Evaluation Advisory Committee and the project director, who will use the feedback obtained from student and faculty participants to "fine-tune" and improve the operation of the program.

In addition, upon completion of the program, each faculty mentor will complete a student evaluation survey. Additionally, the student fellows will agree in writing to maintain current addresses on file with the department for six years following completion of the Minority Fellowship Program, and to complete an existing evaluation survey upon receipt of their doctorates, as well as a three-year follow-up survey and a six-year follow-up survey. The data obtained from these surveys will be compiled and analyzed to evaluate the effectiveness of the program in meeting the primary objective of increasing the number of minority individuals entering university teaching and research in electrical and computer engineering.

Observations of the participants would be valuable to the Science Agency in establishing similar programs in the future. Further, comparing national and departmental data can assess the program. The success of the program will be determined based on the grade point averages of the minority fellows, the quality of their dissertation research, the number and quality of their publications, the percentage of minority fellows completing the program, the number of minority fellows actually beginning university teaching careers, the starting salaries of the minority fellows, the quality of the institutions they join and, finally, the progress of their careers after three and six years in the profession. The results of these studies will be reported in the literature after completion of the program, and again after three and six additional years.

Example 3

A child care development proposal submitted to a private foundation:

Evaluation. An outcomes-directed evaluation plan means collecting data to document the extent to which objectives and activities were achieved. Evaluation feedback will be used to modify child care programming, trainings, and technical assistance to improve the likelihood of accomplishing project goals. To ensure that the evaluation is objective, meets rigorous standards of research, and is sensitive to ethnic and cultural differences, we will subcontract with external evaluation consultants, Dilworth & Associates, Inc. Methodologically, they will set up appropriate systems to collect, analyze, and report progress on:

1. **Structural measures**: the environment and settings in which services occur, e.g., licensing, accreditation, group size, adult-child ratio, staff experience and turnover.

2. **Process measures**: the type, intensity, and frequency of services provided, e.g., nurturing caregiving, length and quality of teacher-student interactions, responsiveness to children's needs, and cultural- and age-appropriate materials and activities.

3. **Outcome measures**: the effectiveness in achieving goals and end results, e.g., cognitive, social, emotional, physical, and language development improvements in children.

Dr. Katrina H. Davidson, Director of Outcomes Evaluation, will assess the program for usability, satisfaction, and efficacy, including a sophisticated return-on-investment analysis for the community at large and individual participants. Evaluation measures will be practical, efficient, consistent with NAEYC Accreditation Standards, and mirror the Healthy Children Foundation's national evaluation of "Excellent Childcare Centers."

Dissemination is essential to project success because education has a multiplier effect. Consistent monitoring and reporting of evaluation measures will improve children's development, help shape program direction, ensure sustainability, and promote program replication. The intended outcomes of dissemination effort are to affect the knowledge, attitude, and behavior of parents and providers relative to child care principles and practices.

STEPS IN THE EVALUATION PROCESS

Evaluation is essentially a four-step process. As you will see, if the objectives and methodology sections of your proposal are precise, you are well on your way to completing the evaluation protocol.

1. **Identify precisely what will be evaluated.** If you wrote measurable objectives, as specified in Chapter 8, you already know what to evaluate.

2. **Determine the methods you will use to evaluate each objective.** More precisely, you will need to describe the information you will need and how you propose to collect it. These details will be found in the methods section of your proposal, as discussed in Chapter 9.

3. **Complete your evaluation design.** Specify the analyses you plan to make and then carry out your evaluation by collecting and interpreting the data needed for each objective. Your evaluation design may be simply to observe the behavior of a particular population or something more complex like

a rigorous experimental and multiple control group design.

4. **Summarize the resulting data analysis and indicate its use.** Consider including mock data tables that show what your resulting data might look like.

Note that of these four steps, the first two are completed as you write the objectives and methods sections of your proposal. In other words, you are halfway done with the evaluation section before you start.

WRITING TIPS FOR THE EVALUATION SECTION

1. Make sure that you include a separate evaluation component for each project objective. Designing an evaluation section for each objective forces you to examine the clarity of your objectives, the ease with which they can be measured, and the possibility of their being achieved.
2. If outside consultants are used, identify costs, credentials, and experience.
3. Evaluation sections are less likely to be included in NSF and NIH basic science research grants. Therefore, to include an evaluation section in a research proposal may give you a competitive edge. Replicability is the primary evaluation criterion in most basic science research proposals.
4. Strengthen the credibility of your evaluation section by citing examples of surveys, questionnaires, data collection instruments, data analysis forms, and other evaluation methodologies.
5. Be sure you consider all types of evaluation in your proposal, and use terminology that is familiar to your sponsor.
6. Web sites that might help you plan you evaluation protocol include www.innonet.org/resources/overview.cfm and www.recudsa.gov.

REJECTION REASONS

Some reviewers' comments concerning poor evaluation sections include the following:

1. Evaluation strategy is weak; much of it is yet to be developed with the help of unidentified consultants.
2. An overall summative or formative evaluation plan is not specific. Evaluation plan expressed in broad terms.

3. The evaluation section belabors obvious problems in reliability of measurement but is thin on specific procedures directly relevant to the purposes of the proposal.
4. Although a commitment to evaluate each objective is stated, no project evaluation plan is presented. How will direct and indirect impact be assessed in terms of quantitative and qualitative goals?
5. Although evaluation is tailored to individual objectives, specific outcomes are rarely mentioned. Much of the evaluation plan is philosophical rather than describing methodology.
6. Program evaluation funding, representing 2 percent of the total budget, is inadequately low to carry out a quality evaluation that looks at process and outcome measures across multiple collaborators, and to participate in a national evaluation.
7. The proposal does not describe methods, objectives, and instruments to measure and evaluate clinical quality.
8. One of the projected results of this project is "to redirect savings to the architecture of this delivery system," yet the narrative does not describe a method by which partner agencies will identify and track "savings" from project efficiencies in order to reinvest monies back to the project.
9. The self-evaluation plan does not include process measures to ensure that systems and procedures are working properly. What methods of evaluation will be used to gather process data, e.g., surveys, focus groups, interviews?
10. The proposal does not identify a specific expert or organization to conduct the evaluation. What are the evaluator's qualifications?
11. The proposal does not describe how data collection will be standardized across partner agencies so that evaluation results will be meaningful.
12. The proposal does not provide examples of the types of data that partner agencies are currently collecting.
13. The sample size of subjects is inappropriate to produce reliable and valid results.
14. The design of this project fails to evaluate important gender, age and racial/ethnic population differences.
15. This project employs a weak evaluation design to be executed by an inexperienced evaluation staff.
16. Lack of clarity and definition of goals and objectives makes it difficult to create an evaluation plan.

Because grantmakers are increasingly insisting on an evaluation component in proposals, you need to have a strong evaluation section in your proposals. Be sure you avoid problems such as those cited above. If you lack evaluation expertise, call your nearest university grants office and ask them to help you select a professor with a specialty in your area.

Clip File Action Item #16
Evaluation

These suggestions will help launch your Evaluation clip file.

- Secure copies of successful evaluation strategies used in other similar proposals.
- Collect names and resumes of potential project evaluators.
- Retrieve examples from projects you have successfully evaluated in the past.

CHAPTER 11
Dissemination

A crank is someone with a new idea—until it catches on.
Mark Twain

PURPOSE OF DISSEMINATION

You want your ideas to "catch on" so others can learn about and share in your results. Dissemination is the means by which you tell others about your project: its purpose, methods, and results. It's also a way for sponsors to get "more bang for their buck." As grants become increasingly competitive, dissemination of project outcomes results takes on increasing importance. No longer is it sufficient to say, for instance, that you will submit a journal article or present a paper at a professional society meeting. At a minimum, specify the tentative titles, target journals, and submission dates. Likewise, indicate which meetings will be attended, including dates and locations for presenting papers.

Some agency application forms may treat the dissemination portion as part of the methodology section. Whether separately or as part of the methodology section, give serious consideration to dissemination if you want to construct a highly competitive proposal. Among beginning proposal writers, this section is one of the last to be planned; the tendency is to minimize or ignore its significance. A particularly innovative and exciting dissemination strategy may be the deciding factor in securing funds for a project that in all other respects is similar to other applications received.

Project dissemination offers many advantages, including increasing public awareness of your program or project, soliciting additional support, locating more clients, alerting others in your field to new ideas, and adding to the stockpile of knowledge. You may need to use different dissemination techniques for different audiences. Remember to justify the budgeted costs of dissemination to the sponsor.

KEY QUESTIONS TO ANSWER

As you write the dissemination section, answer these key questions. Does your proposal do the following:

1. Indicate why dissemination activities are important to your project?
2. Clearly identify the intended results of the dissemination effort?
3. Include a feasible and appropriate plan for dissemination?
4. Succinctly describe any products to result from the dissemination effort?
5. Demonstrate that you understand dissemination principles and practices?
6. Provide sufficient detail to justify your dissemination budget request?
7. Include imaginative and practical dissemination?
8. Specify precisely who will be responsible for dissemination and why they are capable?
9. Discuss internal as well as external project dissemination?
10. Evaluate the effectiveness of the dissemination efforts and products?
11. Indicate how and when the audiences will get timely and useful information?
12. Invite a follow-up proposal to disseminate the results of the current project?

DISSEMINATION STRATEGIES FOR PROPOSALS

Project results can be distributed verbally or visually. The visual/verbal distinction emphasizes how you—as project director—choose to communicate your project results to your target audiences. Additionally, your project dissemination strategies can be active or passive. The active/passive distinction refers to your target audiences and the role they play in processing the visual or verbal information you present. If you choose to write up a report of your project results, you have chosen a visual channel of communication to which the reader responds passively, since reading is a passive process. On the other hand, you may involve the target audience in a hands-on demonstration of project results. Here the results are presented verbally and the target audience is actively involved. While the visual/verbal and active/passive distinctions are not wholly discrete, Exhibit 38 illustrates how the more common dissemination strategies might be classified.

In most proposals, you will want to use an appropriate mix of active/passive and verbal/visual dissemination strategies. Although the categories may overlap in some instances, they do reflect differing emphases. The active/passive distinction is a relatively new concept to grantwriters. Active dissemination strategies are those that place the project results directly in the hands of the target audience, whereas passive techniques are those in which the audience must seek them out. If the dissemination process is active, the audience is passive; conversely, if the dissemination process is passive, the audience is active, as Exhibit 38 illustrates. Any given dissemination strategy may be either active or passive, depending on the relationship between the sender and the receiver. For example, if we e-mail our final project report to you, that's an active dissemination process, assuming that you read it. On the other hand, if we post our project report on our Web site and wait for you to find it, that's passive dissemination.

As a proposal writer, you should write "generic" versions of each dissemination strategy, about two paragraphs long, and store them in your clip file (see Chapter 1), ready for final editing in your next proposal. A "generic" two-paragraph example follows for each dissemination strategy, one that can easily be adapted to your specific situation. The examples arise from the same theme and assume a proposal is being submitted to develop some training materials in bioethics that would be used to train members of Institutional Review Boards, committees that approve the use of human subjects in research experiments. Obviously, not all examples would be used in any one proposal.

We begin our example with an orienting paragraph:

Dissemination of project activities is essential because education has a multiplier effect. The intended results of the project's dissemination

effort are to affect the knowledge, attitude, and behavior of health care providers within the hospital system relative to ethical principles and practices. Accordingly, the project will use the following dissemination strategies:

Active Verbal Dissemination Strategies

1. **Conferences and Seminars** are hosted for individuals or groups that might be interested in project results. What regular forums exist that would be attracted to your project findings?

During the final quarter of the project period, we will sponsor a Midwest Regional Conference on Bioethics, tentatively titled "Managing Change with Fewer Resources: How to do More with Less—Ethically." Dr. Roberta Griff from the Kennedy Bioethics Institute, a nationally recognized expert in Bioethics, has tentatively agreed to present a keynote speech entitled "Application of Ethical Principles to Bioethical Decision Making." Concurrent breakout sessions will use the case study approach to apply ethical principles in specific patient situations.

Conference invitations will be sent to all central hospital administrators, all department heads, and Institutional Review Board members in a five-state area, representing approximately 2,500 health professionals; a minimum audience of 250 is anticipated. No registration fees will be charged, although participants will be asked to pay $25 for two lunches during the two-day conference, which will be held at the Wingspread Conference Center. Dr. Howard Thornberg will serve as conference observer and write a conference evaluation report, a role that he has repeatedly fulfilled over the past decade. Resumes for Drs. Griff and Thornberg are included in the proposal appendix.

2. **Demonstrations** illustrate techniques and materials developed by the projects. Will you develop instructional materials to be shared?

To increase distribution of the *IRB Bioethics Training Manual*, a 10-minute video demonstration tape will be prepared to highlight its contents and applications. More specifically, typical clinical scenarios will be presented to show the complexity and impact of bioethical decision-making. Appealing to adult learning styles, the demonstration video will emphasize the practical applications of ethical theory. In essence, the demonstration video becomes a marketing tool for Woodgrain Publishers to stimulate

Process	Verbal	Visual
Active	Conferences and Seminars Demonstrations Site Visits Web Casts+Chat Rooms Teleconferences	Courses/Seminars Displays/Poster Sessions Commercial Distributors Instructional Materials Web Sites Video Conferences
Passive	Convention Papers Staff Presentations	Books and Manuals Computer Disks Executive Summaries Interim Working Papers Journal Articles National Information Sources Newsletters + Listservs Pamphlets Press Releases

COMMON DISSEMINATION STRATEGIES

EXHIBIT 38

sales; Woodgrain will underwrite all costs associated with preparation of the video.

The video will be shot in standard VHS format and be of commercial broadcast quality. Woodgrain will use its production studio to shoot and edit the video, once the script storyboard has been prepared. Woodgrain has used this marketing approach with 10 other products in the past two years and found it very successful. The sponsor's role in funding the entire project will, of course, be properly acknowledged.

3. **Site visits** are arranged for representatives of key professional associations or organizations. Could you host a site visit, a special briefing that allows key representatives to capture your enthusiasm and results firsthand?

During the final project year, a series of four "Bioethics in Action" site visits will be held for key officials, including central hospital administrators, IRB chairs, health care advocates, and governmental officials. Our objective of the site visits—frankly—is to have the visiting administrators and policy makers see the personal and practical consequences of bioethical decision

making. This information, in turn, should have a positive impact on future ethical policies upon which these decision makers must act.

Each site visit will include the following activities during its daylong schedule: Overview of policies and implementation strategies, brief case history reviews, a grand rounds tour of pertinent patients, observation of an IRB meeting, interviews of select patients and families, and a question-and-answer session. Preparatory materials will be sent to the site visitors one month in advance of their arrival at our facility.

4. **Web Casts** are similar to TV broadcasts over the Internet. Could you broadcast your project results over the Internet? The Internet offers suggestions regarding conducting Web casts, which are often followed up with a live **Chat Room**. Plug the phrase "web casts" into your favorite search engine (chapter 17) to learn more.

The widespread use of the Internet offers new dissemination strategies. One novel technique growing in popularity is Web casting. With this approach, one literally broadcasts a program over the Internet much like a television show is broadcast. The technological requirements are minimal. At the broadcast's end, a camera is attached to a personal computer, which, in turn, is logged on to the Internet. At the receiver end, one needs only a free software program like Real Player or Quick Time, to receive the broadcast.

Our broadcast, Bioethics 101, will be available to anyone worldwide who can access the Internet. Simple instructions for accessing the broadcast will be posted on our Web site two weeks in advance of the broadcast. Participants can download handouts in advance of the presentation. An e-mail address will be used for participants to send in questions and receive answers during the broadcast. A Chat Room will be created so participants can continue their electronic discussions in real time after the Web cast.

5. **Teleconferences** are group telephone conference calls. Should you hold a group conference call about your project results?

Teleconferences are one of the most cost-effective and time-efficient dissemination strategies available. Live, real-time interactive audio communications occur no matter where the key participants are located, whether they are participating on their cell phone or in a large group on a speaker phone.

One objective of this project is to disseminate the results to policy makers. The strategy is to hold a teleconference call with the staff members in each congressional office that handles health and aging issues. A one-page Results Fact Sheet will be faxed to the participants one week in advance of the teleconference. At the agreed upon conference hour, participants will dial in to the central number and be connected so that all parties can hear each other. The project director will present a 10-minute summary of the major project results that have significant policy implications. Next, a 30-minute question-and-answer period follows. Finally, a 20-minute list of potential legislative policy action items will be generated and subsequently shared with all federal legislators in the state through their key staff members.

Passive Verbal Dissemination Strategies

1. **Conference Papers** are delivered at regional or national conferences, conventions, trade shows, or professional society gatherings. Which conferences? Where and when?

The project results will be presented at the National Bioethics Society Convention to be held

in San Diego on July 1, 2002. The convention has an average attendance of 1,500 bioethics professionals from throughout the United States. The tentative working title of the conference paper is "Avoiding the Horns of Ethical Dilemmas: The Midwest Agency Experience."

The main thrust of the paper is to disseminate project results to the leading national bioethicists. Through the case study method, we will explain how the rather abstract principles of ethical decision making apply in some very concrete ways to people with seriously impaired health status. Copies of our paper will also be placed on our Web site at www.artseducation.org for those individuals wishing copies; our Web site home page receives approximately 1,300 hits per month. A Web counter will tally the number of hits on the conference paper page, and we will include this information in our final project report to the sponsor.

2. **Staff Presentations** are given at local, state, and national meetings. Can you and your staff proactively reach out to various professional forums?

Dissemination of project results is a project priority. Among the multiple dissemination strategies used in this project, key staff members will use their existing networks to make presentations at local and regional meetings. To ensure quality and uniformity of presentations, the project director will oversee the development of a Powerpoint presentation, approximately 30 minutes in length, that can easily be adapted for different audiences. A minimum of one presentation per month is planned.

The content of the presentation will mirror the manual and training video—namely, ethical principles, bioethical practices, and case studies. While all key staff members are experienced in making public presentations, the chair of the Speech Department at Midwest University will present a short inservice workshop to ensure quality field presentations.

Active Visual Dissemination Strategies

1. **Courses and Seminars** show how the information resulting from the project can be explained to others in a formal instructional setting. Does the nature of your project warrant creation of a special course?

The instructional materials that result from this project form the basis of a continuing education course that could be presented either in person or via the Internet. If presented as a course or seminar, the project director would, working in conjunction with the hospital Director of Continuing Education, arrange for Continuing Medical Education credits (CMEs) to be awarded, thereby satisfying certification requirements. An all-day (eight-hour) seminar would permit sufficient coverage of the topic. The hospital administers approximately 75 CME programs per year and brings a prior history of success in coordinating similar seminars.

If the seminar proves successful after several presentations, then it would be converted to a Web-based format and be available online, on demand; that is, health professionals with access to the Internet could interact with the training program at their convenience. The Office of Continuing Education has instructional designers and Web technology experts who can adapt the content of the training materials to this electronic format that allows for self-paced learning.

2. **Displays and Poster Sessions** at appropriate meetings and conferences. Which meetings? Where and when?

Besides presenting a paper at the National Bioethics Society Convention on July 1, 2002, we will also conduct a poster display of our major project results. The poster display will be entitled "Avoiding the Horns of Ethical Dilemmas: The Midwest Agency Experience." More precisely, a case study will trace the bioethical issues and their effective resolution. Poster sessions offer the advantage of one-on-one interaction with interested convention participants.

Beyond disseminating information about the project results, the poster display represents an opportunity to build our newsletter mailing list and identify new collaborators who share our project values. In particular, we will be seeking other organizations in different geographic locations who might like to replicate our project results, thereby increasing its generalizability.

3. **Commercial Distributors** agree with other agencies to produce or market project results. Do you anticipate using a commercial vendor to produce and distribute your project products?

All resulting tangible products—the training manual, demonstration video, and training video—will be produced and distributed by Woodgrain Publishers, who has a 25-year history of successful marketing of biomedical training materials. A preliminary draft of a marketing and licensing agreement has been approved in principle by all parties and now awaits formal completion of the training manual.

One key feature of the marketing agreement sets minimum sales thresholds. Should Woodgrain fail to meet those minimums for whatever reason, we have the option to cancel our agreement and change distributors. Although this seems unlikely in actual practice, it is an important contract mechanism to insure widespread distribution of the intended project results.

4. **Instructional Materials** include such things as films, slide shows, filmstrips, videotapes, or television programs. Will audiovisual materials be produced internally or commercially?

Beyond the demonstration video for marketing purposes, Woodgrain will prepare and distribute a videotape companion to the *IRB Bioethics Training Manual*. The videotape will supplement, not supplant, the text. More specifically, it will show typical IRB case studies and invite viewer comments based on pertinent bioethical principles prior to showing the actual IRB result.

The final video will be approximately 45 minutes long and of commercial broadcast quality. To insure the appropriateness of the content, two separate focus groups will view the draft cuts and offer suggestions for final editing. The training manual and the videotape will be marketed as one companion unit and not sold separately. The resulting royalties will be used to continue the project beyond the grant period.

5. **Web Sites** are international electronic libraries. Can your project results be filed in the world's electronic library—the Internet?

It is axiomatic that the project results will be filed on our Web site. This offers multiple advantages. It is not appreciably constrained by length. It can easily be updated. It represents the latest technology trend in information dissemination. It is a familiar and friendly communication tool for the end users.

Hosting the report on our Web site is a necessary but not a sufficient condition of information dissemination. Equally important, the report must be structured to attract the major search engines e.g., Google, HotBot, AltaVista, Northern Lights, and so forth. This is done by registering the site with the major search engines and "loading" the report with key words that will facilitate search engine identification. Without belaboring details, we have the technological expertise to attract top search engine "hits."

6. **Video Conferences** are televised versions of telephone conference calls. It is particularly useful in

those instances when participant visual feedback is important to disseminating information.

Videoconferencing uses television to join people in live interaction. Its applications range from live video lecturing to large audiences, to a point-to-point, individual-to-individual desktop PC chat. In essence, it integrates the best of distance and convention information exchanges as participants get together on a virtual basis.

One of the target audiences for the project results is health professionals and bioethicists in the 147 Veterans Administration Medical Centers located throughout the country. Accordingly, a two-hour teleconference, entitled Bioethics: Nice Solutions to Nagging Problems, will be held for this audience. A satellite relay system involving one-way video and two-way audio will connect all VAMC locations; each has the necessary send-and-receive technology and, indeed, has been involved in videoconferencing for the past six years. The teleconference will focus on three main topics: major project finds, clinical applications, and two case studies, including a question-and-answer period, all coordinated by the Project Director.

Passive Visual Dissemination Strategies

1. **Books and Manuals** can be issued by your organization, the sponsor, or commercial publishers. Do you anticipate textual material to be published for public consumption?

The primary result of this project is to produce a training manual for use with Institutional Review Boards as they consider complex bioethical issues. The leading publisher in the field is Woodgrain Publishers, who has expressed strong conceptual interest in publishing our IRB Bioethics Training Manual after review of two initial chapters and the table of contents. Because of their national reputation as a publisher of biomedical books, they have the marketing distribution channels and networks necessary to insure a reasonable market penetration.

A 200-page training manual is envisioned and will consist of three parts: Ethical Principles, Biomedical Applications, and Case Studies. We will provide appropriate text and references, while Woodgrain will handle graphics and illustrations in addition to marketing. In the event Woodgrain decides against publication, three other publishers in the bioethics field will be contacted. A text delivery date of November 2002 is anticipated.

2. **Computer Disks** can be used to disseminate project reports instead of the more traditional printed reports. Could you prepare an electronic report that could be produced inexpensively and shared with other computer users?

We propose taking a cost-effective approach to the dissemination of our final project report. Rather than spend valuable project dollars printing a more traditional, four-color report with fancy graphics, we propose to prepare our report on a computer disk that can be widely disseminated at low cost. The final report consumers are extensive computer users and will find great convenience in being able to read and search the report for items of special interest to themselves.

Since the report consumers have different electronic platforms—some have personal computers while others are Macintosh users—it is important to prepare the final report in a universal electronic format. The Rich Text Format (RTF) satisfies this requirement because any computer can read it. Accordingly, the final report will be prepared using RTF files. The final project report cost will be approximately 30 cents per disk.

3. **Executive Summaries** of project results can be faxed to appropriate persons. Are there significant professionals who would appreciate a brief but very timely abstract of your project results?

The ubiquitous fax machine is an ideal communication tool to disseminate executive summaries of project results. Timely project summaries will be distributed to top hospital administrators, IRB chairs, and policy makers. Taking advantage of skim reading techniques—bulleted lists, bolded headers, and short sentences—the executive summaries are intended to keep the project and its results foremost in the minds of executives.

To meet this goal of high visibility, the content emphasis has to focus on how the project results impact the daily lives of executives, e.g., selection of members to local IRBs, ethical treatment of patients, mediation of ethical disputes, and new regulatory agency requirements. The overarching principle is to add value to the executives' understanding of bioethics.

4. **Interim Working Papers** can be used to describe those portions of project findings of most immediate interest to other audiences. Do you have significant provisional findings to share with various publics?

Since our project work progresses in distinct phases, we plan to issue interim progress report—to be called "White Papers." These White Papers will briefly summarize project results to date and concentrate on the findings from each ethical principle and its application; that is to say, since the project involves six different ethical principles, six different White Papers will be issued, each within 30 days after the completion of each project phase.

Each White Paper will follow the same general format. Following introductory remarks, a basic principle of ethics will be described from its philosophical roots, followed by a discussion of some practical applications of the principle. An annotated bibliography will conclude each White Paper, which is projected to be about 10 pages long. All White Papers will, of course, also be posted on our Web site in addition to being distributed to key policy makers.

5. **Journal Articles** can be submitted to scholarly, professional, or trade journals. Which publications? What tentative article titles?

Bioethics professionals read two major journals: *The National Journal of Bioethics* and the *Bioethics Society Journal*. Each has a circulation in excess of 1,000 subscribers, consisting of theoreticians and practitioners alike. Our first submission will be to the *National Journal of Bioethics* no later than August 1, 2002. Since this journal encourages a more theoretical perspective, our tentative working title is "Theoretical Perspectives on Bioethics: The Midwest Project." In our, 1,500-word article, we shall trace the ethical roots of the major decision-making principles that confront bioethicists. If accepted for publication without revision, Summer 2003 would be a reasonable publication date.

The article for the *Bioethics Society Journal* requires a slightly different approach. Since its readers are primarily practitioners and clinicians, our tentative working title is "Practical Applications of Ethical Principles: The Midwest Project." In this, 1,200-word article to be submitted by October 1, 2002, we will emphasize how this project has taken basic ethical principles and applied them to complex biomedical problems. Barring major changes, a Fall 2003 publication date is expected."

6. **National Information Sources** like the National Technical Information Service can be used as a repository for reports and raw data. Can you make your data and major reports available to a nationwide information service?

Our primary source data and major project reports will be filed with the National Technical Information Service (NTIS), a branch of the U.S. Department of Commerce. This information warehouse makes federal grant data available to interested individuals. More precisely, other professionals concerned with bioethics will be able to learn the project title, name of the project director, information about our organization, and a detailed description of the project along with the resulting data.

We anticipate filing the NTIS documents no later than August 1, 2002. Our entry will then be included in their electronic catalog within two weeks, thereby making the project results instantly available, as opposed to waiting a year or more for an article to be published in a professional journal. Our newsletters and poster displays will direct interested professionals to NTIS for more project details. NTIS averages more than 400,000 information requests annually.

7. **Newsletters** can be circulated to selected organizations and individuals in the field. Who are the influential decision makers that share your concern for this project?

To disseminate the results of this project, we will publish a monthly electronic newsletter entitled Bioethics Briefings, with the tagline "Tips, Ideas, and Techniques to Promote Bioethics among Health Professionals." The target audience includes central hospital administrators, all department heads and Institutional Review Board members from all participating hospitals. Feature columns include From the Editor's Desk, Practically Speaking, Ethically Speaking, Clinician's Calendar, Field Focus, and Medicolegal News. Since health professionals are very busy, it will be written for newsletter skimmers: short copy, highly practical, boldface text for emphasis, white space, and bulleted lists. Readers can skim, skip, surf and flip through the text quickly.

The newsletter will emphasize four features under the direction of Robert Hopkins, director of Staff Communications:

1. It will tell people who we are, where they can find us, and what we can do for them.
2. It will draw people into the newsletter by showing that we can provide what the readers need and that we have expertise in the area.
3. It will give specific features and reasons why readers should follow the principles of ethical behavior.
4. It will tell the readers what action to take—attending a seminar, joining a study group, participating in a focus group, or discussing cases with colleagues.

8. **Pamphlets** describe available project products and their potential use. Do you anticipate a tangible, marketable product?

> One major result of this project is the development of training materials in bioethics that are specifically targeted to Institutional Review Board members. Since IRB training is now federally mandated, an identifiable need and market exists. The budget requests $5,500 to publish and distribute a brochure that would announce the availability of the training materials.
>
> Since our organization lacks the capacity to publish attractive but reasonably priced pamphlets and brochures, this production item will be outsourced to the Midwest Brochure Publishing Company. For a cost of 75 cents per pamphlet, they can produce and mail a three-fold, four-color document. In total, 3,000 pamphlets will be distributed nationwide. The resulting income from product sales will be used to continue the project beyond the grant period.

9. **Press Releases** can be issued to the media. Do you have the necessary resources to issue quality press releases?

> The project staff has 84 years of cumulative experience in issuing successful press releases. Over time, the following rules of writing press releases have become clear: Press releases attract attention when they emphasize the relevant. Include all of the who-what-when-where-why-how facts. Write in simple sentences. Don't jam too much into a sentence. Make the lead paragraph strong.
>
> Writing strong press releases is only part of the job; the other part is distributing it to the right targets. The first rule of trash-can avoidance is don't send trash. Take the time to do a good job, but don't bury the recipients in a paper blizzard. The case study applications of bioethics have strong human interest appeal and will be the focus of mass media press releases.

INTERNET SEARCH TIPS

The above list of 22 different dissemination strategies represents the more common ways that successful grantseekers tell their good-news story. Look at the boldface words that introduce each dissemination approach. These are the key words that you can begin your Internet search to garner additional information.

For example, if you decide to issue a press release, using the phrase "press release" in your favorite search engine will identify a wealth of useful information, including tips for writing a press release, writing mistakes to avoid, an ideal length, suggestions on where to send the release, and examples of good press releases.

As another example, assume you want to host a conference on your project topic. Conducting a successful conference requires attention to myriad details, many which are overlooked by inexperienced conference conveners. Entering a phrase like "conference planning" in your favorite search engine will take you to multiple sites that offer tips on such things as gathering mailing lists, confirming speakers, choosing a conference format, signing contracts for facilities and services, coordinating volunteers, handling registration, arranging food, evaluating protocols, and disseminating conference proceedings.

As a final illustration, you may wish to write a more technically detailed use of video conferencing, specifying band width and compression features. Simply enter the phrase "video conferencing" in your favorite search engine to get useful background information for a more complex discussion.

WRITING TIPS FOR DISSEMINATION

As you write your dissemination section of your proposal, consider these guides that will enhance your credibility.

1. If the proposal guidelines do not request a dissemination section, you may weave it into your methods section, explaining how the results of your methods with be transmitted to interested personnel.
2. Include sufficient detail to let reviewers know you have developed a well-written, carefully reasoned approach to sharing your project results.
3. Incorporate active/passive and visual/verbal dissemination strategies.
4. Develop generic examples of various dissemination strategies and include them in your clip file, so you can quickly add appropriate ones to your next proposal.

REJECTION REASONS

Some reviewer comments from rejected proposals include the following.

1. The project is unique but lacks an effective strategy for disseminating some potentially significant results.

2. This proposal contains no plans for translating the results in a highly readable form, drawing practical implications, and getting this information into a dissemination network.

3. Unfortunately, the proposal advances no mechanism to share the project results with influential policy makers.

4. While the proposal offers some novel dissemination strategies, the costs of dissemination are not addressed in the budget.

5. The resumé of the project director is silent on his technical capabilities to handle videoconferencing as a dissemination strategy. Before funding can be recommended, the project director should either document his technology expertise, especially as regards bandwidth, or agree to hire a consultant in this area.

Clip File Action Item #17
Dissemination

To build your Dissemination clip file, follow these suggestions.

- Each day, pick one of the dissemination strategies cited above and write a "generic version" for your organization: proper names, project titles and dates can be inserted later. In one month, you will have a smorgasbord of dissemination strategies that can be called upon when needed.

- Garner examples of successful dissemination strategies used in other proposals.
- Explore the search engine suggestions cited above to strengthen your clip file offerings.

Time Saver Tip #15
Interruptions

To manage interruptions, consolidate your interactions with the few people who interrupt you the most. Arrange a 15-minute coffee break with Jon and Jane; hold a conference call with Fred and Susan. Jot down an agenda to use when you want to talk to with them: it will hasten your meeting.

Time Saver Tip #16
Interruptions

To manage interruptions, postpone the interrupters by asking them if you could talk later; then set up a time. In this way, you control your own time but still honor their needs.

CHAPTER 12
Budgets

There are no price objections, only value questions.
Helen Feden

PURPOSE

A project budget is more than a statement of proposed expenditures. It is an alternate way to express your project, establish its credibility, and appraise your project's value. Reviewers will scrutinize your budget to see how well it fits your proposed activities. Incomplete budgets are examples of sloppy preparation. Inflated budgets are signals of waste. Low budgets cast doubt on your planning ability. In essence, your budget is as much a credibility statement as your project narrative.

In addition to the size of your budget, your distribution of expenditures gives important clues about your organization's commitment to the project. For instance, with training or service grants, don't ask for all the money up front with a vague promise that you will share the costs in subsequent years. Instead, when preparing multiyear budgets, show that you will pick up an increasing amount of the costs each year. In doing this, you communicate your intent to continue the project after the sponsor's funds are gone. Further, you are developing your capacity to fund the program. In this way, you demonstrate that you will be a good steward of the sponsor's funds. Future funding is not apt to be an issue in most research grants, which may have limited time spans.

Preparing proposal budgets can be a bedeviling experience for beginning writers. The starting point is to understand the different types of costs included in budget building. Some key budget terms are discussed below: direct costs, indirect costs, and cost sharing.

Direct Costs

Direct costs are explicit project expenditures listed as line items in the budget. Direct costs are usually categorized into personnel (people) and nonpersonnel (things) components. Personnel costs include such items as salaries, wages, consultant fees, and fringe benefits. Nonpersonnel costs include such items as equipment, supplies, travel, and publication charges. Usually, such cost figures are easy to pinpoint. For example, grant-funded salaries are calculated as a percentage of the time and effort devoted to the project relative to one's annual salary. As another illustration, travel costs can be computed on the basis of reimbursement costs per mile or round-trip airfare, as appropriate. Space and utilities may be reflected either as direct costs or included as part of your indirect cost rate, which is described next.

Indirect Costs

Indirect costs represent other project costs not itemized as direct costs. Typically, grant budgets don't list all of the costs associated with a project because some costs are hard to pin down, e.g., payroll and accounting, library usage, space and equipment, and general project administration. Do you include in your proposal budget the costs associated with preparing payrolls or the time your boss spends talking with you about your project? Although you could cost out those factors, and others, with some effort, they are more difficult to quantify. At the same time, they are real project costs, e.g., someone has to write your payroll checks. Rather than calculating a strict cost accounting of these nebulous factors, many sponsors allow you to compute them as a percentage of your direct costs and add it to your budget request as an indirect cost item.

Federal Indirect Costs

Semantically, the federal government uses the term "indirect costs" to refer to these additional project operating costs. Sometimes called "facilities and administration costs," these grant costs are usually calculated on a percentage figure assigned to you by the federal government as a result of an indirect cost audit. The percentage figure may be based on either the total direct costs or a percentage of the total project salaries and wages. To illustrate, assume the federal government assigned you an indirect cost of 45 percent of total direct costs. This means that for every dollar you receive in federal direct costs, the government would give you an additional 45 cents to administer that dollar expenditure.

Organizations regularly receiving federal grants have an approved federal indirect cost rate that is included in the budgets of federal proposals; it consists of two major component categories: facilities and administration. "Facilities" is defined as depreciation and use allowances on buildings equipment and capital improvements, interest on debt associated with certain building, equipment and capital improvements and operations and maintenance expenses. "Administration" is defined as general administration and general expenses such as the director's office, accounting, personnel, library expenses, and all other types of expenditures not listed specifically under one of the subcategories of "Facilities."

If you plan to periodically submit federal proposals and do not have a federal indirect cost rate, your federal program officer can refer you to the appropriate federal agency to find out how you negotiate a federal indirect cost rate for your organization. Alternatively, you can get started by visiting the Office of Management and Budget Web site, www.whitehouse.gov/omb/grants/attach.html#cost.

Foundation Indirect Costs

Foundations often use the term "administrative costs" rather than "indirect costs" when referring to additional project operating expenses, although the terms are interchangeable. Foundations vary considerably in their policies regarding administrative costs. Some will pay administrative costs on grants, and their application guidelines specify the allowable percentage of total direct costs. For instance, one health-related foundation has a fixed administrative cost rate of 20 percent; to submit a budget, you add up all of the direct costs and add an additional 20 percent to the total to cover your operating expenses.

Other foundations will say explicitly in their application materials that they do not fund administrative costs. In those instances, you have two options: (1) absorb those operating costs within your organization's budget, or (2) itemize those operating costs as direct costs within your proposal budget and recover those costs as direct line-item costs.

For instance, if you think you will need five percent of your boss's time to provide updates on your project progress, include that five percent time as a direct proposal cost. If you choose the first option of absorbing those costs, at least show it as a cost-sharing component to your project, as discussed below. If you choose the second option of direct-cost itemization, you are, in reality, taking your administrative (or indirect-cost) rate apart and budgeting it as a direct cost item. Many nonprofit organizations fail to realize they can recover these operating costs if only they would ask for them. Administering a grant should not cost your organization any money.

Although some private foundations permit charging administrative costs and others don't, the majority of the foundations remain silent on this budget issue; that is, their application materials do not specify what their policy is, and yet they have administrative costs themselves. Somebody has to pay their utilities, payrolls, insurances, and other operating costs. In such instances, the preference is to request of private foundations the same indirect cost rate that they are paying themselves. To do that, look at a foundation's tax returns, annual reports, or description in the Foundation Directory (see Chapter 3) and identify two figures: (1) the total amount of grants awarded, and (2) the total expenditures for the year. For instance, recall that the Ramsey Charles Foundation (from Chapter 3) spent $17,221,933 during their fiscal year, including $16,032,149 in grants. What happened to the other $1,189,784? That amount (7 percent) represented their operating costs. Accordingly, when submitting a budget to the Ramsey Charles Foundation, you might include this language:

> In addition to the direct costs of $10,000, we are requesting 7 percent (or $700) in administrative costs, the same rate that the Ramsey Charles Foundation incurred in your last fiscal

year, according to your tax records. Our total project investment is $10,700.

Corporate Indirect Costs

In contrast to governments and foundations, corporations use the term "overhead" to mean the same thing as administrative or indirect costs. As business professionals, they are accustomed to the concept of overhead and are apt to have a high overhead rate themselves.

In most instances, the corporate application materials do not specify a policy regarding the payment of overhead. Unlike foundations, you do not have access to their tax records to request a comparable corporate rate for your project, but you do have three other options for determining a reasonable overhead rate to include in your proposal.

First, if they are a publicly held company, you may be able to determine their overhead rate by studying the latest annual report. Second, some corporate officials might be willing to tell you or one of your advisory members what their overhead rate is as a percentage of their total costs. Third, if you have no basis for calculating their corporate overhead, you can use your federally negotiated indirect cost rate since it is an audited figure. If none of these three options is acceptable, your fallback position is to list everything as direct cost items.

Cost Sharing

The costs that your organization will contribute to the total project costs are called shared costs. You may contribute partial personnel costs, space, volunteer time, or other costs toward the total project expenses. Your cost sharing may be in the form of a "hard" dollar match or one of in-kind contributions—costs not requiring a cash outlay to your organization, although they would represent real dollars if you had to pay for services rendered, e.g., the value of time contributed by volunteers. Use a fair market value to calculate in-kind contributions; simply determine what it would cost you if you had to buy those volunteered services or goods outright. For example, if teens are helping you stuff envelopes as part of a direct mail campaign, you might use a minimum wage figure to show cost sharing. On the other hand, if you have a volunteer attorney giving you *pro bono* services to evaluate a new rental contract, you would use that person's hourly billing rate multiplied by the number of donated hours as a cost sharing budget item.

Because expectations about cost sharing vary considerably, check with your program officer to determine their preferences. In fact, preproposal contact (Chapter 4) is essential to determine the value that cost sharing carries in evaluating budgets. Many sponsors still look upon cost sharing as evidence that your organization is committed to your proposed project to the extent that you are willing to absorb some of its expenses. Some sponsors will require a minimum amount of cost sharing, as indicated in their proposal guidelines. For instance, most equipment grant proposals to the National Science Foundation require a 50 percent cost sharing effort on the organization's part. On the other hand, some sponsors don't place a high value on cost sharing, even to the extent of insisting that the cost sharing be dropped from the proposed budget as a condition of awarding a grant. Sponsor attitudes towards cost sharing vary widely, so ask your program officer.

Mandatory vs. Voluntary Cost Sharing

Cost sharing may be mandatory or voluntary. Mandatory cost sharing is often referred to as "matching funds;" it is required whereas voluntary cost sharing is optional. Your promise of cost sharing in a proposal budget may be a key factor in a sponsor's funding decision.

Mandatory—as one of the eligibility requirements of the grant, the sponsor requires you to share a certain percent of the total project costs. For example, "Local organizations are required to provide a local match totaling 75 percent of the requested grant funds." In this case, if a sponsor provides $20,000, you must provide an additional $15,000 toward the total project cost of $35,000.

Voluntary—you offer cost sharing in your proposal as an incentive to get the grant award. For instance, a sponsor may indicate, "Consideration will be given to organizations with in-kind contributions." In response, you may offer 20 percent cost sharing of personnel time toward the total project cost of $150,000. This means the sponsor would contribute $125,000, and you would provide $25,000 of the total project costs. However, you can cost share too much: for some agencies, higher levels of cost sharing require more administrative monitoring on their part, something program officers may wish to avoid. Accordingly, check with your project officers to see if they have a "preferred level" of voluntary cost sharing.

Cash vs. In-Kind Cost Sharing

Cost sharing may be in the form of a cash match (hard dollars) or an in-kind contribution (soft dollars).

Cash—your organization contributes so-called "hard dollars" toward your proposed project. Perhaps you were planning to purchase some equipment with your regular internal budget. Those dollars can be allocated toward your project. Usually, you had already planned to spend the money; now, in a tactical budget building mode, you link those planned expenditures to your proposal.

In-kind—these "soft dollars" do not require a cash outlay by your organization, yet they represent real dollars you would have to pay if the costs were not absorbed elsewhere. Personnel effort is perhaps the most common form of cost sharing; it can include salaries, fringe benefits, and associated indirect costs. To illustrate, Ida Know, Project Director, may allocate 50 percent of her time (salary and fringe benefits) to a project grant, yet request sponsor funding for only 10 percent effort. Ms. Know's institution would cost share the remaining 40 percent of her salary and fringe benefits. As a further example, you can also cost share indirect costs. So, if your organization has a 26 percent indirect cost rate and your sponsor allows only a maximum reimbursement of 20 percent on direct costs, you can show the 6 percent difference as cost sharing.

Internal vs. External Cost Sharing

Assuming you've decided to cost share on your proposed budget, the funds may come from either internal or external sources—or both.

Internally—you may allocate a portion of your direct or indirect costs to your proposed project. These shared costs may take on the form of cash or in-kind contributions. Consider this internal cost sharing example. Assume you decide to cost share 20 percent of the project director's salary for your proposed project. This means that instead of your project director receiving 100 percent of her salary from your agency personnel budget, she will now receive 80 percent from that source and the remaining 20 percent from the cost sharing account on the grant; you merely reallocate a portion of her salary; her income remains the same. The source(s) of income are changed on the bookkeeping records.

Externally—you may allocate extramural dollars from other sources to the project, as indicated in the following three examples.

- You have a matching grant from another sponsor.

- A wealthy philanthropist has given you unrestricted dollars that can be earmarked to this project.

- Revenue is generated from another fund-raising activity, e.g., golf outing income can be directed to this project.

In each case, you can redirect dollars from those sources to help support the total costs of your proposed project, thereby showing your sponsor you are financially committed to supporting your proposal.

Cost Sharing Example

If your sponsor requires or strongly encourages cost sharing, then you obviously should do this. But where do you find the cost sharing dollars, particularly if your organization has a modest budget? Cost sharing is often done through a portion of salary, fringe benefits, and indirect costs. For instance, assume that a project director will spend 20 percent of her time on the project, but is requesting the sponsor to fund only 10 percent of that effort. The other 10 percent of the project director's salary can be shown as cost sharing. In addition to the cost sharing on salary dollars, additional cost sharing can be shown on the fringe benefits and indirect costs associated with the salary dollars, as Exhibit 39 shows.

In essence, this cost sharing portion of the overall budget tells your sponsor that your organization is willing to absorb one-half of the personnel costs, provided the sponsor will pay the other half. Once funded, your organization uses the grant funded salary dollars ($3,000 in this example) to pay the project director. In turn, your organization can use the deobligated salary dollars ($3,000 in agency dollars) to hire someone else part-time to do those tasks that the project director is surrendering during the course of the funded project. The project director will still receive the same salary. Instead of 100 percent of the salary coming from the organization, now 90 percent will come from the organization and 10 percent from the grant.

If your project personnel are not spending 100 percent of their time on the grant, you should identify how the remainder of their time will be spent. For example, the one-year budget shown in Exhibit 40 suggests that the project director will be spending 40 percent of her time on the grant. Among other things, that means she must "give up" doing 40 percent of her current activities in order to devote 40 percent of her time to the grant. In turn, 40 percent of her agency salary is now "deobligated" and can be used to hire someone else part-time to pick up those duties that were relinquished by the project director in order to administer the grant.

Item	Amount Requested	Cost Sharing	Total Amount
Project Director ($30,000/yr × 1 yr × 20% effort)	$3,000	$3,000	$6,000
Fringe Benefits (28% × $6,000)	$840	$840	$1,680
Indirect Costs (30% of salaries)	$900	$900	$1,800
Totals $	$4,740	$4,740	$9,480

SAMPLE COST SHARING

EXHIBIT 39

Exhibit 40 shows how one budget could be put together, but one size does not fit all. There are many variations in assembling meaningful grant budgets. Looking at past winning proposals and talking with your program officer will help clarify expectations. The following Web addresses will suggest other budget models that may be adapted to your situation.

- http://web.indstate.edu/OOR/resource/budgetf.htm A sample university-based budget page
- http://grants.nih.gov/grants/funding/phs 398/phs398.html. NIH budget page for research grants, including whole application
- http://www.neh.gov/grants/guidelines/collaborative.html. NEH collaborative research budget form
- http://www.whitehouse.gov/omb/grants/sf424.pdf. Generic grant application and budget forms used by many federal agencies—including Department of Education (ED), Environmental Protection Agency (EPA), Department of Commerce (DOC), Department of Labor (DOL), and others—in the absence of especially prepared application kits
- http://www.rwjf.org/app/rw_applying_for_a_grant/ bgtguide.pdf. Robert Wood Johnson Foundation budget with detailed information on how to fill out a multiyear budget, including a comprehensive budget narrative
- http://tram.east.asu.edu/forms/budget.pc.html. Perhaps the most comprehensive source of grant budget forms on the Internet
- http://www.grantmakers.org/common/common appform.html. A common application form used by multiple private foundations in Rochester, NY
- http://www.cooperfoundation.org/Com_App.html. A common application form used by private foundations in Nebraska
- http://www.marquette.edu/fic/common.html. A common application form used by many private foundations in Milwaukee
- http://www.cnjg.org/ComApHTM.htm. A common application form used by many private foundations in New Jersey

To look for other budget models, use the phrase "grant budget forms" in your favorite search engine.

Public and private sponsors vary within and among themselves regarding the cost categories they use on budgets. Some require more detail than others. Occasionally, a sponsor may request a list of other sponsored support or a copy of your most recent independently audited financial statement.

KEY QUESTIONS TO ANSWER

Use these key questions to prepare your next grant budget. Does your proposal do the following:

1. Follow all pertinent guidelines governing your project's budget?
2. Provide sufficient resources to carry out your project?
3. Include a budget narrative that justifies major budget categories?
4. Present the budget in the format desired by the sponsor?
5. Show sufficient detail so reviewers know how all budget items were calculated?
6. Separate direct costs from indirect costs and describe their components?
7. Include sufficient flexibility to cover unanticipated events?
8. Relate budget items to project objectives?
9. Specify the type and amount of any cost sharing?

Budget Item	Requested from Sponsor	Cost Shared by Applicant	Total
Personnel			
➢ **Salaries**			
Jane Doe, Project Director $30,000/yr x 1yr x 40% effort	$6,000	$6,000	$12,000
Carol Wooden, Survey Coordinator $20,000/yr x 6 mo x 50% effort	$5,000		$5,000
Emily Johns, Secretary $15,000/yr x 1 yr x 25% effort	$3,750		$3,750
10 Volunteers @ 100 hours each $8/hr x 100 hr x 10 volunteers		$8000	$8,000
➢ **Fringe Benefits**			
Jane Doe, Project Director 30% of salary	$1,800	$1,800	$3,600
Carol Wooden, Survey Coordinator 25% of salary	$1,250		$1,250
Emily Johns, Secretary 20% of salary	$750		$750
10 Volunteers 20 % of salary (entry level)		$1,600	$1,600
➢ **Consultants**			
James Ball, Project Evaluator $300/day x 5 days	$1,500		$1,500
➢ **Personnel Subtotal**	$20,050	$17,400	$37,450
Nonpersonnel			
➢ **Physical Facilities**			
Space Rental $700/month x 12 months	$4,200	$4,200	$8,400
Utilities (Gas, electric) $125/month x 12 months	$1,500		$1,500
➢ **Equipment**			
Pentium IV Laptop Computer	$3,000		$3,000
LaserJet 6 Plus Printer	$4,000		$4,000
Annual Maintenance Contract Laptop ($300) + Printer ($400)		$700	$700
➢ **Supplies**			
Basic Office Supplies $300/person x 3 people	$900		$900
Survey Printing and Mailing $1.27/survey x 1500 surveys	$1,905		$1,905
Long distance phone + fax charges $50/month x 12 month	$600		$600
➢ **Travel**			
Local mileage: Smith (1000 miles) + Wooden (500 miles) @ 33.5¢/mile	$502		$502
Volunteers 300 miles x 10 volunteers x 33.5¢/mile		$1005	$1005
Smith R/T Airfare ($400) + Per Diem ($125/day x 3 days)	$775		$775
➢ **Subtotal Nonpersonnel**	$17,382	$5905	$23,287
Total Direct Costs (Personnel + Nonpersonnel Subtotals)	$37,432	$23,305	$60,737
Indirect Costs (30%)	$11,230	$6,692	$18,222
Total Project Costs	$48,662	$30,297	$78,959

SAMPLE ONE-YEAR COMPLETE BUDGET: FEDERAL HEALTH EDUCATION PROJECT

EXHIBIT 40

Budget Narrative

This proposal requests a sponsor investment of $48,662, 62 percent of the total project costs. The remaining 38 percent will be cost shared by the applicant as evidence of its commitment to the project. The requested funds will be used to supplement, not replace, existing operating funds. The following comments further clarify the basis for calculation of budget items. Volunteer wages were calculated on the basis of fair market equivalent replacement costs. Our agency has three levels of fringe benefits, depending on employment tenure. All employees receive, health, life, and social security benefits. After one year, vision and dental insurance is added. After two years, retirement contributions are added. Office supplies are based on best reasonable estimates and include laser cartridges, printer paper, stationery, folders, and general items such as paper clips, pens, and staples. Equipment costs are based on actual vendor quotations. Local travel costs are based on IRS allowable mileage rates. The economy domestic round-trip air travel costs are to the American Institute of Nutrition Conference, November 1–3, 2003, in St. Louis, Missouri. Indirect costs are calculated on the basis of 30 percent of total direct costs, a rate approved by our cognizant agency, the Department of Health and Human Services, effective July 1, 2002. The results of this project will directly impact 6,000 frail minority elderly and result in a cost of six cents (6¢) per hour of nutrition instruction per individual over a five-year period.

SAMPLE ONE-YEAR COMPLETE BUDGET: FEDERAL HEALTH EDUCATION PROJECT

EXHIBIT 40 (continued from p. 137)

10. Include any attachments or special appendixes to justify unusual requests?
11. Identify evaluation and dissemination costs?

WRITING TIPS FOR BUDGETS

These tips will help you plan and write your next budget.

1. Show the basis for your calculations. Fuzzy: Travel = $384. Specific: Local mileage for Project Director, 100 mi/mo @ $.32/mi × 12 mo = $384; if attending conventions, indicate name, location, and date.
2. Desktop supplies (pens, pencils, paper clips, and so forth) average $300 year/key person. It is not necessary to itemize these costs; just indicate that this is an estimate.
3. Tell sponsors the components of your fringe benefit rate. Indicate if it includes FICA, health, life, retirement, dental and disability insurance, and other benefits.
4. In university-originated proposals, separate graduate student stipends from tuition.
5. In multiyear budgets, allow for yearly increases; indicate annual percentage increases. Ask your

program officer what percentage increases are currently being approved in multiyear budgets.

6. Include a budget narrative immediately following your budget figures to explain or justify any unusual expenditure items, even if one is not specifically requested (see Exhibit 40).
7. Include your organization's overall budget, if requested, showing how the grant budget request fits into your general operating budget.
8. If you have applied for or received other funding, say so. It will enhance your credibility, for your proposed sponsors will recognize your commitment to supporting your project.
9. Check agency regulations for indirect costs and your approved rate, if applicable.
10. Some grant budgets require cost sharing; that is, the sponsor and you must co-pay for the project. If so, distinguish between your cost sharing and the sponsor's share.
11. Itemize the budget and justify each item, such as travel, equipment, personnel, and other major expenses. Don't lump costs together. You can either round numbers to the nearest $10 or show exact numbers, as Exhibit 40 indicates, to let the sponsor know you are using "measured" numbers.
12. If the project is to occur in phases, identify the costs associated with each phase.

13. Don't overlook budget support for such things as service or maintenance contracts, insurance, shipping, or installation. If you anticipate training costs associated with the purchase of new equipment, include those costs in your budget as well. Your budget clip file should contain basic financial information needed in preparing proposal budgets, such as fringe benefit components, and indirect cost rates. Use your computer spreadsheet to draft various versions of your budget.

14. All costs must be incurred during the proposed project period. You cannot prepay someone for follow-up work that will be performed before or after the grant. All costs must be auditable.

15. Budgets should be close approximations of what you plan to spend. You do have some flexibility in the expenditure of funds and often it is possible to reallocate dollars between certain cost categories. For example, one federal agency will allow up to a 25 percent cost transfer between supplies and equipment. If you need to shift more than 25 percent of your supply budget to equipment, prior written approval is required. Your award notice will indicate the flexibility you have in rebudgeting your grant dollars. If you are uncertain about budget flexibility, ask your program officer for a copy of their grant administration guidelines *before* you submit a proposal.

BUDGET SIZE

"How much should I ask for?" is a common question asked when preparing a grant budget. Your prospect research will reveal typical sponsor award amounts and represent one important clue in establishing your target budget, but use it only as a guide. If your organization is new to the sponsor or lacks an established track record, you may want to request something less than their average grant size. On the other hand, if your needs are well documented and you have strong credibility, you may wish to exceed the average amount awarded by the sponsor. Remember, nobody gets an "average" grant. "Average" is a mathematical concept, and organizations continually receive grant awards above or below the average.

If you need bigger dollars than your sponsor typically awards for a grant, you may wish to take your larger project and divide or "chunk" it up into smaller but logical segments, thereby inviting the sponsor to fund a phase of your overall effort. If phase one funding for them proves to be successful, they are reasonable candidates for phase two funding. As another alternative, you can approach multiple sponsors, requesting each to fund part of your project. Although this can be done, it is difficult to do because it requires an extensive amount of marketing and intersponsor coordination on your part. Experienced grant-getting organizations seek partial funding from multiple sponsors only as a last resort; their preferred alternative is to target a different sponsor, one who is capable of giving the entire amount.

SUPPLEMENT OR SUPPLANT FUNDS

Most grantmakers want to be sure that you use their money to supplement, not supplant, existing funds. In other words, they don't want to have their money used to replace—supplant—existing dollars. Said differently, they generally don't want to provide money for regular operating support. Instead, they want their money to supplement or expand projects, programs, or services. Accordingly, you may wish to include a sentence like the following in your budget narrative: "The requested funds will be used to supplement, not replace, existing internal budgets." They want their money to be used as an "add-on" instead of a substitute for existing dollars. In essence, they want their funds to be used for project support, not operating support.

ALLOWABLE BUDGET ITEMS

What can you include in your budget? Answer: usually every reasonable expense associated with the project. Unless sponsor regulations indicate otherwise, you can include such cost components as indicated in Exhibit 41.

Occasionally, a sponsor's guidelines will prohibit a specific budget item, e.g., computers or equipment. Program officers can provide useful reactions to draft budgets.

The budget exhibit and narrative are meant to persuade the reviewer that sufficient funds are requested to achieve the project goals and objectives in a cost-effective manner. The budget in Exhibit 40 is for one year only. If it were requesting multiyear funding, it would look the same, except that three additional columns per year would be added on the right side of the ledger—namely, amount requested, cost sharing, and total. First-year funding is usually higher because of inevitable start-up costs, whereas subsequent funding levels decrease over time.

USING COMPUTER SPREADSHEET PROGRAMS

Spreadsheet programs, such as Lotus 1-2-3 or Excel, enable you to manipulate numbers and automatically recalculate whenever you change a budget figure. As a result, they are particularly helpful in preparing grant budgets. With a spreadsheet program, you could extend the budget over multiple years, showing what would happen as salaries rise and year one start-up costs drop. Multiyear budgets are easy to calculate. If you plan to submit a three-year budget request, you need to prepare four budgets: one for each year separately and the fourth for a cumulative total. Similarly, consortium budgets can detail figures for each strategic partner as well as a collective budget total.

Spreadsheet numbers can be sorted, extracted, or merged with other spreadsheets. You can display your values as pie charts or graphs. Consider attaching to your proposal budget a bar graph that shows the requested and cost-shared amounts each year over a multiyear grant; many sponsors will respond favorably if you can systematically increase your cost-sharing portion over time.

When reviewing grant funding histories, many sponsors report their average grant size. That "average" may be misleading for organizations like yours. Consider entering funding histories from a targeted sponsor onto a spreadsheet, sorting out the organizations that are like yours, and computing averages and ranges on this narrower information. It may give you an entirely different picture of how much to request in your proposal.

FUTURE FUNDING PLANS

Some sponsors expect you to continue funding your project after the grant expires. If you have a financing plan for future funding, briefly outline it. Forecast your future budget needs for this project and indicate whether those dollars will come from internal or external support. Mention other sponsors that could become involved in your project. If government funding is unavailable, state that fact, because it is especially important to corporation and foundation proposals. Other methods to raise money include, but are not limited to, these described below.

Special Events

Special fundraising events should follow these basic principles:

- Be restricted to ones that your organization can effectively carry out
- Bring in significant revenue for the efforts of paid and volunteer staff
- Attract new volunteers and new money
- Provide positive community relations
- Be followed up for future volunteer and donor support
- Be evaluated each year to determine your future involvement

Among the options for special events: antique shows, auctions, balloon races, beach parties, bingo, book signings, business openings, car shows, casino nights, celebrity appearances, chili cookoffs, concerts, cooking demonstrations, costume parties, cow chip bingo, dances, dine-arounds, golf outings, home tours, pancake breakfasts, races, radiothons, raffles, runs or walks, sidewalk sales, telethons, and tournaments. The following example presents some future funding grant language, using a dinner as the special event.

To sustain this project after the initial grant period, we plan to initiate an annual fundraising event called "Dinner with the Docs." The dinner will feature local prominent physicians who support our project outcomes or other individuals who are well-known in the community. The main purpose of this special event is to raise funds and heighten attention to volunteer service opportunities. Briefly, one high-profile physician will be selected as "head waiter" and will assist in recruiting other physician-waiters. All waiters will personally invite their own guests to fill a 10-person table or provide a list of colleagues and friends to which invitations could be sent. Additionally, they will choose a theme to decorate their table and be in a costume to match the theme. Finally, they will entertain their guests as they wait on their tables, competing during the evening for tips. A four-course gourmet meal will be served at a leisurely pace, allowing ample time for waiters to dream up new ways to work for their tips, e.g., serve meals in bedpans. Finally a Master of Ceremonies will auction off the head waiter's apron autographed with the signatures of all CEO waiters.

While many special events can be a financial disaster, this one has the elements of success. The event is great fun and the volunteers love to be involved with no begging. Ticket sales are

Accounting	Indirect costs	Renovation
Advertising	Instruments	Rent
Audiovisual instruction	Insurance	Repairs
Auditing	Legal services	Salaries and wages
Binding	Maintenance	Security
Books	Periodicals	Subcontracts
Computers	Postage	Supplies
Consultants	Publications	Telecommunications
Dues	Recruitment	Travel
Equipment	Registration fees	Tuition
Fringe benefits	Relocation	Utilities

ALLOWABLE BUDGET ITEMS

EXHIBIT 41

generally nonexistent; most often the waiters invite their own table guests. Decoration committees are not needed, as the waiters select their own themes and decorations. The Celebrity Waiters provide most of the entertainment for their table. The event is repeatable every year. The event stimulates natural competition between visible leaders in the community. Our past experience has shown that people are more likely to donate to a cause in a competitive social event than to respond to direct, one-to-one solicitation.

Fee-for-Service

We believe it would be ethically irresponsible to initiate the important social services described in this proposal and then abruptly terminate the services at the end of the grant period. That notion flies contrary to our mission of helping people help themselves. The support requested in this proposal seeks start-up funding to establish the awareness, systems, and service delivery procedures. Once beyond the three-year implementation phase, services will be sustained on a fee-for-service basis. Even using a sliding scale fee schedule based on patient income, our business plan analysis suggests this service can be self-funded, as evidenced by the budget and expenditure projects included in

the appendix. Our patient surveys reaffirm not only the need for this service but the willingness of patients to sustain it. Their bottom line message: the nearest comparable service is more than 100 miles away.

Membership Fees

Once the Biomedical Research Institute is established and fully operational within the three-year grant period, it will continue its activities by charging corporate membership fees. Within a two-hundred-mile radius of the Institute, there are 247 different manufacturers of biomedical equipment. They will be offered different membership levels and benefits.

Basic Membership: $1,500/year
- Discounts for attending seminars and workshops
- Publications, including the institute newsletter, seminar and workshop materials, and membership directory

Executive Sponsors: $10,000/year
- All basic membership privileges
- Opportunity to do projects with center staff
- Participation in center program activities
- Referral of qualified personnel for internships and recruitment
- Service on Institute Advisory Board

- Contributions to newsletter
- Participation in collaborative activities with other members

Corporate Sponsors: $25,000/year
- All above privileges
- Company name listed prominently on Institute letterhead, the banner in the center newsletter, and all press releases
- Speakers in program activities
- Unlimited access to Institute-initiated project reports
- Staff presentations to sponsor clients or prospects once at no charge

Grants

For years, grants have been the lifeblood of our organization. As a result, we have established long-term relationships with major grantmakers. More than two-thirds of our annual budget over the past decade has come from grant-funded support. While one cannot run a program on grants forever, our grantmakers recognize us as a responsible steward of their funds. Once the funding for the demonstration phase of this proposed project ends, other grantmakers will be approached for implementation funding. In that sense, the demonstration funding requested in this proposal will become a magnet to attract follow-up support. Preliminary conversations with two community foundations have been encouraging; more precisely, both foundations reacted favorably to our preliminary proposal and have expressed interest in jointly funding the next project phase.

Direct Mail

Our direct mail campaign has four main goals:

- To acquire new donors
- To encourage prior donors to increase their giving size
- To renew lapsed donors
- To bolster public relations

We are particularly interested in acquiring new donors because our experience shows that 50–80 percent will donate again.

An effective direct mail campaign involves multiple mailings. For purposes of sustaining the project after the grant funds lapse, we plan to initiate quarterly mailings during the final project year. The most crucial element in a direct mail campaign is the quality of the mailing list. Beyond mailing to prior donors, new donors will be identified by consulting with a mailing list vendor to target people who live in upper-income geographic areas, meet minimum income levels, and subscribe to magazines compatible with our overall mission. A preliminary check of individuals living in the 532XX zip code range with family income levels exceeding $75,000 and subscribing to the *Strengthening Family Values* Magazine identified 938 mailing targets. The Project Director will oversee the direct mail campaign, which will be crafted with the help of board member Joyce Kunkel, who is director of advertising for Zigfried and Associates, a leading advertising and public relations firm with more than 200 cumulative years of experience in direct mail advertising.

Planned Giving

Planned giving integrates personal, financial, and estate planning with the individual donor's plans for lifetime giving. Through bequests or other planned gifts, donors have the capacity of funding a charitable gift annuity with relatively small investment. Planned giving is an intricate long-term fundraising strategy that requires special training in financial planning and tax laws. Although no staff members have this type of training or expertise, we are fortunate that Attorney Terrence Case, Trust Officer at the Wells Fargo Bank, is an active member of our Board and has volunteered to lead a planning giving campaign on behalf of our organization. His interactions with potential donors will include bequests, charitable gift annuities, charitable remainder trusts, life estate contracts, life insurance policies and revocable trusts.

Phone-a-Thons

Telephone solicitation is a powerful fundraising strategy. While the idea of telephone solicitation does generate some negative semantic reactions—people don't like to be bothered—our experience has shown that relatively few people are annoyed by telephone solicitations from well-respected charities. Universities, for example, use phone-a-thons with great success.

Using the facilities at a local telemarketing firm, we will conduct a phone-a-thon by having volunteers call people and solicit donations.

This approach enables us to reach out to people who don't give on a regular basis. Additionally we can encourage regular donors to give more. Our primary target audience will be current and past donors. The key is the training of volunteers, who will undergo a six-hour program that will consist of two parts: (1) the carefully scripted opening, and (2) the follow-up question-objection-ask sequence. Because telephone solicitations are most effective when conducted by a peer of the prospect, the volunteers will come from backgrounds that match as closely as possible those of the prospects. No paid solicitors will be used. Since the phone banks are donated for this project, no up-front money is required.

Other Options

Some of these options will be appropriate for your organization, whereas others will not. Here are some questions to help you identify some more viable options.

1. Can your organization absorb future funding in your general operating budget over the next few years?
2. Can your project be supported on a fee-for-service basis?
3. Could you contract with a third party to subsidize your services to clients?
4. Could your future expenses be covered as a part of a nongrant fund-raising program?
5. Do you have another profitable service or activity that can be expanded to cover costs of running your new project in the future?
6. Could the financial responsibility for your project be transferred to some other organization?

Proposal reviewers are not looking for an ironclad guarantee that you can provide future project funding. Rather, they want specific evidence that you have a tentative plan in place. Such a plan also shows that you have an extensive project network of support, thereby enhancing your credibility. Some types of research grants may not need extensive funding beyond the grant; nevertheless, this proposal section may be used to lay the groundwork for future support requests.

Example of Future Funding Plan

Proposal seeking minority fellowship support from a national science agency:

"Midwest University is committed to continuing this program after completion of agency funding. To help sustain the program, we have identified the following sources of future funding:

1. *Summer Employment in Industry.* The College of Engineering will use its strong partnership with industry to arrange summer employment for future participating students. Through such employment, students will gain practical experience and financial support.
2. *Consortium Membership Support.* As noted in Section V.B.1.b, the College of Engineering is part of the Midwest Engineering Consortium, which includes the membership of several local companies and three engineering colleges. (See Appendix E.) Funds generated from membership fees will be targeted for future program participants.
3. *Training Grants.* The College of Engineering, working in close cooperation with the Development Office, will aggressively seek extramural funding from private sources, including corporations and private foundations, to continue the proposed Minority Fellowship Program.
4. *Engineering Fellowship Funds.* The College of Engineering will give future and continuing program participants first priority for fellowships from funds received each year from its Engineering Fellowship Fund. These funds average more than $30,000 per year.
5. *Graduate Research and Teaching Assistantships.* The Department of Electrical and Computer Engineering will supplement support generated from the four sources above with research and teaching assistantships. Currently, the Department has 27 university-funded assistantships.
6. *Online Fund Raising.* Since the department has thousands of graduates spread throughout the country, many in high-paying jobs, a Web site will be established to encourage on-line giving. Electronic donations will be encouraged through the College's quarterly alumni newsletter.

Together, these six sources of future funding will continue the program beyond the agency grant period. Nevertheless, agency support is needed, as detailed in the budget proposal, to establish the Minority Fellowship Program.

REJECTION REASONS

Here are some reasons why reviewers have rejected proposals based on inadequate budgets.

1. The applicants' claim that "we will continue to look for alternative sources of support" does little to inspire confidence.
2. No systematic funding plan beyond the termination date is presented.
3. The budget is too high for the expected results.
4. The principal investigator is asking the sponsor to carry costs normally borne in his institutional operating budget.
5. While full funding of this project cannot be recommended, given its highly innovative nature, pilot support should be provided.
6. The budget request is unusually excessive, not justified, and not linked to specific project objectives.
7. Without adequate justification, the proposal appears to request support for resources already in place.
8. The budget is not sufficiently explained or justified.
9. The budget does not seem to reflect costs associated with the marketing of the newly proposed services.
10. The budget does not identify personnel full-time equivalents.
11. The budget does not identify sources or amounts of in-kind contributions.
12. Is it realistic for the project director to dedicate 50 percent effort in year one and only 20 percent effort in years two and three, especially when year two proposed to expand into new and larger communities?
13. The budget request for project evaluation seems inadequate given the magnitude of the evaluation plan.
14. Are there unidentified matching dollars being used to make up any difference?
15. The budget does not appear to include a line item for project evaluation, nor does the budget narrative identify an evaluator. Who is doing the evaluation and how much will it cost?
16. The proposal doesn't identify who will be doing the project evaluation or indicate what will be evaluated, so how do they know that the evaluation will cost 5 percent of the budget?
17. The budget does not identify the fringe benefit rate or its components.
18. The federal share of the project funding decreases over the five-year period, but there is no discussion of who is picking up the expense. Do partner agencies have the capacity to integrate project costs into their operating budgets?
19. The proposal narrative does not discuss a sustainability plan for this specific project.
20. The proposal narrative identifies potential sources of future private and federal government funding; however, no firm commitments of cash or in-kind funding dedicated to sustaining services exist yet.
21. The proposal's plan to secure sustainability funding is weak. Many agencies will not be able to absorb project costs to maintain efforts. A more comprehensive plan might include examples of private foundations and corporations to approach for support.
22. If they have a federally negotiated indirect cost rate, they should say so in the narrative and include a copy of it in the appendix.

 **Clip File Action Item #18
Budget**

Consider these action items to build your Budget clip file.

- List all of the items included in your fringe benefit package.
- Get a copy of your current indirect cost rate.
- Include a copy of your overall organizational operating budget.
- Write generic versions of the future funding options cited above, ones that are applicable to your organization.

 **Time Saver Tip #17
Procedures**

As an efficient procedure, use a telephone headset. It allows you freedom of movement to express your ideas with your entire body; it also frees up your hands to clear the desk clutter when you're on hold.

 **Time Saver Tip #18
Procedures**

As an efficient procedure, return calls during lunch hour that require only a short answer or when you're posing a simple question. Many people will be away from their desks and you'll reach voice mail. Be specific in your call. This way they can leave you a complete, detailed answer.

Time Saver Tip #19
Procedures

As an efficient procedure, group your calls. Place a flurry of calls in the morning, then block out time to do busywork created by the calls, such as mailing or chasing down answers.

Time Saver Tip #20
Procedures

As an efficient procedure, "power block" your time in intervals where you do nothing except what you schedule yourself to do. Make an appointment with yourself to work on the next step in developing your proposal.

CHAPTER 13
Appendixes

Great minds must be ready not only to take opportunities,
but also to make them.

C. C. Coulton

PURPOSE OF THE APPENDIXES

Proposal appendixes are opportunities waiting to be finished. They contain supportive secondary information that will further strengthen your proposal narrative. As a writer, you may need to include appendix items such as those listed in Exhibit 42.

Some grantmaking agencies do not circulate copies of appendixes when transmitting proposals to reviewers, a practice you should clarify with your program officer. As a consequence, essential proposal information should go in the narrative. Nevertheless, the use of appendixes is recommended, especially when sponsor page limits are constraining. Each item listed in Exhibit 42 represents a valuable addition to your clip file.

KEY QUESTIONS TO ANSWER

Ask yourself these key questions as you plan your appendixes:

1. Could reviewers evaluate the proposal without any appendix information?
2. Have you included strong letters of support and commitment?
3. Are assurances of cooperation provided in instances of interagency support?
4. Are resumés included for all key project personnel and consultants?

WRITING TIPS FOR APPENDIXES

Follow these tips in planning your appendixes:

1. Judicious use of appendixes can overcome agency constraints on page limits.
2. Use appendixes for presentation of secondary supporting material.
3. Put long charts, graphs, tables, formulas, and other forms of visuals in the appendixes.
4. Make sure all resumés reflect expertise essential to your proposed project.

CONSORTIUM AGREEMENTS

A consortium grant or contract is an award made to one institution (known as the lead institution) in support of a project that carries out programmatic activity in collaboration with other organizations, which are separate legal entities, administratively independent of you. Your selection of coalition partners for a consortium grant should be guided by these principles. The collaborators should be able to do the following:

1. Include an appropriate cross-section of members
2. Build on existing strengths and resources.
3. Develop and pursue concrete, attainable goals and objectives.
4. Partner on activities and evaluation.
5. Share in both processes and outcomes of the coalition.
6. Promote a learning and empowering process.
7. Disseminate findings and knowledge to all partners.
8. Foster mutual respect, understanding, and trust.

When submitting a consortium proposal to a sponsor, you should include a copy of the agreement that all

Agency publications	Maps of service area	Reprints of articles
Certifications	Organizational charts	Resumes
Consortia agreements	Organizational fiscal reports	Significant case histories
Definitions of terms	Past success stories	Subcontractor data
Letters of support	Publicity material	Tabular data
Lists of board officials	Recent annual reports	Vendor quotes

POSSIBLE APPENDIX DOCUMENTS

EXHIBIT 42

agencies would sign, an agreement based on these eight principles that binds the agencies together for a common cause. The preferred approach would be to have the agreements formally executed prior to proposal submission and to include them as an appendix item. If that is not possible, the fallback position is to at least include a draft of the consortium agreement in the appendix and indicate that it is the type of document all parties would sign once the grant award is made.

In consortium agreements, a separate, detailed budget for the initial and future years for each institution is submitted, as well as a composite budget for all institutions. The lead institution must approve any major rebudgeting requests from collaborating institutions; additionally, the collaborators must provide the lead institution with appropriate reports (progress reports, expenditure reports, invention statements) in order to fully comply with sponsor requirements.

Following are two examples of consortium affiliation agreements often found in proposal appendixes. Exhibit 43 involves two agencies collaborating on a federal grant. Exhibit 44 involves the same two agencies collaborating on a private foundation grant. These exhibits are meant to represent common examples but they should be modified to conform to specific sponsor requirements.

PHANTOM COLLABORATIONS

Successful grantseekers know that true collaborations must be genuine, not phantom-based. To illustrate, a local grantmaking agency recently announced its intention to fund a health-related project, but with a catch. Only one proposal would be funded per geographic area, and all interested applicants in the county should get together, join forces, and submit a collaborative proposal. The sponsor's well-intended but conceptually flawed idea was to create a grant opportunity that would automatically guarantee interagency collaboration.

Here's what happened. The lead applicant agency asked other collaborators to submit a one-page outline of what they could contribute to the proposal. On the basis of those one-pagers, the lead applicant crafted a proposal and sent it in without further collaborations. The other collaborators requested meetings to talk about the content and format of the proposal. Their request for collaborative meetings was denied.

To no one's surprise, the proposal didn't get funded. The lead applicant agency didn't recognize the characteristics of successful collaborative proposals. Consider these key ideas:

1. Collaborators talk about the strategic planning process used to develop the proposal.
2. Collaborators identify the contributions of each participant and how it contributes to the "big picture."
3. Collaborations usually contain an advisory board with representation from the major participants.
4. Collaborators include a draft consortium agreement showing how they will cooperate administratively, fiscally, and programmatically.
5. Collaborators schedule progress reports that involve the major players.

This proposal had none of these characteristics. As the reviewers will quickly determined, this was not a "real" proposal; rather, it was a phantom proposal. Phantom collaborations don't get funded.

The elements of a successful collaboration include the following:

Consortium Grant Agreement between Alzheimer's Basic Care Agency and XYZ Agency

This Consortium Agreement is entered into this first day of May, 2002, by and between Alzheimer's Basic Care Agency (hereinafter called ABC) and XYZ Agency (henceforth XYZ).

Whereas, ABC was awarded a single grant (HRSA-09214-8421-0672) from the U.S. Department of Health and Human Services (hereinafter called "Sponsor") and this single grant involves multiple agencies; and

Whereas, XYZ proposes to provide support for this project;

Therefore, ABC and XYZ mutually agree on the following programmatic, fiscal and administrative considerations.

Programmatic Considerations

1. **Project Director.** Ms. Jane Smith is the Project Director for ABC. In the event she cannot perform in this capacity for any reason, ABC retains the right to appoint an alternative Project Director of its choice, subject to Sponsor approval.

2. **Project Co-Director.** Mr. Jon Jones will serve as Project Co-Director for XYZ. Any personnel change will require prior written approval from ABC and Sponsor.

3. **Scope of Work.** The scope of work to be conducted by Ms. Smith and Mr. Jones and project associates is described in the award entitled "Evaluation of Service Delivery Models for the Frail Elderly," which is incorporated herein by reference referred to as the "Grant Awrd." Ms. Smith and Mr. Jones are responsible for directing and monitoring the grant effort as described in the Grant Award.

4. **Performance Standards.** XYZ will use reasonable efforts to accomplish work in the Grant Award following generally accepted standards of professional skill.

Fiscal Considerations

1. **Allowability of Costs.** ABC will determine the allowability of direct costs in accordance with applicable Sponsor policies and guidelines. If fiscal policies and practices at XYZ differ from those of ABC, the policies of the institution where the costs are generated will apply, provided any such policies are in compliance with those of the Sponsor.

2. **Indirect Costs.** Indirect costs for XYZ will be 8% of the total direct costs, as specified in the Grant Award.

3. **Excess Cost Reimbursement.** Any cost reimbursement to XYZ in excess of its budget award will require prior written agreement from ABC.

4. **Billing Schedule.** ABC shall pay XYZ on a monthly basis, provided invoices and vouchers are in such form and reasonable detail to verify the allowability of costs in accordance with Sponsor grant administration guidelines.

5. **Payment Schedule.** ABC shall pay XYZ no later than thirty (30) days after the receipt of each invoice or voucher, unless Sponsor delays its funding to ABC.

6. **Rebudgeting.** XYZ can rebudget up to 10% of its Grant Awards funds at its sole discretion, provided Sponsor requirements are not violated. Rebudgeting in excess of 10% for XYZ must have prior written approval of ABC.

7. **Financial Records.** XYZ agrees to provide ABC and Sponsor access to records supporting grant-related costs upon reasonable demand. Further XYZ agrees to preserve its records for five years after the expiration of the Grant Award.

Administrative Considerations

1. **Effective Date and Duration.** This Agreement becomes effective when signed by duly authorized representatives of ABC and XYZ and ends upon the project completion of May 20, 2005, unless otherwise stipulated in writing.

2. **Inter-agency Collaborations.** ABC and XYZ agree to cooperate, communicate, and collaborate in the manner and detail described in the Grant Award.

3. **Title to Equipment.** Title to all equipment purchased with funds under this Agreement resides with ABC. However, ABC may wish to make such equipment available to XYZ for an indefinite period of time, provided Sponsor guidelines allow it and XYZ agrees to furnish ABC with reasonable and appropriate inventory control information.

CONSORTIUM AGREEMENT INVOLVING GOVERNMENT GRANT

EXHIBIT 43

4. **Project Dissemination.** ABC and XYZ shall make reasonable efforts to disseminate project results through research reports and other print and electronic distribution mechanisms.

5. **Compliance.** In accepting this Agreement, XYZ agrees to comply in all applicable federal requirements, including but not limited to the following citations or their successors:

   a. **Employment Authorization.** All project personnel must be authorized for employment as stipulated in the Immigration and Reform Control Act of 1986.

   b. **Civil Rights and Equal Employment Opportunity.** XYZ affirms that they have filed assurance of compliance regarding the Civil Rights Act of 1964 and the Rehabilitation Act of 1973.

   c. **Projection of Human Subjects.** Interactions with human subjects comply with 45 CFR Part 46, assuring individual rights are protected and no one is put to undue risk.

   d. **Drug-Free Workplace.** XYZ will comply with regulations implementing the Drug-Free Workplace Act of 1988.

   e. **Scientific Misconduct.** XYZ will comply with 42 CFR Part 50 governing reporting procedures dealing with possible misconduct in science.

   f. **Patents and Inventions.** XYZ will comply with Sponsor regulations on patents and inventions. If the Sponsor declines ownership of any intellectual property arising from this Agreement, disposition of such rights will be determined by the policies of the inventor's employer.

6. **Amendments.** ABC and XYZ may amend this agreement upon written approval.

7. **Entire Agreement.** This Agreement, the Proposal, and the Grant Award constitute the entire understanding of XYZ and ABC; any oral understanding shall be without effect.

In Witness Herewith, ABC and XYZ warrant they are empowered to execute this agreement.

ABC Agency	XYZ Agency
By _____	By _____
Adam Q. Quinkleberry	Murgatroyd Grivlovitch
President	President

CONSORTIUM AGREEMENT INVOLVING GOVERNMENT GRANT

EXHIBIT 43 (continued from page 148)

1. A clear statement of goals, objectives, and outcomes to which all partners subscribe
2. Clear identification of each partner's roles and responsibilities
3. Regular meetings to provide feedback and share or exchange information
4. Concrete benchmarks to monitor progress and maintain focus
5. Patience to survive periods of frustration and seeming lack of progress
6. Open, effective channels of communication between partners

STRATEGIC PARTNERING WITH ACADEMIA

Looking for a strategic partner? Consider partnering with a nearby college or university. They are place-bound and their futures depend on the social and economic vitality of their regions. Institutions of higher education are ecological connections to their local communities. No longer can academics expect to thrive by being aloof from the conditions, needs, and opportunities of their neighbors. Academia is shifting philosophically from the concept of the academy as a

Consortium Grant Agreement between Alzheimer's Basic Care Agency and XYZ Agency

This Consortium Agreement is entered into this first day of May, 2002, by and between Alzheimer's Basic Care Agency (hereinafter called ABC) and XYZ Agency (henceforth XYZ).

Whereas, ABC was awarded a single from the We Care Foundation (hereinafter called "Sponsor") and this single grant involves multiple agencies; and

Whereas, XYZ proposes to provide support for this project;

Therefore, ABC and XYZ mutually agree on the following programmatic, fiscal and administrative considerations.

Programmatic Considerations

1. **Project Director.** Ms. Jane Smith is the Project Director for ABC. In the event she cannot perform in this capacity for any reason, ABC retains the right to appoint an alternative Project Director of its choice, subject to Sponsor approval.

2. **Project Co-Director.** Mr. Jon Jones will serve as Project Co-Director for XYZ. Any personnel change will require prior written approval from ABC and Sponsor. Mr. Jones will coordinate the institution-specific functions and activities with the overall project and serve as liaison between ABC and XYZ.

3. **Scope of Work.** The scope of work to be conducted by Ms. Smith and Mr. Jones and project associates is described in the award entitled "Evaluation of Service Delivery Models for the Frail Elderly," which is incorporated herein by reference referred to as the "Grant Award." Ms. Smith and Mr. Jones are responsible for directing and monitoring the grant effort as described in the Grant Award.

4. **Performance Standards.** XYZ will use reasonable efforts to accomplish work in the Grant Award following generally accepted standards of professional skill.

Fiscal Considerations

1. **Allowability of Costs.** ABC will determine the allowability of direct costs in accordance with applicable Sponsor policies and guidelines. If fiscal policies and practices at XYZ differ from those of ABC, the policies of the institution where the costs are generated will apply, provided any such policies are in compliance with those of the Sponsor.

2. **Indirect Costs.** Indirect costs for XYZ will be 8% of the total direct costs, as specified in the Grant Award.

3. **Excess Cost Reimbursement.** Any cost reimbursement to XYZ in excess of its budget award will require prior written agreement from ABC.

4. **Billing Schedule.** ABC shall pay XYZ on a monthly basis, provided invoices and vouchers are in such form and reasonable detail to verify the allowability of costs in accordance with Sponsor grant administration guidelines.

5. **Payment Schedule.** ABC shall pay XYZ no later than thirty (30) days after the receipt of each invoice or voucher, unless Sponsor delays its funding to ABC.

6. **Rebudgeting.** XYZ can rebudget up to 10% of its Grant Awards funds at its sole discretion, provided Sponsor requirements are not violated. Rebudgeting in excess of 10% for XYZ must have prior written approval of ABC.

7. **Financial Records.** XYZ agrees to provide ABC and Sponsor access to records supporting grant-related costs upon reasonable demand. Further XYZ agrees to preserve its records for five years after the expiration of the Grant Award.

Administrative Considerations

1. **Effective Date and Duration.** This Agreement becomes effective when signed by duly authorized representatives of ABC and XYZ and ends upon project completion on May 30, 2005, unless otherwise stipulated in writing.

2. **Inter-agency Collaborations.** ABC and XYZ agree to cooperate, communicate, and collaborate in the manner and detail described in the Grant Award and further elaborated upon below.

CONSORTIUM AGREEMENT INVOLVING PRIVATE FOUNDATION GRANT

EXHIBIT 44

a. Participate in the Evaluation Advisory Board by designating two representatives, one of whom shall be an Assistant Director.

b. Work with Project Director in organizing and offering two multidisciplinary workshops of one day's duration for health professionals at ABC.

c. Designate guest lecturers to participate in the project's Speaker's Bureau.

3. **Title to Equipment**. Title to all equipment purchased with funds under this Agreement resides with ABC. However, ABC may wish to make such equipment available to XYZ for an indefinite period of time, provided Sponsor guidelines allow it and XYZ agrees to furnish ABC with reasonable and appropriate inventory control information.

4. **Project Dissemination**. ABC and XYZ shall make reasonable efforts to disseminate project results through research reports and other print and electronic distribution mechanisms.

5. **Amendments**. ABC and XYZ may amend this agreement upon written approval.

6. **Entire Agreement**. This Agreement, the Proposal, and the Grant Award constitute the entire understanding of XYZ and ABC; any oral understanding shall be without effect.

In Witness Herewith, ABC and XYZ warrant they are empowered to execute this agreement.

ABC Agency
By _____
Adam Q. Quinkleberry
President

XYZ Agency
By _____
Murgatroyd Grivlovitch
President

CONSORTIUM AGREEMENT INVOLVING PRIVATE FOUNDATION GRANT

EXHIBIT 44 (continued from page 150)

cloister to the academy as a public space directly linked to the life of society.

Bluntly, academia needs partnerships with nonprofit organizations. If you don't have a point of contact in a nearby academic institution, call the nearest one and asked to be connected to the Grants Office or the Development Office and explain your interest in collaboration. As a nonprofit organization you can provide opportunities to enrich the educational experiences of students, focus on areas of shared concern that offer the prospect of mutual benefit, and create a "town-gown" community that values all members. Communication is the staple of any successful partnership. You'll be borrowing their credibility that will, in turn, strengthen you next proposal and increase your likelihood of getting funded.

LETTERS OF SUPPORT AND COMMITMENT

Letters of support are important appendix enclosures. Strong letters help establish your credibility and document that you have a solid base of support for your project. Your strong letters of support should go be-

yond the customary "This is a great project" endorsement and spell out what commitment is being made to the project, e.g., personnel time, space, physical facilities, financial resources. To get a strong commitment letter, provide the targeted letter writers with a draft copy of your proposal and a draft copy of the letter you would like them to sign. They can make whatever changes they feel are warranted and have it printed on agency letterhead.

When considering letters of support, grantwriters often wonder if they should solicit endorsements from congressional officials. Although congressional officials will usually provide such letters when requested, use them sparingly; that is, save congressional "muscle" for big projects, not routine ones. For example, one hospital follows the "two-comma" policy for getting congressional support letters; that is, the requested budget must have two commas in it, i.e., be greater than one million dollars. When you judge that such a letter is appropriate, contact a staff officer, explain your situation, and request a support letter. Offer to send background information about your organization as well as a draft of the letter you would like to receive.

A letter of commitment or support is usually short, less than one page. The following five sample paragraphs endorse various projects. Each paragraph came from a separate letter. Typically, these letters contain a polite opening and closing paragraph and one more substantive, or operative, paragraph, as exemplified here:

Support Letter #1:

I am pleased to lend official support from our agency to your project. I welcome this opportunity to blend our interests with your very real needs. I enthusiastically endorse the involvement of my agency. All will profit from this cross-pollination of ideas. I know from experience that multiple viewpoints are needed to traverse the milieu you face.

Support Letter #2:

I have just finished reviewing your proposal. Your emphasis will certainly be of benefit to your agency and ours. Bringing together the interdisciplinary expertise you have assembled in this proposal can only augment the richness of your project. I enthusiastically endorse the involvement of our agency and will personally assure the administrative support required to reach your project objectives. We eagerly await the formal beginning of your project.

Support Letter #3:

For more than a decade, our agencies have worked cooperatively on a variety of social service projects. In that context, I see your current proposal as a systematic continuation of our past joint efforts. The human and physical resources are in place—and have been for years—to achieve your desired project objectives.

Support Letter #4:

Thank you for the opportunity to review your proposal. You have identified some very significant local problems. As you address these problems in your agency, I am particularly pleased that we can contribute our organizational strength. [specify]. Our agency personnel have a demonstrated concern for and proven expertise in this area. In total, you have assembled an excellent interdisciplinary cadre of professionals to make this project quite promising. I want you to know that this project has the highest levels of support and commitment to success. We eagerly await active participation.

Support Letter #5:

I enthusiastically support your proposal. Its interdisciplinary approach to addressing the ever-increasing challenges we face promises valuable guidance. Your leadership role provides you with unique experience and insights with which to direct this project. Your past efforts will serve as an indispensable resource to professionals and enrich the delivery of services. Your proposal has my strong support, and I will continue to allocate time for my personnel to participate in your project activities.

In contrast to these kernel paragraphs that attempt to communicate some degree of enthusiasm, commitment, and support for the project, notice the uninspired "flatness" of this letter of support (?), recently seen in one proposal:

> I will be pleased to participate in your project. I look forward to the possibility of collaborating on this exciting and important project.

That was it! The whole letter. The letter belies the description as an "exciting and important project."

RESUMÉS

Format

Your organization should settle on a standardized format for proposal resumés so that they all look similar. The choice of formats is not as important as the fact that all of your organizational resumés match. The format you ultimately choose should emphasize the skills that are essential to conduct your proposed project. Update your resumés at least every six months.

Information Sources

Three main sources of information exist to help prepare resumés. First, your nearest public library will offer many books and examples of resumé formats. Second, for examples of resumés and tips on writing them, query your favorite search engine and enter key words like "sample resumés," "resumé examples," and "writing resumés." Third, most computers now come loaded with software that has "wizards," which enable you to customize your resume. For example, Microsoft Windows 98 contains three different formats to follow.

Common Mistakes

Your resumé is a window to your experience, expertise, and education. Be honest. Don't oversell or undersell. Ask others to review your resumé. Human resources professionals cite the following most common resumé mistakes:

- Wrong focus: instead of focusing on yourself, emphasize the skills you have that will strengthen the project.
- Inappropriate length: too long or too short.
- Disorganized: scattered information.
- Poorly reproduced: unprofessional, inconsistent spacing and type styles.
- Poorly written: substandard use of language.
- Poor description of experiences: unclear presentation of responsibilities.
- Irrelevant personal information: height, weight, marital status, etc.
- Overenthusiasm: fancy typesetting, binders, exotic paper stock.

TRANSMITTAL LETTER

Although the transmittal letter is not an appendix item, it often emerges as a last-minute detail when the proposal narrative and appendixes are assembled. Accordingly, it is included here because of the sequence in which proposals are assembled.

Your transmittal letter should tell who you are, what your proposal is about, how much money is requested, and the grant program to which it is targeted. You want to transmit your proposal so it is reviewed by the "right" program. If you have preproposal contact with a program officer about this project (see Chapter 4), then mention that:

- "This proposal culminates the preliminary discussions I have had with Dr. Jane Wingert, Program Officer in Cellular Biology."

Besides the proposal copies you send to a central receiving center, send another copy under separate cover directly to your program officer. It may take weeks between the time you send it to a central receiving station and the time it is forwarded to program officers, who usually appreciate an early review opportunity so they can begin to think about the selection of appropriate reviewers.

If you are submitting a proposal to the National Institutes of Health (NIH), consider this tip. Before you submit your proposal, ask your program officer to send an internal Awaiting Receipt of Application (ARA) notice to the Center for Scientific Review, the entry point for NIH proposal review. This will flag your proposal internally at NIH so it is forwarded to the study or review section of interest to your program officer. Further indicate in your transmittal letter that

"You should have on file an Awaiting Receipt of Application (ARA) notice regarding this proposal from Dr. Kelby Merrick, Cellular Biology Program, National Cancer Institute."

Transmittal letters for proposals to private sponsors follow the same general approach but place greater emphasis on institutional support for the project, even to the point where a chief executive officer and/or board member should countersign the proposal. An example of a transmittal letter follows in Exhibit 45.

REJECTION REASONS

Although proposals are seldom rejected because of shortcomings in the appendixes, the reviewers nevertheless do expect to see certain information items properly presented. If their expectations are not met, then your proposal may be downgraded. These reviewer comments suggest weaknesses in proposal appendixes.

1. The proposal does not provide evidence of formal structures or relationships binding collaborators.
2. The proposal does not identify or describe the qualifications of the project director to lead this collaborative venture.
3. The resumés of key project personnel do not demonstrate that they have the capability and experience to administer a million dollar grant award.
4. The applicants need to acquire greater familiarity with the pertinent literature.
5. The problems to be investigated are more complex than the applicants realize.
6. The applicants propose to enter an area of research for which they are not adequately trained.
7. The principal investigator intends to give actual responsibility for the direction of a complex project to an inexperienced co-investigator.
8. The investigators will be required to devote too much time to teaching or other non-research duties.

Clip File Action Item #19 Appendixes

To build your Appendixes clip file, return to the beginning of this chapter and begin collecting as many of the items in Exhibit 42 as possible. Encourage others to contribute as well. One organization, for example, requires all people attending staff meetings to come with a clip file contribution in hand.

Today's Date

Ms. Beau Tribblehorn, President
Black Foundation
19800 18th Street, N.W.
Washington, DC 20555

Re: Proposal Title
Your Name
Your Institution

Dear Ms. Tribblehorn:

On behalf of Midwest Agency, California's most comprehensive health provider agency for the displaced Hmong population, I am transmitting the referenced proposal for your review and consideration.

The proposal requests $150,000 for a three-year project to improve the delivery of health care among the elderly Hmong, a population facing limited choices, lost aspirations, and cultural linguistic barriers.

Ms. Laura Bennett, Project Director, has reviewed with me in detail the proposed project plans, and I can assure you that it will receive our highest organizational priority because it is central to our institutional mission of serving worthy, deserving, and needy populations.

I invite you to contact Ms. Bennett at (619) 555–1234 to answer any programmatic questions you may have. If you have any administrative questions, please call me directly at (619) 555–6789.

Sincerely,
Your Name
Your Title

PROPOSAL TRANSMITTAL LETTER

EXHIBIT 45

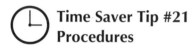 **Time Saver Tip #21
Procedures**

As an efficient procedure, take time to organize. Organization is being able to find what you're looking for—getting things done—being in control of your life. If you are disorganized, your life isn't working for you.

 **Time Saver Tip #22
Procedures**

As an efficient procedure, establish a telephone time during which you make all necessary calls. By making them in one sitting you are more likely to stay with the task at hand rather than to digress and chat with someone. An office support person can explain: "The boss is tied up right now but will be returning calls at 11:30 A.M."

 **Time Saver Tip #23
Procedures**

As an efficient procedure to get people off the phone, warn them your time is limited:

- "It sounds interesting, but I've got to leave in five minutes."
- "Can you tell me about it briefly?"
- "I really can't spend a lot of time on the phone. Let's make plans to meet for lunch instead."

CHAPTER 14
Abstracts

No one objects to how much you say, if you say it in a few words.

Martha Lupton

PURPOSE OF THE ABSTRACT

Successful grantseekers follow Lupton's advice: say much in a few words. The abstract is usually the first read and last written section of your proposal. It provides a cogent summary of your proposed project. It should offer a quick overview of what you propose to do and a rapid understanding of the project's significance, generalizability, and potential contribution. Project outcomes should be clearly identified. Often, proposal reviewers must write up a summary of your project for presentation to a larger review panel. If you do a first-class job on your abstract, program officers may use it as a basis for their proposal review, thereby simplifying their job. If your abstract is poorly written, their job is more difficult and your funding chances diminish.

Components

A thorough yet concise abstract includes the following information elements:

- **Subject**: What is the project about?
- **Purpose**: Why is the project being done? What is the problem or need being addressed?
- **Activities**: What will be done? What methods will be used?
- **Target Population**: What special group is being studied or served?
- **Location**: Where is the work being performed?
- **Outcomes**: What types of findings will result? To whom will these be useful?

KEY QUESTIONS TO ANSWER

1. Does my abstract effectively summarize the project?
2. Does it place appropriate emphasis on the various proposal components?
3. Does it enumerate project outcomes?
4. Does it comply with length or word requirements of the sponsor?
5. Does it use key subheadings to highlight proposal sections?

EXAMPLES OF ABSTRACTS

Example 1

The following is a project abstract statement for a corporate internship program to a manufacturer of industrial brushes. Most sponsors prefer relatively short abstract or summary statements. The traditional approach is to use a paragraph narrative, as indicated in this example:

> This proposal describes an Internship Program that involves the collaborative efforts of the State Department of Vocational Rehabilitation and the Ace Brush Manufacturing Corporation. Internship activities are principally aimed at identifying and utilizing a rational method for the design of filament brushes, leading to the development of advanced brushing tools that exhibit superior machining performance when used in an automated environment for deburring and surface conditioning operations. The availability of compliant machining tools can facilitate successful implementation of automated secondary machining operations and, therefore, have a beneficial impact on manufacturers that are engaged in reducing the large cost associated with manual deburring and surface finishing processes.

A classical approach is employed in developing a design critical for brushing tools and is based upon evaluation of brush force and filamentary stresses that are encountered during inservice brushing conditions. Advanced concept brushing tools are subsequently developed by employing the stated design criteria in conjunction with recently documented information from high speed and strobe photography on the nature of filament-workpart interaction during actual brush operation.

The proposed Internship Program would support three graduate students over 10 months with a budget of $30,000.

Example 2

The following is a project abstract statement for a federal minority fellowship program:

The Midwest University Department of Electrical and Computer Engineering proposes to establish a Graduate Engineering Education (GEE) program of study, research, and academic support for students from underrepresented backgrounds. All aspects of the program will be focused directly upon the timely completion of a doctoral degree in signal processing, and the preparation and motivation for a career in university teaching and research in electrical and computer engineering.

The program will rely on the department's strong academic program, quality faculty, state-of-the-art facilities, partnership with industry, and on Midwest's strong tradition in successfully educating minority students, women students, and students with disabilities. The proposed five-year GEE program will provide financial, academic, professional, and personal support for eight GEE Fellows in each program year. It is anticipated that students will complete their degrees in three to five years, allowing room for new participants in year four. As its key components, the program provides financial assistance; nurtures academic success and professional growth through mentorship, advising programs, and role models (including three female and one African-American faculty members); offers cutting-edge research experiences and special resources in signal processing; fosters university teaching as a career; and provides opportunities for both teaching and industrial work experience.

Example 3

The following is a project abstract statement for private foundation support for a parent training center.

This abstract is presented twice: first as it was originally written and second as it was rewritten.

At the conclusion of extensive long-range planning, the Parent Training Center has defined its priorities for the next decade. To implement its plan, the Center has undertaken a comprehensive multiyear development program to generate funding for its highest priorities and aspirations. The New Parent Training Program is one of the special programs for which support is sought. To date, a training curriculum has been created and a parent advisory board and a lending library were begun. The Program is proposing activities that include parenting classes, a parenting clinic with further agency referral, and an annual one-day parenting convention. Six sites have been chosen for training sessions for more than 100 parents between January and April 1999. A three-year budget and explanatory narrative are attached delineating the fund-raising goal for the Program. Because the Foundation has evidenced a strong concern for families and children and because of the need for a New Parent Training Program in the metropolitan area, the Parent Training Center is requesting a $30,000 grant, payable over three years, to assist in addressing a pervasive problem in our society.

In contrast, consider this rewritten version that uses bold headings and white space to improve the readability of this abstract for the same proposal.

Overview. The Parent Training Center, the only nonprofit agency in the State exclusively dedicated to teaching parenting skills, is seeking $30,000 to establish a new program to train teenage parents.

Need for Training Teenage Parents. Child abuse and neglect have grown dramatically, up 18% in the four-county area over the past two years. Although the growth occurs across all socioeconomic levels and races, the greatest rate of growth is occurring in families with teenage parents. These parents are poorly informed about child development and often favor corporal punishment as a means of managing their children.

Objectives of Teenage Parent Training Program

- Conduct parenting classes for teenage parents
- Establish a clinical program for serious problems
- Disseminate information about teenage parenting

Methods for Implementing Teenage Parent Training Program. A four-week series of parenting classes will be offered at sites that serve high-risk, teenage parents. Instructional techniques include discussion, videotapes, handouts, and parent support groups. Two clinical psychologists will conduct the Teenage Parent Training Program and, through their linkages with other appropriate agencies in the community, create a referral network.

Annually, a one-day parenting convention will present informative sessions and speakers on a variety of topics, e.g., toy safety, young children's literature, health issues. Additionally, exhibits will also show relevant community resources, e.g., hospitals, day care centers, preschools.

Outcomes for Teenage Parent Training Program. The effectiveness of the program will be measured through consumer satisfaction questionnaires and pre- and posttests of parenting knowledge and skills to be developed. Pilot data suggest that culturally sensitive training materials will have a positive impact on parental behaviors. The one-day conference will heighten community sensitivity to this issue.

WRITING TIPS FOR PROPOSAL ABSTRACTS

1. Don't write the abstract until you have completed the proposal.
2. Unless otherwise indicated, limit your abstract section to between 250 and 500 words.
3. Include at least one sentence each on problem, objectives, methods, and outcomes.
4. Use major subheadings in the abstract: Need, Objectives, Methods and Outcomes.

REJECTION REASONS

Weak proposal abstracts have caused reviewers to raise the following concerns:

1. The applicant raises points in the abstract that are not explained in the proposal narrative.
2. The abstract was unclear and raised questions at the outset that were subsequently confirmed upon reading the narrative. This proposal simply is not well-reasoned.
3. The applicant ignored the 100-word limitation on the abstract. In fact, the entire proposal is rather verbose.

Clip File Action Item #20
Abstracts

Following are some action items to build your Abstracts clip file.

- Gather sample abstracts of successfully funded proposals, regardless of subject matter.
- Collect examples of document design principles that will enhance your abstract: use of subheads, white space, and layout.

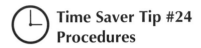

Time Saver Tip #24
Procedures

As an efficient procedure, cordless telephones extend your phone range in your office—as do cell phones, which are useful everywhere. Other telephone devices also make good timesaving sense: caller ID, call waiting, speed dialing, speaker phone, automatic redial, mute button, and conference calling.

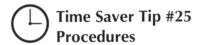

Time Saver Tip #25
Procedures

As an efficient procedure, voice mail can receive calls when you're not there. Callers are now accustomed to it, but change your message frequently to update callers on your schedule.

Time Saver Tip #26
Procedures

As an efficient procedure, swap times with a colleague when you can answer the phone for each other. Each of you gets some uninterrupted work time.

Time Saver Tip #27
Procedures

As an efficient procedure, when you leave a message for someone, give a time that you will be available in order to avoid phone tag.

- "John, I'll be at my desk between 2:00 and 4:00 P.M. today."
- "Sara, please call me tomorrow between 8:00 and 10:00 A.M."

PART IV
The Final Steps

At this point in the proposal development process, you have identified potential sponsors (Chapters 2–3) and selected one who might be interested in supporting your project (Chapter 4). It's now time to put your thoughts and ideas on paper—or the computer screen.

Establish some reasonable writing objectives. Don't try to do everything at once. Chunk it up. Write your first draft down as quickly as you can. It doesn't have to be good, just get it down in writing. Successful grantseekers estimate they spend 25 percent of their time writing the first draft and 75 percent of their time editing it. Editing is a multistage process: edit for only one feature at a time. The multiple loops through the proposal ensure that all elements are presented with punch and persuasion.

Chapters 5 through 14 offered many key questions that you should be asking yourself as you write a particular proposal section. Additionally, review the examples for ideas on things to do and the rejection reasons for things to avoid.

The four chapters in Part IV offer many concrete tips on how to write your first draft (Chapter 15) and how to do an effective editing job (Chapter 16). Some of your writing will rely on using search engines effectively (Chapter 17). Finally, you need to understand what happens to your proposal, once it is submitted (Chapter 18).

CHAPTER 15
Writing Techniques

No grantsmanship will turn a bad idea into a good one, but there are many ways to disguise a good one.

William Raub

PURPOSES OF GOOD PROPOSAL WRITING

There are many ways to disguise a good idea. All too often, proposals do just that—they cleverly mask, albeit unintentionally, a novel idea that reviewers ultimately reject. As a proposal writer, your job is to write a highly readable proposal, one that is stylistically appropriate, free of jargon, and persuasive. More precisely, your proposal should analyze a significant problem, propose an effective solution, and communicate your credibility. A well-written proposal will always have a competitive edge. Skill in proposal writing cannot compensate for a weak project, but it can provide the extra measure of quality that distinguishes a high-quality proposal from its competition.

GETTING STARTED

Getting started in writing a proposal is a straightforward process. Begin by reading some examples of the type of proposal you plan to write. Experienced grantwriters offer this advice: "The first draft is for getting down, not for getting good." Rewriting is easier than original writing. Nothing is etched in stone. Create an outline to get started. Obtain a copy of the reviewer's evaluation form from your program officer, if one is available. Use it as a basis for creating your proposal outline, along with any application guidelines.

If you experience a bad case of writer's block, or are groping for the perfect word or phrase, insert a *** at the place that is giving you trouble and keep on going. When you have completed the first draft, activate your word processor's "find" command and let it identify the triple-asterisked places. Don't try to do it all in one sitting or in an intensive manner; you'll lose the benefit of two processes that are important to good writing. One is the perspective that can come only with percolation time. If you go away from the project for 24 hours, you will have a clearer view when you return to it. The second process is that of testing a limited part of the project against the overall project structure. That happens when you force yourself to consider only one segment of the project at a time. Work on your idea in small pieces.

Avoid overreliance on a committee when you are writing. Although you should seek reactions to proposal drafts from many readers, one person should be responsible for writing the proposal and have the authority to make final decisions when inevitable contradictory suggestions emerge. Further, not all committee members will share your timeline responsibilities; failure to get timely feedback demoralizes proposal writers, especially when writing under deadline. Use a committee to critique your proposals, but let it be known clearly where the "buck stops."

PROPOSAL WRITING TIPS

Set Computer Defaults Before You Start Writing

Successful grantseekers prepare to start writing by first setting the default commands on their computer. Attention to basic proposal format considerations at the outset will simplify the later editing process. Unless your proposal guidelines specifically direct you to use other settings, follow these default guidelines.

Line Spacing. Use single spacing within paragraphs and double spacing between paragraphs. Novice grantwriters sometimes attempt to overcome page limitations by using a line spacing less than a single line. Although word processing programs enable you to do this, the text appears jammed together to the reviewer and makes it harder to read.

Margin Width. Set all margins (left, right, top, bottom) at one inch. This allows for thumbspace; that is, with one-inch margins, you should be able to hold any sheet of paper in your proposal and your thumbs should not cover up any type on the page. Additionally, the one-inch white-space border around your proposal helps to frame the text and set it off much like a mat border accentuates a framed oil painting.

Paragraph Indentations. Use indented rather than block paragraphing. The five-space indentation at the beginning of each paragraph is another visual clue to the reader that a new thought is being advanced.

Ragged Right Margins. Adjust your margin alignment for a ragged right margin, not a right or double justified margin. The ragged right margin is easier to read than one that is fully justified because the proportional spacing of the letters slows readability. It is easier for the reader's eye to track from the end of one line to the beginning of the next line when the right-hand margin is jagged.

Type Style. Apply a serif typeface for your proposal text and a sans serif typeface to titles and headings. Serif typefaces have small strokes that finish off the main stroke of a letter and make it easier to read. Three serif typefaces with high readability are Courier, Garamond, and Times Roman.

Courier: ABCDEFGHIJKLMNOPQRSTUVWXYZ abcdefghijklmnopqrstuvwxyz

Garamond: ABCDEFGHIJKLMNOPQRSTUVWXYZ abcdefghijklmnopqrstuvwxyz

Times Roman: ABCDEFGHIJKLMNOPQRSTUVWXYZ abcdefghijklmnopqrstuvwxyz

Sans serif typefaces, which do not have the small finishing strokes, are ideal for titles and headings because they stand off from the body of the text. Three effective sans serif typefaces are Arial, Bell Gothic, and Universal.

Arial: ABCDEFGHIJKLMNOPQRSTUVWXYZ abcdefghijklmnopqrstuvwxyz

Bell Gothic: ABCDEFGHIJKLMNOPQRSTU VWXYZabcdefghijklmnopqrstuvwxyz

Universal: ABCDEFGHIJKLMNOPQRSTU VWXYZabcdefghijklmnopqrstu vwxyz

Experienced grantwriters will use their favorite serif type style for the main text of the proposal narrative and a contrasting sans serif font for the headings and subheadings to help emphasize new sections of the proposal. Whatever type style you select, avoid using ornate ones, which are hard to read and distract from the content of the proposal. Three type styles inappropriate for proposals are Aurora, Cloister Black, and Freestyle Script.

Aurora: **ABCDEFGHIJKLMNOPQRSTUVWXYZabcde fghijklmnopqrstuvwxyz**

Cloister Black: ABCDEFGHIJKLMNOPQRSTU VWXYZabcdefghijklmnopqrstuvwxyz

Freestyle Script: ABCDEFGHIJKLMNOPQRSTUVWXYZabcdefghij klmnopqrstuvwxyz

Type Size. Adjust your word processing program for a 12-point type style. With the graying of America, including proposal reviewers, 12 point text is easily readable. Increasingly, sponsors stipulate 12-point text as a minimum requirement. Text smaller than 12-point becomes more difficult to read and makes the reviewer's job harder, something you obviously want to avoid. Examples of Times Roman 12-, 11-, 10-, 9-, and 8-point text follow. Rather than reducing type size to make all your ideas fit on the page, try tightening sentences and editing wordy phrases (Chapter 16).

Times Roman 12 point text: ABCDE FGHIJKLMNOPQRSTUVWXYZabcde fghijklmnopqrstuvwxyz

Times Roman 11 point text: ABCDE FGHIJKLMNOPQRSTUVWXYZabcde fghijklmnopqrstuvwxyz

Times Roman 10 point text: ABCDE FGHIJKLMNOPQRSTUVWXYZabcde fghijklmnopqrstuvwxyz

Times Roman 9 point text: ABCDE FGHIJKLMNOPQRSTUVWXYZabcdefghijklmnopqrstu vwxyz

Times Roman 8 point text: ABCDE FGHIJKLMNOPQRSTU VWXYZabcdefghijklmnopqrstuvwxyz

While You Are Writing

Successful grantseekers emphasize the importance of quickly completing the first proposal draft so that most of their writing time is actually spent on editing—polishing the proposal. Write your first draft quickly and spend much more time on editing and revising. Some suggestions for writing your first draft are indicated below; they deal with how to get started, how to emphasize your text style, reminders about punctuation, word choice, and use of lists. Editing suggestions are found in Chapter 16.

Getting Started

Where do you begin your writing? There are no "hard and fast" rules. Getting something—anything—down is more important than where you start. Nevertheless, successful grantseekers usually begin with the statement of the problem (Chapter 7). Because the need, or the gap, provides the rationale for the entire proposal, you could begin with this section first. If you cannot write a convincing need statement, then the justification for the whole proposal collapses. See page 81 for the complete sequence to follow in writing your proposal.

Emphasizing Text

You have your choice of **four** *different* special EFFECTS—as this sentence illustrates. Use boldface type when you wish to emphasize your text, because **boldface** is easier to read than *italics*, underlining, or all-CAPITAL letters. Boldface is less likely to slow down the reviewer's reading rate than italics, underlining, or all caps. Use bold type to emphasize only the key words or phrases that truly need emphasis; excessive bolding loses its meaning and wears on readers.

The First Mention

Most professionals exist in a sea of alphabet soup. We use abbreviations and jargon because they are timesaving conveniences and because we assume their referents are well known. To avoid any possible reviewer confusion, always define or translate terms the first time they are mentioned in your proposal.

> *Jargon*: Our hospital complies with all JCAHO requirements.
> *Plain*: Our hospital meets all requirements of the Joint Commission on Accreditation of Healthcare Organizations.
> *Jargon*: The final prototype will exceed OSHA ergonomic mandates.
> *Plain*: The final prototype will satisfy requirements of the Occupational Health and Safety Administration for safe and comfortable repetitive wrist movements.
> *Jargon*: All project employees will first sign NDAs with the company.

> *Plain*: All project employees will first sign nondisclosure agreements with the company to protect their intellectual property.

Pronouns

Which pronouns do you commonly use in writing proposals? First person (I, me), second person (we, our), or third person (they, them, it)? For most sponsors, the days of the formal third person have faded away in favor of the second person.

> *First person*: I invite the investment of the Free Speech Foundation in this proposal.
> *Second person*: We invite the investment of the Free Speech Foundation in this proposal.
> *Third person*: The Loose Tongue Society invites the investment of the Free Speech Foundation in this proposal.

Colons

Use colons when you write to carry your reviewer's interest forward from introduction to main subject, from cause to effect, from premise to conclusion.

> "The proposal methodology contains three main steps: selection of subjects, administration of survey instrument, and interpretation of results."

In this example, the colon acts as a pointing finger, alerting reviewers to the organization of the methodology section and signals probable subheadings.

Commas

The comma, with its mortarlike ability to build complex sentences, enlarges upon thoughts, joins them to further thoughts and afterthoughts, and binds in extra information. When writing proposals, slim down on the use of commas without going overboard.

Excessive commas: "Some institutions have discovered, as a result of careful deliberations, including the use of focus groups, and faculty surveys, that major curriculum reforms are needed, but lack the funding, personnel, or technological hardware such as T3 connections, and Internet access, to make the needed reforms."

That sentence needs comma reforms, not technology reforms.

Corrected commas: "Some institutions have examined carefully their views on e-learning. The results of focus groups and faculty surveys affirm that major curriculum reforms are needed. However, three barriers must be overcome: budget support, trained personnel and technological capacity."

Limit each sentence to a maximum of two commas. Excessive commas slow down reading rate.

Dashes

Dashes are versatile punctuation tools. Dashes can **interrupt** a sentence—as they are doing now—or they can **extend** a sentence—like this. However, too many dashes can jar and irritate reviewers—both mentally and visually.

Some rules for using dashes:

- Don't use dashes in adjoining sentences (as above).
- Restrict the use of dashes to one pair per page.
- Avoid using the dash as an all-purpose punctuation mark.

Graphs and Charts

Include graphs and charts in the narrative only if they are absolutely essential to the central body of the proposal; otherwise, include them as appendix items. If used, the graphs and charts should be simple bars, lines, or pies. Complicated displays merely disrupt the reader's fluency.

Make reviewers' jobs easier by describing where in the proposal they should look to find graphs, charts, or tables, rather than just numbering each illustration. The following are examples of "original" and "revised" sentences:

Original: See Exhibit 3.
Revised: Exhibit 3 on page 12 illustrates the proportion of philanthropic giving to health, education, and the arts.
Original: Table 4-2 gives details about chronic health conditions in our state.
Revised: The table below, "Chronic Health Conditions in Our State," details rates per condition per thousand.
Original: We've included a graph that compares enrollment data from the last three years.
Revised: The graph on the following page compares enrollment data from the last three years.

Bulleted Lists

Grant reviewers favor bullet points, especially when they must skim-read proposals. Proposal writers use bullets five different ways:

- Summarize clearly a series of facts or conclusions.
- Signal to the reviewers "Here are the essentials."
- Encourage brief rather than long sentences.
- Capture readers who skip solid text blocks.
- Make the proposal appear readable.

Use a bulleted list when items are all equally important (as above):

- Cluster lists into groups of five to nine items.
- Use only words, phrases, or short sentences.
- List comparable items in parallel structure.
- Capitalize the first word in each item.
- Punctuate list items consistently; if you punctuate some, punctuate all.
- Don't end a list with a comma or semicolon.
- Set off the list with extra white space.

Numbered Lists

Numbered lists help get messages to the reviewers with a sense of immediacy without being wordy. Use a numbered list when items need to be examined in a specific sequence. Furthermore, because numbered lists are easy to skim, they convey chunks of information quickly. Rather than writing long prose paragraphs, use lists to indicate the following:

1. Steps in a sequence
2. Materials or parts needed
3. Items to remember
4. Criteria for evaluation
5. Conclusions
6. Recommendations

KEY QUESTIONS TO ANSWER

As you review your proposal, do you do the following:

1. Use language and editorial style appropriate to the sponsor?
2. Establish your credentials to successfully complete the project?
3. Use language that communicates to the nonspecialist?
4. Emphasize key points with headings, boldface type, spacing, titles, and interim summaries?
5. Include enough detail, based on preproposal feedback?
6. Address the review criteria of the funding source?
7. Identify anticipated problems and indicate how these will be handled?
8. Make appropriate use of diagrams, charts, and other visual displays?
9. Include appropriate references to prior research, related literature, or comparable programs?
10. Provide all of the information requested by the sponsor in the required format?
11. Reflect content requested in both the guidelines and the reviewer's evaluation form?

Writing Aid	Web Site Address
Dictionary	www.m-w.com/dictionary.htm
Thesaurus	www.m-w.com/thesaurus.htm
Elements of Style	www.bartleby.com/141
Foundation Center Writing Guide	fdncenter.org/learn/shortcourse/prop1.html
Foundation Proposals	www.mcf.org/mcf/grant/writing.htm
Non-Profit Grant Writing Guide	www.npguides.org/grant/index.html
Technology Proposals	www.wested.org/tie/granttips.html
Corporation for Public Broadcasting Writing Guide	www.cpb.org/grants/grantwriting.html
Zip Code and Address Information	www.usps.gov/ncsc

WRITING AIDS ON THE INTERNET

EXHIBIT 46

USING COMPUTERS TO WRITE PROPOSALS

You do not need special grant-related computer software programs to write your next proposal. Rather, you can take existing computer programs and adapt them to your requirements. For instance, word processing programs such as WordPerfect or Microsoft Word integrate text and simple graphics so you can create professional-looking proposals. They automatically take care of page numbering, renumbering, formatting, and placement of footnotes or endnotes. Often they can automatically generate tables of contents or allow you to merge information from several sources into a single document, such as capturing important statistics on the Internet and inserting them directly into your text for further editing. Usually you can preview your proposal document on the computer screen to see exactly what it will look like on the printed page.

Spell checkers hunt for typographical and spelling errors, and a thesaurus helps you select the "right" word. The cut-and-paste feature enables you to resequence segments to increase proposal fluency. Most important, editing a proposal (discussed in Chapter 16) becomes an easy task. As a result, once a proposal is written and submitted to a sponsor, it can easily be modified and sent to other sponsors, thereby increasing the number of proposals you submit.

Beyond spell checkers, most word processing programs now include a grammar checker that counts the number of words, sentences, and paragraphs; computes average sentence length; and determines readability quotients. Although the field of computational linguistics still lacks precision, these computer tools can help spot simple errors that are often overlooked under the pressure of deadlines.

Beyond grammar checkers on personal computers, the Internet has some writing aids that can simplify the proposal writing process. Exhibit 46 shows common resource tools such as English and foreign-language dictionaries, thesaurus, grammar-check, and proposal writing guides.

One computer-based topic remains to be discussed, namely, search engines. These are "word magnets" that rapidly scan the Internet and pick up keywords that you specify. Because the Internet is growing so rapidly, the volume of information available in electronic form is truly staggering. Search engines enable you to comb these electronic libraries and select only the information you want. Because skill in the use of search engines is so important to successful grant seeking, Chapter 17 is devoted exclusively to this topic.

SOME FINAL WORDS

Grantseeking is an increasingly competitive process. Most sponsors receive many good ideas. You will submit a good idea, but so will others. As a result, sponsors sometimes make funding decisions on the basis of secondary factors. One important factor is proposal appearance. Using the practical tips in this chapter should help your proposal stand out from the competition.

If you'd like to try your hand at grantwriting just for practice, the Environmental Protection Agency (EPA) has an interesting Web site where you can practice writing a grant without submitting it. Their "Mock Grant Writing" Web site allows you to practice writing a grant proposal one step at a time. The site provides actual grant proposal examples for you to follow and compare with your own. If you'd like to draft a mock grant application before you actually do the real thing, go to *http://www.epa.gov/seahome/grants.htm*. Perfect practice makes perfect.

Clip File Action Item #21
Proposal Writing

Although each suggestion in this chapter represents a potential clip file action item, perhaps the starting point is to have complete examples of successful proposals on hand. They become important reference points as one considers such things as organization, structure, and level of detail. The best way to obtain copies of successful proposals is to swap with past grant winners.

Time Saver Tip #28
Procedures

For efficient office procedures, you can do the following:

- Use the answering machine to screen morning calls so a conversation that could be held later doesn't bog you down.
- Set the clocks ahead a few minutes for the chronically late.
- Keep only one daily calendar so you don't forget to transfer information.

- Choose the type of calendar you feel most comfortable with: electronic, Palm Pilot, daily planner, or other.
- Record key decisions and action items so you don't clutter your mind with details.
- When using your calendar to record an appointment, write down the address, phone number, and directions in the place next to the appointment. You have the ability to verify details, such as local mileage for tax records.
- Invest in a computer antivirus program or download one from an online vendor.
- Invest in a good computer backup system that is easy to use. Ask for recommendations from your nearest computer software store or use "computer backup system" as a phrase in your favorite search engine.
- Organize your desk so you can quickly find what you are looking for. A clean desk is a sign of an organized mind.
- Process each paper (do, delegate, or discard) as it comes in; don't let papers pile up. Handle each piece once.
- Refile papers, either chronologically or alphabetically.
- Use a paper or electronic tickler file to keep track of deadlines.
- When your desk is a disaster, clear the space you want to organize, make a big pile of papers, and then evaluate each one.
- Staple rather than paper-clip relevant things together; "lost" papers are less likely to stick together.

CHAPTER 16
Editing Techniques

Vigorous writing is concise.

William Strunk

Congratulations! You've gotten your first draft down on paper. The hardest part is now behind you. If your high school English teacher were to give it a letter grade now, you'd probably receive a D, right? But that's okay, because this is your first draft, not your final draft. This chapter shows you how to turn that "D" grade into an "A+" and increase your chances of getting funded—by writing vigorously and concisely.

INITIAL EDITING TIPS

Below you will find a number of editing tips that are usually overlooked in the initial proposal drafting. Collectively, these suggestions can significantly strengthen your proposal.

Headings

Headings and subheadings act like a table of contents placed directly in your proposal text; that is, at a glance they reveal the main ideas and the organization of your proposal to the reader. Ask your program officer for a copy of the reviewer's evaluation form, and use those same headings and subheadings in your proposal. If a reviewer's evaluation form is not available, use headings and subheadings that are specific to your proposal. Generic headings such as "Introduction," "Background," "Materials," "Methods," "Results," "Conclusions," and "Recommendations" are not unique to your proposal. Short, specific headers such as these will have more impact on your readers:

- **The Problem: Overcoming Distance Barriers**
- **Eliminating the Shock Waves**

- **Our Credentials: 125 Years of National Experience**
- **Benefits of Youth Programming**
- **Capabilities: 75 New Volunteers**

Specific headings give reviewers an overview of your entire project, even if they are merely skimming your proposal. Note that the headings are in a different type style (Arial Boldface in the above examples) than the proposal text (Times New Roman, in this paragraph).

Levels of Organization

You can use vertical and horizontal white space to create up to three levels of organizational headings. Do not use more than three levels of headings, because you may lose the reader in the structural detail of your proposal. Effective use of white space sets off headings and enhances readability.

- Level one headings should be centered, with boldface type and key words capitalized; triple-space before further text follows.
- Level two headings should be left justified, boldface, and with key words capitalized. Double-space before further text follows.
- Level three headings should be indented; capitalize key words, boldface subheadings, punctuate, and continue with paragraph copy.

Exhibit 47 is an example of all three levels of headers.

Line Length and Margin Width

Lines approximately 65 characters long are preferred from the standpoint of readability. Physiological studies

THIS IS A LEVEL ONE HEADING

The rest of the proposal would continue here.

This Is a Level Two Heading

The rest of the proposal would continue here.

This Is a Level Three Heading. The rest of the proposal would continue here.

Note the spacing between the three heading levels. This visual chunking strategy is highly readable and facilitates reviewer skimming.

LEVELS OF HEADINGS

EXHIBIT 47

of the eye suggest that this line length is comfortable to read without inducing fatigue. The line length relates to the standard one-inch margins used in proposals. Although smaller margins allow more words per page, the proposal narrative becomes too difficult to read.

Needless Qualifiers

The following words are needless qualifiers; that is, they do not add to the meaning or understanding of your proposal. Use your computer's "find" command to locate these qualifiers, and then rewrite those sentences to make them more specific. Look for these common qualifiers: "many," "partially," "really," "rather," "seldom," "sometimes," "somewhat," "important," and "very."

Vague: Many therapists believe that violent behavior begins in the home.

Better: More than 90% of the therapists surveyed agree that violent behavior begins in the home.

Vague: In order to preserve our natural watershed habitats for future generations, it is very important that factories stop dumping chemicals into our streams, lakes, and rivers.

Better: Factories must stop dumping toxic chemicals into our streams, lakes, and rivers if our natural watershed habitats are to be preserved for future generations.

Sentence Length

Sentence length varies, but try to limit each sentence to 15 words or fewer on the average. Any sentences over 30 words are too long to track easily. Hold your draft copy in your hand and walk around the room at a fast pace while reading it aloud. If you have to fight for breath in the middle of any sentence, it is too long.

Too Long: The elastic fabric surrounding the circular frame whose successive revolutions bear you onward in space has lost its pristine roundness.

Better: You have a flat tire.

Sexist Language

Use nonsexist language to prevent excluding others. Pronoun problems with "s/he" or "his or her" can usually be avoided by shifting the entire sentence to the plural form: "they" and "them." Write with a sense of dignity, equality, and appropriateness for both sexes.

Sexist: S/he plans to use his or her computer.
Nonsexist: They plan to use their computers.

"Iffy" Words

Beware of "iffy" and "hopeful" statements. They do not inspire confidence. Be as positive as you can. Use your computer "find" command to locate words like "may," "might," and "hope"; replace them with stronger words like "can," "will," and "expect."

Transitional Words and Phrases

Transitional expressions—words and phrases that signal connections among ideas—can help you to achieve coherence in your writing. Each expression is a signal to the reader that explains how one idea is connected to the next. Business writers suggest that the use of transitions makes the difference between average and persuasive copy. Common transitional words and phrases can indicate the following:

- **Addition:** *also, in addition, again, and, and then, too, besides, further, furthermore, equally important, what's more, next, then, finally, likewise, moreover, first, second, third, last, indeed, more precisely, what is more*
- **Comparison:** *similarly, likewise, in like manner, in the same way, in comparison*
- **Concession:** *after all, although this may be true, at the same time, even though, of course, to be sure, certainly, naturally, granted*
- **Contrast:** *but, yet, however, on the other hand, nevertheless, nonetheless, conversely, in contrast, on the con-*

trary, still, at the same time, after all, although true, and yet, in spite of, notwithstanding

- **Example**: *for example, for instance, thus, as an illustration, namely, specifically, in particular, incidentally, indeed, in fact, in other words, said differently, that is, to illustrate, of note*
- **Location**: *in the front, in the foreground, in the back, in the background, at the side, adjacent, nearby, in the distance, here, there*
- **Restriction**: *despite, contrary to, although, while, provided, in case, if, lest, when, occasionally, even if, never*
- **Result**: *therefore, thus, consequently, so, accordingly, due to this, as a result, hence, in short, otherwise, then, truly, that caused, that produced*
- **Sequence**: *first, second, third, next, then, finally, afterwards, before, soon, later, during, meanwhile, subsequently, immediately, at length, eventually, in the future, currently, after a short time, as soon as, at last, at the same time, earlier, in the meantime, lately, presently, since, temporarily, thereafter, thereupon, until, when, while*
- **Summary**: *as a result, hence, in short, in brief, in summary, in conclusion, finally, on the whole, to conclude, to sum up, thus, therefore, as a consequence, at last*

Transitional Sentences and Paragraphs

To ensure that your proposal reads smoothly and fluently, use transitional sentences and paragraphs, that blend separate proposal segments into one continuously flowing copy. Insert them wherever you are making major content shifts within your proposal.

These overview paragraphs provide signals that the current ideas are shifting to something else; often they summarize what was just read and foreshadow what is coming next.

1. A transitional bridge from a problem section to a solution section in the proposal:

> In sum, a combination of school and community poverty, health disparities, and shortage of health care providers are preventing children from leading healthy lifestyles. School-based health centers can bridge these gaps in order to provide comprehensive primary and preventive health care to this medically underserved community.

This transition paragraph reminds reviewers of the problems as a prelude to discussing solutions.

2. An introductory statement to a methodology section: "This section summarizes our plans and is supplemented with concise statements that provide the motivation behind this plan of action." This sentence does two things: it foreshadows for the reviewer what

the upcoming proposal section is all about, and it alerts the reviewer that the rationale for selecting this particular methodology section will be explained, an important inclusion that is often overlooked.

3. A proposal section that helped to establish the credibility of the project co-directors:

> One added value of the co-directors is that they have experienced the challenges associated with managing multifaceted projects; they know what works and doesn't work. Based on this experience, and a concern that reviewers might feel the co-directors are already "overextended," considerable thought has gone into this carefully crafted project organizational structure, which includes strategic highly trained professionals as key support personnel.

This section tells the reviewers that the key project personnel are not only experienced project managers but are also not overcommitted.

4. A proposal section that alerts the reviewer to the structure of the methodology section:

"Each of these activities is written in a way that is consistent with the agency scoring system."

This sentence signals the reader that the proposal writers obtained a copy of the reviewer's evaluation form from the Program Officer and followed it in their discussion of the methods section, thereby simplifying the reviewer's task.

5. These proposal writers had a pretty good idea who their competition might be and wanted to posture themselves favorably against it:

> Our plan of activities is built on a careful reading of the RFP priorities and of activities of the existing center at the XYZ Institute. Although their activities are appropriate, we believe that we have the infrastructure in place that enables us to aim higher.

In a very professional manner, this section says, "We're better than our competition."

Verb Choice

Use action verbs instead of forms of "be" and "have" whenever possible. Select active sentences over passive sentences. Passive-voice verbs add variety to your sentence structure. However, if you use too many of these, your proposal becomes dull, weak, hard to read, and filled with useless words. Passives use a form of the verb "to be" and a past-tense form of another verb.

Passive: The homeless are little appreciated by people today.

Active: Today, people don't appreciate the homeless.

Passive: By the year 2010, half of this population is projected to be 75-plus, according to the Census Bureau.

Active: The Census Bureau estimates that one-half of the elderly will be over age 75 by the year 2010.

When you write in passive sentences, readers often "rewrite" the sentence into an active form, thereby slowing reader comprehension.

Passive: The data indicate that this service is used by women and persons living alone.

Active: Women and persons living alone use this service.

Use your computer "find" command to find forms of the verb "to be." Convert passive to active verbs whenever possible, but do not feel guilty about using some passives.

White Space

Use white space to break up long copy. Ample white space makes your proposal appear inviting and user-friendly. In addition, white space gives readers a visual clue to the structure of your proposal. That is, on a page full of print, a block of unprinted lines or white space, stands out immediately. White space can indicate that one section is ending and another is beginning, or that an idea is so central to the proposal that it needs to be set off by itself. Judicious use of white space breaks your proposal into smaller, manageable "chunks" of information. Some grantwriters recommend that up to 50 percent of each page should be white space. To open up white space in your proposal, consider these suggestions:

- Indent five spaces at the start of new paragraphs.
- Limit paragraph length to an average of eight single-spaced lines (or no longer than the distance between the first and second knuckle on your index finger.)
- Double-space between minor proposal segments.
- Triple-space between major proposal sections.

Wordy Phrases

Avoid common wordy phrases; use more concise language, as indicated in Exhibit 48.

Further, when writing proposals, demonstrate the capability to carry out the proposed activities and stress the impact of the project on others. For example, one effective corporate proposal started out:

Fifty-one percent of the community, 58 percent of the company's future workers, and 62 percent of the firm's potential stockholders are represented by the applicant.

Needless to say, this caught the eye of the contributions committee.

USING COMPUTERS TO EDIT PROPOSALS

Line Numbering

When editing proposal drafts, experienced grantwriters use the line numbering feature, whereby each line of text is numbered consecutively. That way, it is an easy matter to pinpoint where questions exist when critiquing text, thereby saving editing time.

Comparing Edited Drafts

Another useful word processing feature involves the "Track Changes" command. When electronically editing a proposal draft, the track changes command enables you to strike through words that should be deleted and add new copy in a different color of type. This way, it is easy to identify precisely the changes that have been made between an original and edited text. Later, you can accept or reject the proposed changes, as you wish. To activate the Track Changes command on the Microsoft Word home page, follow these commands: Tools→Options→Track Changes→Highlight Changes→OK. This feature in Wordperfect is called "Compare." Follow these commands from the home page: File→Document→Add Compare Markings→Enter document name→OK.

Using Your Computer "Find" Command

The "find" command on most word processing programs enables you to locate any word or phase in your proposal and replace it with a substitute, if desired. This simple feature can be a very powerful "low-tech" tool to upgrade the quality of your written proposal. Use it to spot and fix the following sentence structures.

"There is" or "There are"

Sentences that begin with "There is" or "There are" are often weak structures. They prevent the verb from carrying a full sentence load.

Example: There is no easy solution to this problem.

Revised: The problem is not solved easily.

Wordy	Concise
• absolutely perfect	• perfect
• afford an opportunity	• allow
• are of the opinion	• believe
• at a later date	• later
• at this point in time	• now
• came to the realization	• realized
• common accord	• accord
• completely eliminated	• eliminated
• conduct an investigation	• investigate
• due to the fact that	• because
• during the time that	• while
• fewer in number	• fewer
• filled to capacity	• filled
• for the reason that	• because
• furnish an explanation for	• explain
• give a justification for	• justify
• had this to say	• said
• have a preference for	• prefer
• in a great many instances	• often
• in excess of	• more than
• in large measure	• largely
• in order to	• to
• in the majority of instances	• usually
• in the normal course of events	• normally
• it is clear that	• clearly
• a large number of	• many
• on a weekly basis	• weekly
• personal opinion	• opinion
• please don't hesitate to call	• please call
• present a conclusion	• conclude
• qualified expert	• expert
• stresses the point that	• stresses that
• with regard to	• regarding

WORDY AND CONCISE PHRASES

EXHIBIT 48

Experience grantwriters often use sentence starter phrases like "there is (or are)" or "here is (or are)" to quickly generate the first draft copy. However, those structures are weak, so writers use the find command to strengthen the sentences during proposal editing.

Example: As we begin our fifth year, there are several problems facing our agency.

Revised: As we begin our fifth year, three problems face our agency: increasing service demand, decreasing resources, and an inadequate infrastructure.

Use your find command to hunt for such structures and see if they can be revised to eliminate this phrase.

Linking Verbs

Linking verbs join the subject and predicate in sentences. Although they bond the two major parts of a sentence, linking verbs also rob sentences of color, energy, and force.

Example: Our agency has two types of clients it serves.
Revised: Our agency serves two types of clients.

Notice that linking verbs stand alone and are not joined by other verbs.

Example: Mrs. Smith is a volunteer in our clinic.
Revised: Mrs. Smith volunteers in our clinic.

Linking verbs are forms of "to be" (be, being, been, am, is, are, was, were) or "to have" (has, have, had). Sometimes these verb forms appear with other verbs, such as "She was applying" or "He had traveled." Used that way, they are helping verbs, not linking verbs. Limit yourself to using no more than 30 percent of linking verbs in your proposal sentences.

Sacrificing Verbs for Nouns

Many proposal writers weaken their narrative when they sacrifice verbs and bury proposal action in a noun or an adjective.

Example: Parental involvement can be beneficial to implementation of the project.
Revised: If we involve parents, it helps us implement the project.

You add zest when you change a noun or an adjective to a verb.

Example: It is our expectation that we will see an improvement in productivity when the staff learns to use the new computer.
Revised: We expect the staff to produce more when they master the new computer.

Changing nouns to verbs also lets you cut excess words. Use the find command to find words that end in -ion, -ance, -ment, -ence, and -ing. Such word endings often hide verbs and weaken your proposal narrative.

"Make" Verbs

A common offender of the verb phrase is the use of the word "make" (present tense) or "made" (past tense). Examples are shown in Exhibit 49.

Use your find command to locate "make" and "made" verb constructions.

Instead of	Rewrite as
• make a decision	• decide
• made a modification	• modified
• make a determination	• determine
• made a revision	• revised
• make a recommendation	• recommend
• made a suggestion	• suggested
• make a judgment	• judge

CONVERTING NOUNS TO VERBS

EXHIBIT 49

Extra Spacing between Words

With word processors, it is unfortunately too easy to insert an extra space between words (like we did here between *extra* and *space*). Your computer find command can help you spot and fix this problem easily. Search for occurrences of a double space by opening your find command, hitting your space bar twice and executing the search. Of course, some occurrences of a double space are intentional, such as between sentences or indentations. As a consequence, you do not want to delete all double-space occurrences, just those that don't belong.

When Every Word Counts

Whether you are trying to meet the strict application guidelines that limit your abstract to 100 words or the proposal to 25 pages, saving an additional word or two can sometimes make the difference between being disqualified on a technicality and getting reviewed. A few simple edits to prune prepositional phrases can shorten sentence length and increase reader comprehension. Use your computer find command to locate common prepositions: *about, at, by, from, of, through, to, with.*

Original Sentence: Community forums are small, informal educational programs offered *by* our organization at neighborhood centers, churches and community-based organizations.

Revision saves two words: Our organization hosts community forums, small informal educational programs, at neighborhood centers, churches and community-based organizations.

Original: Our consultants can assist us in answering questions *about* our project evaluation.

Revision save four words: Our consultants can answer our project evaluation questions.

Original: Curricula vitae *of* the core staff are included in the appendix.

Revision saves four words: Curricula vitae are included in the appendix.

Original: Nationally, respiratory conditions are the most prevalent chronic health problem experienced *by* children, as reported *by* the Department of Health and Human Services.

Revision #1 saves two words: Nationally, respiratory conditions are the most prevalent childhood chronic health problem, as reported by the Department of Health and Human Services.

Revision #2 saves four words: Nationally, the Department of Health and Human Services reports respiratory conditions as the most prevalent childhood chronic health problem.

PROPOSAL APPEARANCE

Although you will obviously spend much time working on the content of your proposal, you should also pay attention to its appearance or design. Experienced proposal writers believe that appearance may account for as much as one-half of your overall proposal evaluation. Just as clothing is important in the business world for establishing initial impressions, so too is the appearance of your proposal as it reaches the reviewer's hands. The proposal should "look" familiar to the reader. A familiar proposal is a friendly proposal. Look at the printed materials issued by the sponsor. When appropriate, use the same type size and style, layout, white space, and headings as they do.

A good proposal design reduces the likelihood of reviewer errors and misunderstandings about the proposal. As a consequence you will simplify the reviewer's job. A well-designed proposal makes even complex information look accessible and gives the reviewers confidence that they can master your proposal information.

Use these design tips to create visual chunks of information that can be quickly noticed and absorbed.

• Visual devices like headings and white space help reviewers see your proposal structure.
• Use white space to make difficult subjects easier to comprehend by breaking them into smaller units.

Reading Style	Writing Technique
Skimming	• White space • Headings and subheadings • Ragged right margins • Graphs and charts • Illustrations
Search reading	• Bold type • Table of contents • Lists • Examples • Appendixes
Critical reading	• Transitions • Type style • Type size • Line spacing • Case

READING STYLES AND WRITING TECHNIQUES

EXHIBIT 50

- Use the same family of type in a proposal or the same highlight device for similar items.
- Use white space as an active design element to communicate user-friendliness to readers as opposed to a cluttered, tightly packed page that intimidates the readers.
- Major headings should normally appear at the top of a page.
- Never leave a heading on the final line of a page.
- The most effective position for headings and captions is the left-hand outside column, because the outsides of pages are noticed first.

As you learn about your reviewers and consider proposal appearance, try to anticipate which of the following reading styles the reviewer is likely to use: skimming, search reading, or critical reading. Recall that your earlier prospect research from a past reviewer or program officer identified the manner in which your proposal would most likely be reviewed. Reviewers skim proposals when they have many pages to read in a very short time. Reviewers search proposals when they are following an evaluation sheet that assigns points to specific proposal sections. Reviewers always critically read proposals, especially when the reading occurs in the time luxury of a mail review as discussed in Chapter 18. Exhibit 50 shows some of the writing techniques that are particularly appropriate for different reading styles.

Sample Edited Proposal

A sample edited proposal is provided in Exhibit 51. Note the comments in the left-hand margin, which exemplify many of the specific document writing tips outlined previously.

GUIDE TO EDITING

Successful proposal writers agree that effective editing is one key to good writing, but few people know how to edit effectively.

Begin with a one-sentence summary of entire proposal.

White space creates visual "chunks" of information. Double space between minor sections. Triple space between major sections.

Headings are specific to the proposal and help readers to skim or search for details.

Today's Date

Mr. Lee K. Wallet
Executive Director
Deep Pockets Fund
P.O. Box 17971
Anytown, WI 53017

Dear Mr. Wallet:

Our House, a nonprofit community-based agency providing quality educational and recreational opportunities for Anytown's southside, invites your investment in a $25,320 project to prevent drug and gang involvement among "at-risk" youth.

Our House, recent winner of Anytown's Community Development Award, utilizes a self-help philosophy to encourage the growth and development of individuals, families, and a health community. Three years ago, Our House began participating in a federally funded program to prevent the recruitment of at-risk youth into gang and drug activity. During this time, Our House helped more than 120 misguided youth find their way back to being fully functional members of the community. However, dollar-conscious politicians have systematically reduced government funding of critical drug and gang prevention programs. More immediately, neighborhood youth centers, including Our House, face an emergency situation because the government, without notice, terminated federal support funds fourteen months ahead of schedule. Consequently, Our House must identity new and creative ways of continuing to provide quality prevention programs at minimal expense.

Our House: Anytown's Southside Neighbor. Established in 1973, Our House is located in the heart of Anytown's southside neighborhood. Unquestionably, Our House is located in one of the most ethnically diverse areas in Anytown. Neighborhood demographics consist of:

- 54% Hispanic   • 23% European   • 14% African American
    • 5% Native American   • 4% Asian

In addition to being one of Anytown's most diverse neighborhoods, it is one of Anytown's most desperate. The southside neighborhood accounts for over one-quarter of all county AFDC cases, nearly one-third of all General Assistance cases, and over one-fifth of all Children's Court referrals for abuse, neglect, and teen births.

SAMPLE EDITED PROPOSAL

EXHIBIT 51

Pages are numbered, beginning with page 2.

2

For over one-quarter of a century, Our House has provided health alternative activities for Anytown's southside youth. However, Our House can attend to only a limited number of youth. With more than 100 children per square block, it is virtually impossible to provide quality educational and recreational opportunities for everyone. Consequently, Our House is currently focusing its efforts on Anytown's "at-risk" youth population.

Problem: Prevalence of Gangs and Drugs. Without a doubt, Anytown has its share of gangs. In fact, gang membership currently averages 4,000 participants operating in 20–30 gangs. Furthermore, studies indicate:

Arial type style headings match those used in the sponsor's printed material

- Gang members are 15 years old, on average
- 52% of gang members used alcohol in the preceding month
- 72% of gang members have an average g.p.a. of 1.73, "D"

In addition, law enforcement agencies witness that there is a significant link between gangs, drugs, and violence. But perhaps the most revealing assessment of gang activity in Anytown was made by the Juvenile Court Assistant District Attorneys when they asserted that membership in gangs was a way of identifying oneself.

At Our House, we recognize this need to "fit in." Furthermore, we recognize that many adolescents turn to gangs, drugs, and violence as a means of combating boredom and loneliness. Our House provides adolescents with healthy alternatives to gang life. More importantly, the youth who participate in Our House's programs report increased levels of respect, self-esteem, positive peer involvement, and more positive attitudes and behaviors. In other words, at Our House they find a real sense of purpose and belonging.

Times Roman type style matches that used in the sponsor's printed material.

Solution: Youth Programs. Our House currently serves over 120 "at-risk" youth and adolescents between the ages of 10–16. Specifically, "at-risk" youth include those failing in school, in children's court on minor offenses, causing neighborhood distances, or having trouble socializing at home.

Our House, together with a local consortium of churches and residential leaders, has designated a Neighborhood Strategic Plan (NSP) to improve the overall quality and safety of the southside neighborhood community. NSP addresses the particular strengths and weaknesses of the community and outlines policies and procedures for social improvement. Our House has taken a leading role in this project by establishing

SAMPLE EDITED PROPOSAL

EXHIBIT 51 (continued from page 174)

a safe haven where youth and adolescents can get away from the stresses and pressures of street gang life and actively cultivate personal growth through specific programming:

Bulleted list conveys information simply and quickly. List is set off with extra white space above and below.

- Educational: after-school tutoring, ESL tutoring

- Cultural: computer programming, drawing, painting, field trips

- Recreational: basketball, volleyball, pool, Ping-Pong

- Employment: summer work opportunities

More importantly, because students are involved in educational and recreational activities, they gain a new sense of personal identity; consequently, they no longer turn to gangs, drugs, and violence for identification and recreational purposes.

Capabilities: Encouraging Responsible Life Decisions.
Last year alone, there were over 11,500 youth participant visits to Our House's educational and recreational facilities. That averages out to over 200 participant visits a week. More generally, in the past three years, Our House has had many distinguishing educational and recreational successes.

Our House's educational programs have had remarkable participation. In three years, 71 students have earned GED certification—more than any other community-based program in Anytown!

Participation in Our House's recreational programs has more than tripled since its inception three years ago. Specifically, youth and adolescents are active in at least one of three unique Rec Center Programs:

Bold type creates emphasis. Use sparingly to stress what is truly important.

- **The Hang Tough Club**—a drug and alcohol prevention club for teens

- **Girls in the House**—a special club addressing the needs of girls and young women

- **Youth Opportunities Initiative**—a teenage gang prevention club

12-point type size matches use in sponsor's publications.

The goal of each of these programs is to provide youth and adolescents with the skills, foresight, and habits necessary for them to make responsible life decisions. More concretely, as a result of obtaining a more positive self-image, youth and adolescents attend school more regularly, earn better grades, and employ more effective coping strategies in their lives.

SAMPLE EDITED PROPOSAL

EXHIBIT 51 (continued from page 175)

Since this project is still in its formative years, Our House will continue to track the progress and success of these programs to evaluate their effectiveness. Specifically, we will calculate the number and frequency of youth participating in these programs; we will also gather program improvement suggestions from youth and adolescents, their educational and religious leaders, and private consultants. These suggestions will be used to implement any necessary changes in youth programming and determine the feasibility of expanding our services to include other at-risk adolescents.

Budget Request: $25,320. With the demonstrated concern that the Deep Pockets fund has shown for community revitalization programs, Our House requests a grant in the amount of $25,320. Quite frankly, without fiscal government support, this project, extends beyond Our House's financial boundaries. Accordingly, we must now reach out for assistance in what surely is a vital service to Anytown's southside community. In effect, by investing 72¢/day in each of the 120 adolescents who participate in Our House's at-risk youth programs, you will be empowering many youth and families to better combat the issues of gangs, drugs, and violence.

Your support really will make a significant difference. The Deep Pockets Fund will be directly aiding hundreds of children and adolescents who are in desperate need of quality educational and life-skill opportunities, and at the same time you will be making a significant contribution to gang and drug prevention in Anytown. Please contact Lindy Ross, Development Coordinator at Our House, at (414) 876-5039 to answer questions or provide additional information.

Sincerely,

Karen Tilly
Executive Director

P.S. Please come visit Our House and see this important project yourself!

Enclosures: Attachment A: Budget
Attachment B: IRS 501(c)3 status

Ragged right margins are easier to read than right justified margins.

Standard one-inch margins throughout proposal.

SAMPLE EDITED PROPOSAL

EXHIBIT 51 (continued from page 176)

General Editing Suggestions

Put your writing aside for 24 hours before editing to give you a fresh perspective. Edit copy that is double- or triple-spaced; this format invites you to make changes. Be completely brutal with your first draft. Nothing should satisfy you. Delete. Substitute. Re-arrange. Insert. Be especially critical of the first few paragraphs. You probably had not warmed up at that stage. Read aloud for content and style. When it comes to detecting errors, the ear is more efficient than the eye. Don't be the only one to proofread and edit your work. The odds of spotting errors increase with each new pair of eyes.

Don't view editing as a time waster, even when time is tight. Your credibility is at stake whenever you send out a proposal.

As you begin to edit, go through the proposal many times, each time looking for something different. Experienced grantseekers follow a four-step editing process, which looks at content, clarity, mechanics and design.

Editing for Content and Organization

Did you include all of the content information in the order requested in the application guidelines and on the reviewer's evaluation form?

Be sure you didn't leave out major parts that could help reviewers gain a better understanding of your proposal. Did you include a persuasive need statement, measurable objectives, process and product evaluation measures, table of contents, page numbers, appropriate appendixes, including resumés? Does your proposal present a logical flow of ideas?

Editing for Clarity

Is all of the necessary content clear and persuasive?

Purge each phrase of extraneous words. Weed out unnecessary words. Choose concrete words instead of abstract ones whenever possible. Make sure technical terms, jargon, and abbreviations are defined. Avoid vague adjectives. Is your average sentence length about 15–20 words? Does your proposal flow smoothly with the appropriate use of transitional words, sentences, and paragraphs? Have appropriate word, sentence, and paragraph transitions been used?

Editing for Mechanics

Is your proposal structurally unblemished?

Ensure that your writing is mechanically flawless by checking the following: punctuation, spelling, pronoun agreement, verb agreement, numbers, paragraph length ($1\frac{1}{4}$ inch maximum), omitted words, word choice, and passive constructions.

Editing for Design

Does your proposal look inviting to read?

Look at your proposal for appearance. Does it use adequate white space, distinctive headings and sub-headings, and lists to invite skim-reading? Are margins at least one inch? Have appropriate devices been used to indicate proposal structure: headings, bullets, numbers, boldface, indentations, and spacing?

Do not sacrifice proposal design in favor of including more text. Rather than reducing type size or eliminating white space, edit sentences for clarity, eliminating extra words wherever possible.

THE FINAL EDIT

You're nearly ready to send the proposal to the sponsor. It's time for one last pass through all proposal details to make sure everything is complete. Double-check these major last minute items.

Binding. For small-to-medium-size proposals (fewer than 30 pages), staple the proposal once (using a heavy-duty stapler) along the vertical margin of the upper left-hand corner of the proposal. Do not bind serially along the left-hand margin or use "slip-on" binders. Both procedures make it difficult to open up the proposal and read the inside pages. Use a large binder clip for larger proposals, making sure that your agency name and the page number is a header on each page.

Mailing Day. Unless you have a specific deadline date, mail your proposal so it arrives on a Tuesday or a Wednesday. Most people receive less mail on those two days, so your proposal will be better noticed. If you do have a specific deadline date, check to see if it is a receipt date or a postmark date.

Mailing Envelope. Mail the proposal in a manila envelope large enough to accommodate the proposal without having to fold or bend it, even if you have a short letter proposal. It'll be more distinctive than those with folds in the paper.

Page Numbering. Place page numbers on the top right or the bottom center of the pages of your proposal. Start numbering with "2" on the second page of your proposal; do not number the first page.

Paper Size. Use the standard $8\frac{1}{2}$ by 11 inch paper unless the sponsor indicates otherwise.

Paper Color. Use white paper. Do not use colored paper for the proposal text or as a divider between proposal sections.

Paper Weight. Use a 20 weight bond paper, a moderately high-quality and reasonably priced paper that will photocopy or print nicely in a laser or inkjet printer.

Paragraph Style. Indent your paragraphs five spaces because it increases readability.

Printer. Print your proposal on a laser or inkjet printer. Either gives an excellent quality product. Those organizations lacking access to a laser printer can use one for a nominal cost in many stores that specialize in photocopying services.

Proofreading. Proofread your proposal several times in multiple readings, looking for different features on each reading. As you proofread, look at the following:

1. Content and Organization: Does your proposal have enough substance? Are your ideas complete? Is your organization logical?
2. Clarity: Have you included appropriate transitions? Are ideas expressed clearly? Are all acronyms defined?
3. Mechanics: Are words spelled correctly, especially proper names? Are all numbers and computations accurate? Are sentences grammatically correct, including subject-verb agreement? Are sentences punctuated properly?
4. Design: Is the proposal design visually appealing? Did you include ample white space? Are headings specific to your project?

Know your common mistakes. Make one proofreading pass looking exclusively for your common errors, e.g., pronoun-antecedent agreement. Have three different people proofread, including at least one reader who has not been involved with the writing of the proposal.

Use your computer's is spell-checker, but recognize that it will not pick up certain types of errors e.g., misuse of "there" for "their." Existing grammar-checkers are of some value but are still in their linguistic infancy.

To spot typographical errors, start from the end of the proposal and read backwards. By doing this you are not influenced by the syntax; you must read each word independent of the others.

To spot the extra spaces sometimes accidentally inserted between two words, turn the proposal upside down and read the spaces; spacing errors quickly reveal themselves.

Increase the size of your proofreading copy on your computer or photocopy machine; mistakes show up more easily in larger print. Do your proofreading from doubled-spaced copy.

Title. Select an interesting, descriptive title: 10 words or fewer. Avoid cutesy titles or tricky acronyms on the cover page. Poor: *Extinguishing Apollo's Flame*. Better: *Expanding Fire Protection Services in Dallas*.

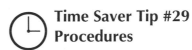

Clip File Action Item #22 Editing

To start your Editing clip file, generate a checklist of potentially problematic words and phrases that you can locate using your "find" command: forms of "be" and "have," "make/made" structures, "there is/are" and "here is/are."

Time Saver Tip #29 Procedures

As an efficient procedure, sort the mail into six categories:

1. To toss: Go through the mail stack quickly, tossing things that aren't worth opening.
2. To ask about: Attach sticky notes to remind yourself what to ask.
3. To file: If you don't need it now, it can be filed.
4. To call: Handle more quickly than by letter.
5. To do: Things that require action.
6. To read: Be selective.

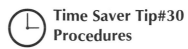

Time Saver Tip#30 Procedures

As an efficient procedure, use colored floppy disks to flag different file types: one color for word processing, another for database files, and a third for spreadsheets.

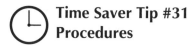 **Time Saver Tip #31**
Procedures

As an efficient procedure, don't get to work "on time." Arrive 15 or 30 minutes early and take control of your day before it takes control of you. Before the phone starts ringing, you'll have a chance to plan your day rather than just reacting to it.

 Time Saver Tip #32
Procedures

As an efficient procedure, think in terms of "project time" when you do things that demand high energy and "maintenance time" when you handle routine tasks.

 Time Saver Tip #33
Procedures

As an efficient procedure, divide your day according to the four Cs: clients, creative work, calls, and correspondence. Deal with clients and creative work during your most productive time, because they demand your best effort. Work on calls and correspondence during off-peak times.

 Time Saver Tip #34
Procedures

As an efficient procedure, choose when to take phone calls and when to make them. Decide how long you should talk, according to the value you place on the call.

 Time Saver Tip #35
Procedures

As an efficient procedure, view your appointment calendar as you would an ad. Just as the ad needs white space so the text or graphics can breathe and attract readers, you need space between activities. Leave some free time to provide you with the flexibility you need to deal with distractions, delays, and emergencies. Without it, your schedule is sure to lead to stress.

CHAPTER 17
Search Engines

The problem with computers is you play with them.
Richard Feynman

OVERVIEW

This book contains hundreds of Web addresses relevant to your grantseeking needs. Because Web pages number in the billions, and with thousands more created each week, it would be impossible to list all grant-related sites, especially because Web addresses change regularly. Search engines are valuable tools that you can use to locate grant-related information quickly.

The depth and accuracy of the information provided by search engines varies greatly, depending on whether you are using a single, meta-, or deep search engine. Frankly, search engines can locate an overwhelming amount of information, thereby inviting you to play with the computer rather than use it as an effective grantseeking tool. Accordingly, this chapter presents strategies for locating and using search engines to strengthen your proposals.

The Internet, the World Wide Web, and Search Engines

Although the media tend to use the terms *Internet* and *World Wide Web* interchangeably, they are not the same. The Internet is an umbrella term for a worldwide network of computer networks. The World Wide Web, like e-mail, is just one component of the Internet. Specifically, the Web is a hypertext interface to the Internet; that is, the Web houses information on the Internet and presents text, graphics, sound, and video together in pagelike collections.

Search engines, then, are "vehicles" that allow you to explore millions of Web pages quickly via key words. Search engines hunt for far more than grant information; they pursue all occurrences of the key words (also

called *search terms*) you provide, whether grant related or not. Search engines are valuable tools to facilitate your grantseeking, and as we offer the following concrete suggestions on how to use them effectively.

USING SEARCH ENGINES

In a sense, using search engines is like hunting for books in libraries. Libraries come in all shapes and sizes, each offering different benefits depending on their resources. Using some search engines is like visiting your local community library; it's small to average in size, contains mostly current or popular information, and has no real frills. These search engines allow you to perform simple key word searches, type in the search terms relating to your project, and the search engine will hunt for any documents containing your key words.

Using other search engines is like visiting the Library of Congress; it's huge, containing a seemingly endless supply of popular and esoteric information, which you can customize to meet your specific needs. These search engines allow you, for example, to search for information by such variables as topic or person.

In order to find books in a library, you use a card catalog. You can locate books by subject, author, and title. Similarly, search engines function like electronic card catalogs. You can find Web pages through key word searches by subject, proper names, and titles. When conducting key word searches, be as specific as possible—it's easier to broaden a search than it is to narrow it. For example, if your organization is interested in the effects of music therapy on autistic children, you might use the key words *"music therapy"* AND *"autism"* to search for information on this subject.

When key words are joined with the Boolean operator *AND*, your results will be more specific because only Web pages that contain all the terms will be returned. (See Chapter 2 for a complete description of Boolean Operators.) Said differently using only one of the individual key words—"music," "therapy," or "autism"—may be too general to locate any pertinent results.

Likewise, you can use search engines to look up information about specific people. For instance, if you were interested in the civil rights movement, you might type the name "Martin Luther King, Jr." into your favorite search engine. Finally, you can look up Web information by title. For example, a key word search for "U.S. Surgeon General's Report" should link you to information about relationships between smoking and cancer.

Because search engines hunt through different size "libraries," they may produce different results, although there may also be considerable overlap among them. In essence, search engines complement each other, enabling you to locate all types of popular and obscure information. Don't limit yourself to using only one search engine any more than you'd limit yourself to using only one library to locate information; computer experts estimate that the average search engine queries less than 20 percent of existing Web pages.

Locating Search Engines

Presently, three different types of search engines are in use on the Web.

- Single Search Engines hunt for the key words in one electronic library.
- Metasearch Engines pursue the key words in several electronic libraries.
- Deep Search Engines track all words and links in one electronic library.

Single and metasearch engines tag key words, whereas deep search engines tag all words in a document. Each type of search engine is discussed below, along with names and addresses of popular Web sites.

Single Search Engines

Each single search engine looks for the key words of all Web pages in its electronic library. While the computer programs used to conduct the searches vary considerably, the single search engines have one common goal: to help you find general information quickly. Each search engine quickly scans through the Web pages in its library, looking for your key words. Exhibit 52 contains the names and Web addresses of popular single search engines.

There is no one "best" search engine for grantseekers. Each one has some unique features; explore them and see which one best fits your needs. Maybe you'll be attracted to Ask Jeeves because it lets you conduct your search by using questions rather than key words. Perhaps you will be attracted to Google because it is one of the largest and fastest search engines currently in existence. Possibly, you'll find HotBot a favorite, especially for its ability to search for people. Conceivably, you'll use Northern Lights because of its unique "folder" feature that supplies phrases to narrow your search, rather than relying on your ability to second-guess the key words used by programmers who create search engines. If you are especially interested in international information, the Voila portal will give you an edge, particularly in France. To find the names of additional search engines, enter the phrase "search engine" in your favorite search engine. Since any single search engine seeks out a small percentage of existing Web-based information, experienced grantseekers usually rely on several search engines—quickly bookmarked—to hunt for grant details.

Metasearch Engines

Beyond the single search engines that explore only one electronic library, metasearch engines can search key words in multiple electronic libraries. Metasearch engines search for surface information from multiple sources; that is, you enter your key words once, and the metasearch engine runs your query on several different search engines, such as Yahoo!, Lycos, Excite, and Altavista. The searches may occur simultaneously, e.g., Metacrawler, or consecutively, e.g., DogPile. The results may be integrated into a single list, e.g., Metacrawler, or contain duplicate entries from different search engines, e.g., DogPile. A few metasearch engines are so sophisticated that search queries can be scheduled to run at regular intervals—daily, weekly, monthly—and the results are downloadable onto your computer. Exhibit 53 presents common metasearch engines.

Since the idea of "a search engine that searches other search engines" is growing quickly, the number of search engines queried is constantly changing. For instance, Metacrawler originally started out exploring four search engines and now probes more than 20.

Deep Search Engines

Both single and metasearch engines troll for your keywords on the surface of electronic libraries. They do not search what is known as the "deep" or "invisible" Web. For instance, the Web contains more than 500 billion documents; approximately 2 billion are on the Web surface.

Single Search Engines	Web Site Addresses
About	www.about.com
Ask Jeeves	www.askjeeves.com
AltaVista	www.altavista.com
Excite	www.excite.com
Fast Search	www.alltheweb.com
FindWhat	www.findwhat.com
Google	www.google.com
Go	www.go.com
HotBot	www.hotbot.lycos.com
Iwon	www.iwon.com
Kanoodle	www.kanoodle.com
LookSmart	www.looksmart.com
Lycos	www.lycos.com
MSN	www.msn.com
NBC	www.nbci.com
Netscape	www.netscape.com
Northern Light	www.northernlight.com
Open Directory	www.dmoz.org
Overture	www.overture.com/d/home
Sprinks	www.sprinks.com
Teoma	www.teoma.com
Thunderstone	www.thunderstone.com
Voila	www.voila.com
Web Crawler	www.webcrawler.com
Yahoo!	www.yahoo.com

SINGLE SEARCH ENGINES

EXHIBIT 52

Metasearch Engines	Web Site Addresses
1Blink	www.1blink.com
Big Hub	www.thebighub.com
C4	www.c4.com
CNET	www.search.com
Dogpile	www.dogpile.com
FuzzyCrawler	www.fuzzycrawler.com
Glooton	www.glooton.com
Go2Net	www.go2net.com
InfoGrid	www.infogrid.com
InfoZoid	www.infozoid.com
Ixquick	www.ixquick.com
Mamma	www.mamma.com
Metacrawler	www.metacrawler.com
MetaEureka	www.metaeureka.com
Metor	www.metor.com
One2seek	www.one2seek.com
QbSearch	www.qbsearch.com
QueryServer	www.queryserver.com
Search Caddy	www.searchcaddy.com
SearchBuddy	www.searchbuddy.com
SearchWiz	www.searchwiz.com
Seek123	www.seek123.com
SherlockHound	www.sherlockhound.com
Sportula	www.sportula.com
SuperCrawler	www.supercrawler.com
SurfWax	www.surfwax.com
Vivisimo	www.vivisimo.com

METASEARCH ENGINES

EXHIBIT 53

The deep Web consists of data that single and metasearch engines generally miss: portable document files, streaming audio, and information storied in databases such as government records. If you are looking for a specific piece of information, such as the incidence of Alzheimer's disease, single and metasearch engines will probably suffice. On the other hand, if you seek detailed data about the incidence of Alzheimer's by various groups or categories of individuals, then a deep search engine, such as those listed in Exhibit 54, may yield more useful information.

Deep search engines index all information on each Web page and convert it into a database; additionally they follow any links and index those pages as well, hence the name "deep" search engines; they represent the "invisible," the billions of pages that don't show up through single or metasearch engines. For most grantseeking purposes, a single or metasearch engine will suffice. If you are unable to find crucial information, then consider using a deep search engine.

Narrowing Your Search

On the World Wide Web, finding the answer you need is a function of asking the right question; that is, you can improve the quality of your "hits" by using increasingly specific key words. Here is a four-step approach to narrowing your search and getting better results, which you can then add to your clip file, your primary means of organizing your search information.

1. **Generate a list of specific key words and phrases.** Brainstorm as many key words as you can think of that are relevant to your project, being as specific as possible; don't limit yourself to the standard vocabulary that your organization uses. Select key words that describe your project by topic area, type, geography, and population served. (See Chapter 1, Clip File Action Item #2, for suggestions on how to refine your grant ideas.) For example, if your organization provides services for people with disabilities, a list of key words could include: *disabled, physically disabled, congenitally disabled, differently abled, special needs, sensory impaired, physically challenged, handicapped,* or *handicapable.*

Most search engines do not recognize the content of Web pages, only key words. Thus, your task is to think in the same terms and use the same key words that particular Web authors' use. Exhibit 55 shows a partial list of sample key words that could be associated with three grant topics: education, health care, and arts and humanities.

2. **Use quotation marks around specific phrases.** Most search engines recognize quotation marks as a sign to look for that set of words in a particular order rather than locating Web pages that contain any of the words in the phrase. That is, a search for "physically disabled" would produce narrower results than the phrase physically disabled without quotation marks, which would search for occurrences of either term, not both together.

3. **Use Boolean Operators.** Many search engines allow you to include operators such as "AND," "OR," and "NOT" to create more complex searches with multiple key word phrases. Key words joined with AND return Web pages that contain all the terms. For example, a search for "physically disabled" AND "vocational training" would produce only results that included both of these specific phrases. Key words joined with OR return Web pages that contain either of the terms. For instance, a search for "neighborhood development" OR "community revitalization" would produce results that contained either key word phrase. Key words joined with NOT return Web pages that contain the first term but exclude pages that contain the second. For example, a search for "captioned video programming" NOT "multimedia" would produce results that contained the first key word phrase but excluded "multimedia." Boolean Operators must be in all caps with a space on each side.

4. **Use a focused approach.** If the results from a preliminary search don't appear to match your expectations, focus on one or two of the more promising Web sites to see if they offer alternative key words for you to use. Then run a new search using those key words to sharpen your topic focus.

WEB SITE CREDIBILITY

Unlike books and journals, which are checked for content and accuracy before they are published, anyone with access to an Internet server can put up a Web site. Said differently, the World Wide Web allows nameless individuals with unknown qualifications to speak authoritatively on myriad topics; the mere fact information exists online does not validate its content. Although the content and organization of Web sites vary considerably, some of the more effective and credible ones share several key features:

- Descriptive title
- Heading of the organization's name

Deep Search Engines	Web Addresses
Complete Planet	www.completeplanet.com
InfoTiger	www.infotiger.com
Invisible Web	www.invisible.com
Planet Search	www.planetsearch.com
ProFusion	www.profusion.com
Scrub the Web	www.scrubtheweb.com

DEEP SEARCH ENGINES

EXHIBIT 54

- Statement of the Web site's purpose
- Information identifying the author
- Date of the last revision
- Information that is complete, accurate, and spell-checked
- Appropriate balance between inward-pointing links within the same site and outward-pointing links to other sites
- Links that are up-to-date
- Contact information for the author or Web master, e.g., e-mail
- Capacity to give visitors the information they need within three or fewer clicks

Although there is not an official yardstick to measure Web site effectiveness, these key features contribute to the quality, reliability, and credibility of Web sites. In addition, answering the following Key Questions will help you to assess the value of Web sites.

KEY QUESTIONS TO ANSWER

As you locate potentially valuable Web sites, answer the following questions.

1. *Who is the source?*
   Government and university sites (domain names ending in .gov and .edu) are among the best sources for valid and reliable information. Private individuals and organizations may have hidden agendas. Even if you start at a credible site,

linking may take you to a site with unknown credibility.

2. *Who is the intended audience?*
   Web sites should explicitly define their purpose and intended audience. That way, you will know up front whether the information will be valuable to you or not.

3. *Does the information sound too good to be true?*
   If so, it probably is. When you find something of interest at a Web site, print it and take it to an authority for corroboration. Also, e-mail the author and ask for further verification.

4. *Is the content up-to-date?*
   Web sites that are not updated regularly may contain information that is inaccurate or incomplete. Information that is complete, accurate, and spell-checked lends to the overall coherence and credibility of the site.

5. *Does the site require an access fee?*
   Before paying an access fee, use a search engine to see whether you can locate the same information somewhere else without paying for it. If you choose to subscribe, what is their policy regarding the confidentiality of data?

Locating information in a library involves a combination of trial and error, experience, timing, and luck. The same is true with Web searching. Because search engines have different strengths and weaknesses, determining which ones will be the most useful to your grantseeking will take some time and practice.

Education	Health Care	Arts and Humanities
Academic achievement	Access to health care	Architecture
Alcohol and drug education	Allied health	Art education
Attrition and retention	Child and maternal health	Cinema and video
Bilingual education	Community outreach	Computer arts
College students	Disease control	Creative writing
Computer literacy	Extended care facilities	Cultural activities
Distance learning	Family health	Dance
Educational administration	Graduate medical education	Design arts
Elementary education	Health care policy	Diplomatic history
English as a second language	Health insurance	Dramatic and theater arts
Financial aid	Home health care services	Folk and ethnic studies
Graduate education	Hospices	Graphic design
High school education	Indigent care	History
Higher education	Medical ethics	Language and literature
Hispanic-serving institutions	Mental health services	Media arts
Historically black colleges	Nursing homes	Music
Instructional programs	Patient care and education	Performing arts
K-12 education	Patient outcomes	Philosophy
Private education	Physician training	Photography
Public education	Public health	Religious studies
Secondary education	Risk management health cares	Spirituality
Teacher education	Rural health	Theology and religion
Undergraduate education	Technology transfer	Visual arts
Workplace literacy	Vital statistics	World history

SAMPLE KEY WORDS FOR EDUCATION, HEALTH CARE, AND ARTS AND HUMANITIES TOPICS

EXHIBIT 55

Very quickly, though, you will see the benefits of having a world of electronic information available at your fingertips.

Clip File Action Item #23
Search Engines

To compare search engines, make a list of six keywords you commonly use: three broad terms (*health, family,* and *social services*) and three very narrow ones (*pediatric asthma, changing family values,* and *welfare-to-work*). Select three search engines and enter your key words. Make a chart to tally the number of hits. Look also at the quality of the citations; give them an appropriate letter grade: "A" through "F." Repeat this five-minute process daily for all search engines to help determine which ones are best for you. When you write you next proposal, you'll know those search engines that will be most helpful.

Time Saver Tip #36
Procedures

As an efficient procedure, schedule an appointment with yourself to make sure you get the uninterrupted time you need to complete a writing task on time. If someone asks to see you at that time, you can honestly say you have an appointment. You'll improve your chances of getting your work done.

 Time Saver Tip #37
Procedures

As an efficient procedure, adopt the "worst-first" policy. Tackle the toughest task early in the day. Even if it's not your highest-priority item, the relief you'll feel when it's out of the way will energize you to handle other work.

 Time Saver Tip #38
Procedures

As an efficient procedure, turn your voicemail on 15 minutes before you have to leave for a meeting or appointment. You'll avoid that irritating rushed feeling you get when you're delayed by last-minute calls you don't want.

 Time Saver Tip #39
Procedures

As an efficient procedure, to remember where you put important papers and other items, create a computer file called "Where is it?" Record the location of each item in that file. If you want to keep the file confidential, use a password.

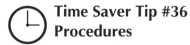 **Time Saver Tip #40**
Procedures

Avoid inefficient and ineffective meetings; insist on seeing an agenda first.

 Time Saver Tip #41
Procedures

Learn how to delegate.

- Decide what to delegate. List the things you do that could be done by someone else.
- Select capable, willing people to carry out jobs. Encourage others to improve their ability to carry out larger tasks unsupervised.
- Delegate complete jobs. Let each individual carry out the whole task; it's more rewarding that way.
- Explain why the job is done, what the expected results are, and how it fits into the overall picture of what you are trying to accomplish.
- Let go. Review only on agreed upon reporting dates. Don't micromanage.
- Give help and coach when requested. Support
- Accept only finished work: delegate to take the workload off you.
- Give credit when a job has been successfully completed.

CHAPTER 18
Grant Review and Funding Decisions

The way to avoid criticism is to do nothing.

Steve Ross

OVERVIEW

This final chapter discusses what happens to your proposals once they are submitted. More precisely, it does the following:

- Stresses the value of submitting your proposal to more than one sponsor at the same time.
- Discusses the different ways in which your proposal might be reviewed.
- Offers tips on what to do if you should be selected for a site visit.

Finally, this chapter suggests follow-up actions you should take, whether or not your proposal is funded. The review and constructive criticism of your proposal—not you—can only strengthen your idea. Beginning grantseekers with eggshell egos can take the advice of a Fortune 500 CEO, Steve Ross, and do nothing, but, obviously, that won't get you funded.

MULTIPLE SUBMISSIONS

Your completed proposal represents an important piece of intellectual property. To receive full value from your efforts, you should submit your proposal to multiple sponsors. This will increase your chances of getting funded.

Beginning grantseekers sometimes wonder if it is ethical to submit a proposal to more than one sponsor at the same time. Our answer is "Yes, it is ethical, provided you advise all grantmakers of your actions." Failure to let sponsors know of your actions would be deceitful—and that is unethical.

Implications

"Will making multiple submissions hurt your chances of getting funded?" ask beginning grantseekers. The question is understandable, but the reality is that making multiple submissions will not jeopardize the likelihood of getting your proposal funded. In fact, it could help, because sponsors with similar interests often form close communication networks among themselves. Grantmakers with similar interests talk to each other. Co-funding is not uncommon in some cases; that is, several sponsors may contribute partially to the total project cost. Furthermore, engaging in multiple submissions communicates to sponsors that you are seriously committed to your project and that you are willing to exert considerable effort to secure funding.

When submitting multiple proposals, present similar but not identical versions; that is, each version should be tailored to meet the varying interests of sponsors as determined by feedback from your preproposal contacts (see Chapter 4). Sponsors expect you will submit similar proposals to other grantmakers. You should name the other sponsors in your transmittal letter. For example, your transmittal letter might include a sentence like this:

> A similar version of this proposal is currently under consideration by the Pain Management Foundation; Mr. John Calder, (414) 234-6789, is the point of contact.

or

> A similar version of this proposal will be will be submitted to the Pain Management Foundation within the next month; preliminary communi-

cations have been held with Mr. John Calder, (414) 234-6789.

Budget Considerations

If you submit multiple proposals, how much money should you request? The total amount you need from multiple sponsors? Partial amounts from each of several sponsors? For example, assume you identified five potential sponsors and want to request support for a $50,000 project. It would be very difficult to get all five sponsors to agree to contribute $10,000. Getting five sponsors to collaboratively support your project is akin to trying to herd cats. Rather, ask all five sponsors for $50,000 each. Funding from any one of them could support your project.

On rare occasions, you may have an "embarrassment of riches" problem whereby several sponsors want to fully fund the same project. To solve this problem, you have two main options. First, you may accept both awards and increase the size or scope of your project, assuming you can handle such a project increase and if both sponsors agree. If you expand the project size, you should keep the budgets separate and not commingle the funds. Second, you may delay the start date from the second sponsor in order to increase the length of the project period; each sponsor will therefore profit from the funds of the other sponsor. Consider making your project bigger or longer before rejecting offered grant dollars. Sponsors will usually be flexible in implementing your project once they have decided that it merits funding.

REVIEW MECHANISMS

Your preproposal contact revealed how your proposal will be reviewed. The review process varies considerably. Your proposal may be reviewed internally by existing staff members or referred externally for evaluation. The external review may be done either by mail (print or electronic) or panel meetings. You need to know how your proposal will be reviewed and by what type of individual, because your proposal should be written to the level of expertise of the reviewer. This audience analysis will help you determine the amount of detail you need to include in your proposal. For instance, if your proposal will undergo mail review by a technical specialist in your field, you will need to include considerable detail and documentation.

On the other hand, if your proposal will be reviewed by generalists who are also reading 15 other

proposals in a three-hour panel review (where they might be able to spend a maximum of 20 seconds per page reviewing your proposal), you would write with all the organizational and skimming mechanisms at your disposal. With an electronic review, your proposal may lose some special features like boldface or italics; as a result, document design considerations (Chapter 16) become critical.

The National Institutes of Health is an example of a federal agency that relies on outside specialists to conduct panel review meetings. In fact, they use a two-tier approach to the proposal review process. The first level of review has specialists evaluate the content or merit of the proposal. The second level of review examines the proposal's relevance to the agency mission. The National Institutes of Health's two-tier approach is illustrated in Exhibit 56.

The job of reviewers is to ask questions about your proposal. Regardless of whether your proposal is being reviewed by a public or private agency, five basic areas are covered, at a minimum:

1. Scope of work
2. Personnel
3. Facilities
4. Track record
5. Budget information

Experienced grantwriters often conduct proposal review sessions within their organizations prior to formal submission.

Although reviewers look for many elements when reviewing proposals, one predominant feature in evaluating service delivery proposals is how many people will be reached by the proposed project. Reviewers often ask, "How many people in the target population will be affected by this project: All? Most? Many? Some?" Proposal writers should use interim summary statements in their proposal sections to highlight how many people will be impacted. Reviewers will be looking for this information. Make their job easier by drawing their attention to things that will boost your proposal ratings.

Electronic Proposal Review

One grantseeking trend is for proposals to be reviewed electronically. Here's what happens: Proposals are e-mailed to reviewers who read them online (but can print hard copies if they wish) and then enter a secured "chat room" to exchange critiques. Some agencies have not overcome the technological challenges associated with electronic review and are resorting to

NIH Dual Review System

First Level of Peer Review by Study Section

- Provides initial scientific review of grant applications
- Rates the scientific and technical merit of the proposal
- Does not set program priorities
- Makes budget recommendations but no funding decisions

Second Level of Peer Review by National Advisory Council

- Assesses quality of Study Section review of grant applications
- Assures compliance with regulatory requirements
- Makes recommendations to institute staff on funding
- Evaluates program priorities and relevance
- Advises on policy

TWO-TIER REVIEW

EXHIBIT 56

CD-ROMs as an interim step. Applicants submit proposals on CD-ROMs that are then passed on to reviewers.

Ask your program officer if your proposal will be reviewed in a panel meeting, by mail, or electronically. If electronically, pay particular attention to document design considerations. Use lots of white space, headings, and subheadings. Find out which computer programs will be used by the reviewers; not all programs handle special effects such as boldface or italics. Send a test copy to yourself to see what it looks like. Remember that the appearance of a proposal accounts for nearly one-half of the reviewer's judgment, according to some experts.

KEY QUESTIONS TO ANSWER

Does the proposal do the following:

1. Show sufficient understanding of sponsor guidelines and priorities?
2. Show a good approach to the problem?
3. Have an efficient time schedule?
4. Indicate probable outcomes?
5. Deal with all clearance requirements?
6. Identify key personnel and their assignments?
7. Provide sufficient information to evaluate key personnel?
8. Allow for sudden changes in the project?
9. Have adequate facilities and equipment?

10. Identify the organization's track record?
11. Specify the organization's field reputation?
12. Propose a reasonable budget?
13. Identify the probable project impact?
14. Address well-documented problems in need of solution?

SITE VISITS

Occasionally, the sponsor may wish to conduct a site visit as part of the evaluation process. This is a good sign that you are on their "short list" of potential grantees. The purpose of the site visit is to see first-hand your organization, its environment and its people. Site visits are held when reviewers want information that is available only at the proposed project site. The information gathered in a single day by a team of reviewers can decide the fate of an application that may have taken months to prepare. Think of a site visit as a "quality control" measure for the sponsor, a way for the sponsor to run a credibility check on you, your organization, and your idea.

Site Visit Survival Strategies

If you are involved in a site visit, you should prepare properly. First, bring all potential project personnel together and review in detail the components of your proposal. Ask the sponsors if they have a particular agenda they wish to follow or if they want to see any special background documents. Arrange a private room in which they can meet and conduct interviews. Your job is to show them, not snow them, that your idea and organization are indeed credible.

Site visits represent a double-edged sword. A poor showing on your part may doom the application. On the other hand, site visits give you a golden opportunity to make up for weaknesses in an application and meet with specialists in the field.

To survive a site visit, follow the three "Rs":

- *Review.* Have everyone reread the proposal, understand, and be able to articulate their contributions, to both your organization and the project.
- *Rehearse.* Conduct practice site visits. The most common mistake in a site visit is for project team members to be unfamiliar with proposal details. It is for this reason that a "dress rehearsal" is crucial, even to the extent of asking outside colleagues to come in and hold a practice site visit.
- *Respond.* Follow the established agenda. Stay on schedule. Don't bombard reviewers with lots of new information. Do provide copies of any specific documents that are requested. Do provide plenty of time to answer reviewers' questions. Give reviewers a "Take Away" folder that includes the agenda, the proposal abstract, contact information for all key participants, any requested documents, written answers to any specific questions raised, and a list of other related projects.

Site Visit Example

Successfully managing site visits is, in large part, a matter of paying attention to many details. The following nuts-and-bolts example came from a recent full-day site visit from a national foundation. A proposal had received favorable initial reviews, and now four site visitors wanted to see the applicant organization firsthand and discuss in greater detail some aspects of the proposed project.

The sponsor provided three weeks advanced notice of the site visit date. They asked the applicant to develop an agenda for the day, which would include a short presentation of the proposal, answers to specific follow-up questions, and time for questions and answers with the project's collaborative partners. A great deal of preparation was done behind the scenes to ensure that the site visit went smoothly. Here's an outline of what happened—and when.

Two Weeks before the Visit

- Review the sponsor's specific follow-up questions.
- Identify key participants—internal staff and collaborative partners.
- Confirm participant availability.
- Have all participants review the original proposal.
- Reserve a conference room for the presentation.
- Begin to develop the presentation.
- Begin to develop the agenda for the day.
- Offer to coordinate hotel and travel accommodations for out-of-town site visitors.

One Week before the Visit

- Finalize the agenda.
- Send the agenda to the sponsor and participants.
- Send a map and driving directions to the sponsor and participants.
- Contact the sponsor and participants to identify any special dietary restrictions.
- Share the presentation with key participants for critique and input.
- Discuss participants' roles and responsibilities during the presentation.
- Practice.

One Day before the Visit

- Print name tags.
- Hang up signs directing site visitors and participants to the conference room.
- Order Continental breakfast, box lunches, and afternoon snacks.
- Copy handouts: (1) agenda, (2) participant list, (3) PowerPoint presentation slides, and (4) answers to specific follow-up questions.
- Check technology: laptop, data projector, Internet, PowerPoint.
- Make sure that the conference room is clean.
- Make sure that the conference room has an adequate number of chairs.
- Have a final dress rehearsal of the presentation.
- Get plenty of sleep.

The Visit

- Look good. Feel good. Think good. Do good.
- Smile.

One Day after the Visit

- Send a thank you note to the sponsor.
- Send a thank you note to key participants.

During the actual site visit, the reviewers asked questions to assess project leadership, accountability, involvement, and communication. Some of their actual questions follow:

- Could you describe your vision for this project?
- Have you secured buy-in from project personnel?
- Do you anticipate ongoing evaluation and feedback during the project: With project participants? With project personnel? With collaborating institutions?
- Do you anticipate that labor shortages will be a problem for staffing this project?
- Have you had difficulties with staff turnover?
- Who will be responsible for data entry?
- Are project personnel familiar with technology, e.g., laptops, Palm Pilots, Internet?
- Can data systems communicate across partnering institutions?
- How do you deal with language and cultural issues?

Since the project under review involved multiple institutions, the site visitors asked questions of project partners about the nature of the collaborative relationships. These questions get at intangible characteristics such as energy, passion, trust, commitment, and ownership.

- How does this project fit in with the work that you do?
- How often do you interface with the project director, lead applicant institution, and other consortium members?
- Have there been previous alliances among your institutions?
- Could you describe the planning process: Who was involved? Why does it work so well?
- What would you do differently?
- Do you see any barriers or challenges to this collaboration that need to be addressed?
- Do you feel the need for formalized administrative and management structures?

The preparation and attention to detail paid off. This proposal was funded.

DEALING WITH GRANT DECISIONS

Plan Ahead

Planned reactions become planned options. How do you plan to behave if your proposal is funded? Rejected? What are your options? When you have a powerful itch, it is almost unbearable waiting to get it scratched! Having to wait to get what you want demands patience and tolerance—unless you have planned options. Patient people turn to other activi-

ties to meet other needs while they are waiting for grant decisions. These activities keep them strong and in control. Strong people wait a lot. It may take many months before the decision on your proposal is made.

Sometimes while you are waiting for a funding decision, you may be asked to supply further information or respond to specific questions from your potential sponsor. Do this in a timely manner, for it means your proposal is under active consideration. Your clip file may be able to provide the requested information.

If You Are Funded

At some point, you will find out if your proposal is successful. Whether your proposal is funded or not, you should do some follow-up work. For example, if you are successful with a proposal, you should request a copy of the reviewer comments, if allowed by the sponsor. Ask the program officer about common mistakes that others have made in implementing a grant so that you don't fall into the same trap. Inquire how you can be a good steward of their money. Ask your sponsors what attracted them to your proposal. The answer provides insights about your organizational uniqueness. Add those uniqueness statements to your clip file and use them in your next grant proposal. Clarify the submission deadlines for technical and financial reports; you can keep your program officer very happy if you submit your reports on time. Invite your program officers to visit you. Add them to your organizational public relations list for news releases about your agency.

If You Are Not Funded

If you are not funded, don't take it personally. Many factors can cause a proposal to be rejected: amount of competition, available budget, geographic distribution, and closeness of match to priorities. Often, these factors are beyond your control. If the sponsor declined your proposal, thank them for reading the proposal and ask what can be done to improve it. Request verbatim written reviewer comments, not summary comments, which are less specific. If you can't get reviewer comments, then request a "debriefing" to go over your proposal over the phone or in person. Learn how your proposal could be more competitive. Ask if you should reapply next year. Use this as an opportunity to build bridges with the sponsor for the next submission cycle. Periodically send them a photocopy of articles or publicity with the "Thought you might not have seen this and might be interested" approach. Invite them to your agency to get to know you better. Avoid the "You only love me at submission time" syndrome.

If You Are Approved but Not Funded

It's a rather inglorious message when you learn that you are "approved but not funded," a reality in grantseeking. This letter of disappointment often uses these words:

> Your application was sufficiently meritorious to warrant a recommendation for approval, but in terms of available funds and the competition for them, it did not receive a priority score high enough to be funded.

This "close-but-no-cigar" communication amounts to a near miss. Usually, it is "good news" information, for it suggests that the reviewers were attracted to your proposal but were concerned about some procedural issues, as opposed to finding the proposal inherently flawed. To use this situation to your advantage, ask the program officer for "verbatim reviewer comments" rather than just summary remarks. Once you learn what the precise issues of concern were to the reviewers, you can decide whether you should revise and resubmit your proposal to this sponsor or seek another funding source. To make this decision, you need three pieces of information: probability estimates, proposal weaknesses, and time frames.

- **Probability Estimates**. Call the program officer and find out where you are on the "alternate" list: first or tenth? Ask how far down the "pay list" the agency has gone in past competitions. Ask about their probability estimate of you getting funded: 10 percent, 50 percent, or 80 percent?
- **Proposal Weaknesses**. Ask for the program officer's reactions to the written reviewer comments. Of the weaknesses cited, which ones were the most significant? Are they easily fixable?
- **Time Frames**. Find out when the next review cycle is. Are you better off to withdraw the proposal, revise and resubmit it as opposed to leaving it in the "hopper?" How soon will the program officer know if additional grant funds might become available?

If you decide to revise and resubmit, your revision should cite the concerns of previous reviews, itemizing them one-by-one and offering appropriate responses, whether you have made changes to accommodate their concerns or rejected their concerns for solid reasons, which you spell out.

DEALING WITH PROPOSAL REJECTIONS

Rejection Letters

Rejection letters from government agencies usually include comments about concerns raised by the reviewers. You are entitled to this feedback and should request it, if it does not accompany your rejection letter.

Private foundations, on the other hand, vary in the extent of their communications. For example, one private foundation provides you with a successful proposal when they turn down yours. Another private foundation commonly provides a funding source book to help you identify alternative sponsors when they reject you. A few private foundations will write detailed rejection letters, spelling out the reason for the turndown.

The most common experience with grant proposals to private foundations is to receive a "form letter" rebuff. The rejection language in four typical foundation letters reads as follows:

- We regret that we will be unable to contribute as the funds available to us are, unfortunately, not sufficient to assist all the worthy organizations which come to us for support.
- Due to numerous requests for gifts and grants and limited funds, we regret we are not in a position to be of assistance to you. We were pleased to have the opportunity of reviewing the proposal, and only regret we will not be able to provide support for your organization.
- We regret to inform you that the Foundation is not in a position to provide a grant for your program.
- We have received your request to our Foundation. In reviewing your proposal, it appears your project is beneficial to certain segments of the community. However, in view of the numerous requests we receive, our limited funds, and the direction in which Foundation funds are applied, it appears we cannot be of assistance.

Occasionally, a reasonable amount of time elapses and you haven't heard anything from a foundation: no funded or declined feedback. This is probably because most foundations lack a support staff to handle such communications; at best, they can only communicate with their grantees. When faced with this situation, you should first attempt to call and see when a funding decision can be expected. If you cannot connect via phone, successful grantseekers usually wait a maximum of one year before sending a letter requesting that their proposal be withdrawn from further consideration. The language of that letter might include something like the following example.

> On July 6, 1999, we submitted a proposal to you entitled "STAR Parent Training Program." Through a fortunate combination of circumstances, we now have the necessary resources to carry out this project. Accordingly, we ask that you withdraw this proposal from further consideration. Since you value the importance of parent training, we will keep you posted on our major project outcomes. Perhaps some future occasion will warrant submission of a different proposal to you.

In most cases, corporations decline grants in a manner similar to foundations; that is, they usually send some short letter announcing their decision without any elaboration of key reasons. A follow-up telephone call may provide further insights. If no response is forthcoming after a reasonable time frame, then you may wish to submit a withdrawal letter, as noted above.

Response to Rejection Letters

Being rejected is the first step to getting funded. Rejection letters present an opportunity to build goodwill with a future potential sponsor. Consider sending them a letter like the following when your proposal has been declined. This letter contains model paragraphs for use with corporations or foundations.

> Thank you for your letter informing us of your decision regarding our request for support for the STAR Parent Training Program. We are, of course, disappointed that the Healthy Baby Foundation cannot support the project. We recognize, however, that there are always more requests than funds, and we are sympathetic with the difficult responsibilities of Foundation officers.
>
> As I reflect on the many achievements of our organization and on the challenges yet to be addressed, I am hopeful that the Foundation will be able to give future consideration to support for us if we submit a different proposal. As a nonprofit organization, we must rely on the generosity of those who value our mission.
>
> We appreciate your consideration of our request. You and your colleagues of the Foundation have our cordial good wishes and our esteem for the conscientious work you do.

In contrast to foundations and corporations, it is not necessary to respond to rejection letters from government agencies for two reasons. First, government funding is more dependent on the merit of your idea and less on its relationship to you. Second, many government agencies are mandated to respond to any communication received from citizens; your letter to them means that they must write back to you. As a result, responding to their initial rejection letter actually makes *more* work for them rather than building a relationship.

Persistence Pays

Like so many things in life, the first "no" is not necessarily the final "no." With federal grants, it is often possible to obtain reviewer comments, revise your proposal, and resubmit. Your funding chances usually improve with resubmissions. In fact, many successful federal proposals are rejected the first time they are submitted. Accordingly, initially declined proposals are revised on the basis of reviewer feedback and resubmitted with a greater likelihood of funding. Lack of prior success is not a solid reason for not trying again.

At the National Institutes of Health, records show that more than one-half of those who apply eventually get funded, if they are persistent and obtain rewrite suggestions from their program officers. Another federal agency reports that the odds of getting first-time funding are one chance in six. Those who are initially rejected but then revise their proposal and resubmit it improve their odds to one chance in three for funding. If the second submission is rejected, the odds improve to one chance in 1.5 for a third, revised submission. Most successful grantseekers switch to a different sponsor after the third declination.

In the world of grantseeking there are no guarantees. Even resubmitting a revised proposal a second or third time does not assure funding, Why? Because review panels change personnel and perspectives. A proposal feature acceptable to one review panel may be unacceptable to another. In reality, this is beyond your control. Successful grantseekers minimize the possibility of changing standards by flagging those components in the revised proposal that respond to the concerns of a previous review panel. In this way, you let the current review panel know that you have taken the previous concerns seriously and have attempted to follow through on them.

Rejection Reasons

Several years ago, the federal government studied 353 research proposals that had been rejected in order to identify some common proposal mistakes. Their review of the rejected proposals yielded the following findings:

- 18% failed to number the pages
- 73% provided no table of contents
- 81% had no abstract
- 92% didn't provide resumés of proposed consultants
- 25% had no resumé for the principal investigator
- 66% included no project evaluation plan
- 17% failed to name the project director
- 20% provided no list of objectives

These are easily correctable mistakes, pitfalls you should avoid. Some people may make these mistakes out of ignorance about the proposal writing process. More people probably make these mistakes out of time pressure and haste. As you write your proposal, you should allow sufficient time to attend to these format issues as well as to your proposal content. Both content and format are important. Together they speak to your overall credibility.

GETTING GRANTS: THE LONG-TERM VIEW

This book has introduced you to the basic reference tools for identifying funding sources. From these potential suspects, you have seen the importance of engaging in preproposal contact in order to maximize the "fit" between your idea and the sponsor's interests. You have read the clip file suggestions that will help you establish your own grant system for developing proposals while saving valuable time. You have dissected the components of public and private proposals. You have learned the importance of being persistent; if you get turned down the first time, revise and resubmit your proposal based on feedback from your reviewer.

We conclude with one final tip: Become a grant reviewer yourself. The "inside look" is very helpful later when you are ready to prepare your next grant. How do you get to be a federal grant reviewer? It's usually a self-nomination process. Once you identify a grant program for which you'd like to become a reviewer, rework your resumé to show related skills and experiences. Send it to the program officer with a cover letter expressing interest that might look like this:

> You and I share something in common: an interest in serving multiple-handicapped children. I'm writing now because, depending on how you are reviewing your grant proposals, there is a possibility my expertise and experience may be of value to you.

As you review the enclosed resumé, you will note the following:

- Six years of experience in the delivery of rehabilitation services to multiply handicapped children
- Hands-on experience with children who have two or more of the following disabilities: hearing, vision, speech, intellectual, emotion, and motor control
- Extensive interactions with diverse rehabilitation professionals
- A bachelor's degree in special education

I'll call you in two weeks to see if you'd like more information or have special application forms to fill out.

Most federal agencies actively seek reviewers and welcome your volunteer efforts. Occasionally, they will respond with a simple form you need to fill out so they can enter demographic information in their reviewer database.

Sometimes the Federal Register will announce an agency's interest in finding new reviewers. A scan through its search engine will identify such opportunities. It is usually not necessary to have a Ph.D. and publish 20 books to become a reviewer. More importantly, your resumé should show that you understand the target problem.

The process in becoming a reviewer for a private foundation is not standardized. We suggest that you contact the program officer and ask if the foundation uses external reviewers. If so, volunteer by sending in your customized resumé.

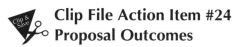

Clip File Action Item #24
Proposal Outcomes

Build your Proposal Outcomes clip file by including following items:

- Sample letters to program officers requesting verbatim reviewer comments, whether your proposal was funded or rejected
- Sample letters to program officers acknowledging their declination notice.

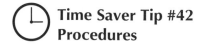

Time Saver Tip #42
Procedures

Get started an extra hour early. Do this for a year and you have effectively created more than five extra working weeks a year.

 **Time Saver Tip #43**
Priorities

To prioritize, you must have a plan; otherwise you lack direction. If you don't set priorities, you are trapped by indecision.

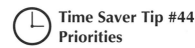 **Time Saver Tip #44**
Priorities

To prioritize, don't start a project without having enough information. That's why, for example, you shouldn't start to write a proposal without having sufficient preproposal contact.

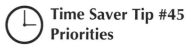 **Time Saver Tip #45**
Priorities

To prioritize, spend 10 minutes each day thinking about what you'll get done tomorrow.

Time Saver Tip #46
Priorities

To prioritize, make your computer password relate to one of your goals, like LOSE10, for losing 10 pounds, or DRAFT3, for drafting three pages of your next proposal. Besides being easy to recall, it can serve as a daily reminder each time you connect to your system.

You have hundreds of tips on successful grantseeking and efficient, time-saving suggestions with which to implement them.

Now, go write your best grant ever!

Bibliography

AIDS Funding. New York: Foundation Center, 1997.

America's New Foundations. Washington, DC: Taft Group, 2000.

Annual Register of Grant Support. New Providence, NJ: R. R. Bowker, 2002.

Arlett, Allan, and Ingrid Van Rotterdam, eds. *Canadian Directory to Foundations.* Toronto: Canadian Centre for Philanthropy, 2000.

Bauer, David G. *The Complete Grants Sourcebook for Higher Education,* 3rd ed. Phoenix: Oryx Press, 1996.

Bauer, David G. *The "How to" Grants Manual: Successful Grantseeking Techniques for Obtaining Public and Private Grants,* 3rd ed. Phoenix: Oryx Press, 1999.

Browning, Beverly. *Grant Writing for Dummies.* New York: Hungry Minds, 2001.

Browning, Beverly. *How to Become a Grant Writing Consultant: A Start-up Guide for Your Home-Based Business.* Chandler, AZ: Bev Browning & Associates, 2001.

Carlson, Mim. *Winning Grants Step-by-Step.* San Francisco: Jossey-Bass, 1995.

Carter, Cheryl, and James Quick. *Grantseeker's Toolkit: A Comprehensive Guide to Finding Funding.* New York: John Wiley, 1998.

Catalog of Federal Domestic Assistance. Washington, DC: Superintendent of Documents, issued yearly.

Chronicle of Philanthropy. Washington, DC: Chronicle of Philanthropy, issued biweekly.

Corporate 500. San Francisco: Public Management Institute, 1995.

Corporate Foundation Profiles. New York: Foundation Center, 2000.

Corporate Giving Directory. Washington, DC: Taft Group, 2002.

Corporate Giving Yellow Pages. Washington, DC: Taft Group, 2002.

Directory of Biomedical and Health Care Grants, 12th ed. Phoenix: Oryx Press, 2001.

Directory of Corporate Affiliations. Wilmette, IL: National Register Publishing, 2001.

Director of Grants in the Humanities, 11th ed. Phoenix: Oryx Press, 2001.

Directory of International Corporate Giving in America. Washington, DC: Taft Group, 2001.

Directory of Japanese Giving. New York: Foundation Center, 1991.

Directory of Research Grants, 23rd ed. Phoenix: Oryx Press, 2001.

Dun and Bradstreet's Million Dollar Directory. Parsippany, NY: Dun and Bradstreet, 2001.

Dun and Bradstreet's Reference Book of Corporate Managements. Parsippany, NY: Dun and Bradstreet, 2001.

Eckstein, Richard M. *Directory of Computer and High Technology Grants.* Loxahatchee, FL: Research Grant Studies, 1999.

Federal Grants and Contracts Weekly. Alexandria, VA: Capitol Publications, issued weekly.

Federal Register. Washington, DC: Superintendent of Documents, issued daily.

Ferguson, Jacqueline. *The Grantseeker's Guide to Project Evaluation.* Gaithersburg, MD: Aspen Publishers, 1999.

Ferguson, Jacqueline, Laurel Drake-Major, and Michael Gershowitz. *The Grantseeker's Answer Book: Fundraising Experts Respond to the Most Commonly Asked Questions.* Gaithersburg, MD: Aspen Publishers, 1999.

Fortune 500 Directory. The top industrial and service corporations are listed in the late May or early June issue of *Fortune* Magazine every year.

Foundation Directory. New York: Foundation Center, 2001.

Foundation Directory Supplement. New York: Foundation Center, 2001.

Foundation Directory: Part 2. New York: Foundation Center, 2001.

Foundation Grants Index. New York: Foundation Center, 2001.

Foundation Grants to Individuals. New York: Foundation Center, 2001.

Foundation Guide for Religious Grant Seekers. Atlanta, GA: Scholars Press, 1995.

Foundation 1000. New York: Foundation Center, 2002.

Freed, Richard C., Shervin Freed, and Joseph D. Romano. *Writing Winning Business Proposals.* New York; McGraw-Hill, 1995.

Funding Sources for Community and Economic Development 1997: A Guide to Current Sources for Local Programs and Projects. Phoenix: Oryx Press, 1997.

Funding Sources for K–12 Schools and Adult Basic Education. Phoenix: Oryx Press, 1998.

Fund Raiser's Guide to Human Service Funding. Washington, DC: Taft Group, 2000.

Fund Raiser's Guide to Religious Philanthropy. Washington, DC: Taft Group, 2000.

Geever, Jane. *The Foundation Center's Guide to Proposal Writing.* New York: Foundation Center, 2001.

Giltin, Laura, and Kevin Lyons. *Successful Grant Writing: Strategies for Health and Human Service Professionals.* New York: Springer Publishing, 1996.

Golden, Susan, *Secrets of Successful Grantsmanship: A Guerilla Guide to Raising Money.* San Francisco: Jossey-Bass, 1997.

Grants, Fellowships, and Prizes of Interest to Historians. Washington, DC: American Historical Association, 2001.

The Grants Register. Chicago: St. James Press, 2002.

Hale, Phale. *Writing Grant Proposals That Win.* Alexandria, VA: Capitol Publications, 1997.

Kenner, Carole, and Marlene Walden. *Grant Writing Tips for Nurses and Other Health Professionals.* Washington, DC: American Nurses Association, 2001.

League, V. C., and Odessa Bethea. *The Proposal Writer's Workshop: A Guide to Help You Write Winning Proposals.* Sacramento: Curry-Co Publications, 1998.

List of Cumulative Organizations. Washington, DC: Superintendent of Documents, 1997.

Locke, Lawrence F., and Waneen W. Spirduso. *Proposals That Work: A Guide for Planning Dissertations and Grant Proposals.* Newbury Park, CA: Sage Publications, 2000.

National Directory of Corporate Giving. New York: Foundation Center, 2001.

National Directory of Grantmaking Public Charities. New York: Foundation Center, 1998.

National Guide to Funding for Children, Youth and Families. New York: Foundation Center, 1999.

National Guide to Funding for Community Development. New York: Foundation Center, 1998.

National Guide to Funding for Elementary and Secondary Education. New York: Foundation Center, 1999.

National Guide to Funding for Libraries and Information Services. New York: Foundation Center, 2001.

National Guide for Funding for the Environment and Animal Welfare. New York: Foundation Center, 2000.

National Guide to Funding for Women and Girls. New York: Foundation Center, 1999.

National Guide to Funding in Arts and Culture. New York: Foundation Center, 2000.

National Guide to Funding in Health. New York: Foundation Center, 2001.

National Guide to Funding in Higher Education. New York: Foundation Center, 2000.

National Guide to Funding in Religion. New York: Foundation Center, 1997.

Orlich, Donald C. *Designing Successful Product Proposals.* Alexandria, VA: Association for Supervision and Curriculum Development, 1996.

Petersen, Susan. *The Grantwriter's Internet Companion: A Resource for Educators and Others Seeking Grants and Funding.* Thousand Oaks, CA: Corwin Press, 2001.

Quick, James A., and Cheryl Carter. *Grant Seeker's Budget Toolkit.* New York: John Wiley, 2001.

Reif-Lehrer, Lianne. *Grant Application Writer's Handbook.* Boston: Jones and Bartlett Publishers, 1995.

Ries, Joanne B., and Carl G. Leukfeld. *The Research Funding Guidebook: Getting It, Managing It and Renewing It.* Thousand Oaks: Sage Publications, 1998.

Robinson, Andy, and Kim Klein. *Grantroot Grants: An Activitist's Guide to Proposal Writing.* Berkeley, CA: Chardon Press, 1996.

Robinson, Judith Schiek. *Tapping the Government Grapevine: The User-Friendly Guide to U.S. Government Information Sources,* 3rd ed. Phoenix: Oryx Press, 1998.

Ruskin, Karen, and Charles Achilles. *Grantwriting, Fundraising, and Partnerships: Strategies That Work!* Thousand Oaks, CA: Corwin Press, 1995.

Standard and Poor's Register of Corporations, Directors and Executives. New York: Standard and Poor's Corporation, 2001.

Standard Industrial Classification Manual. Washington, DC: U.S. Government Printing Office, 1987.

Tammemagi, Hans. *Winning Proposals.* Bellingham, WA: Self-Counsel Press, 1999.

Zimmerman, Robert, and Lehman Zimmerman. *Grantseeking: A Step-by-Step Approach.* San Francisco: Zimmerman-Lehman, 2001.

Index

About the Authors

Lynn E. Miner is Associate Dean for External Relations in the College of Engineering at Marquette University, Milwaukee, Wisconsin. He has been an active grantseeker in academic, health care, and other nonprofit environments for the past three decades and has been affiliated with public and private universities and hospitals as a professor and research administrator. He has served on the board of directors for several private foundations and has helped public and private agencies establish guidelines for awarding grants. Miner regularly reviews proposals for the federal government. He is a partner in Miner and Associates Inc., a leading nationwide grants consulting group that specializes in training successful grantseekers.

Jeremy T. Miner is Director of Government Relations and Sponsored Programs at St. Norbert College, De Pere, Wisconsin. In addition to developing and administering proposals, he has served as a reviewer for federal grant programs and has helped private foundations streamline their grant application guidelines. Miner is a member of the National Council of University Research Administrators. He is a partner in Miner and Associates Inc. and has presented grantseeking workshops nationwide to thousands of grant-getters. His successful grant writing techniques have resulted in the generation of millions of grant dollars for many nonprofit education, health care, and social service agencies.

BAR Code NEXT PAGE

Public Grant Web Sites

Web addresses for the major public grant information sources: enter the URL http://plus the specific domain.

Name	Address
Administration on Aging	www.aoa.dhhs.gov
Advanced Research Projects Agency	www.arpa.gov
Administration for Children and Families	www.acf.dhhs.gov
Air Force Office of Scientific Research	www.afosr.af.mil
Army Research Office	www.aro.army.mil
Bureau of Health Professions	bhpr.hrsa.gov
Catalog of Federal Domestic Assistance	www.cfda.gov
Centers for Disease Control and Prevention	www.cdc.gov
Centers for Medicare and Medicaid Services	www.cms.hhs.gov
Congressional Record	www.access.gpo.gov/su_docs/aces/aces150.html
Civilian Research & Development Foundation	www.crdf.org
Department of Agriculture	www.usda.gov
Department of Commerce	www.doc.gov
Department of Education	www.ed.gov
Department of Energy	www.energy.gov
Department of Health & Human Services	www.dhhs.gov
Department of Housing and Urban Development	www.hud.gov
Department of Justice	www.usdoj.gov
Department of State	www.state.gov
Department of Transportation	www.dot.gov
Environmental Protection Agency	www.epa.gov
FEDIX (Federal Information Exchange)	content.sciencewise.com/index.htm
Federal Acquisition Regulation	www.arnet.gov/far
Federal Business Opportunities	www.fedbizopps.gov
Federal Register	www.access.gpo.gov/su_docs/aces/aces140.html
Federal Research in Progress	www.ntis.gov
FirstGov	firstgov.gov
Fogarty International Center	www.nih.gov/fic
Fund for the Improvement of Postsecondary Education	www.ed.gov/offices/OPE/FIPSE
Grantsnet	www.grantsnet.org
Institute of International Education	www.iie.org
National Aeronautics & Space Administration	www.nasa.gov
National Coastal Resources R&D Institute	www-adm.pdx.edu/user/ncri
National Endowment for the Arts	arts.endow.gov
National Endowment for the Humanities	www.neh.gov
National Institute of Standards and Technology	www.nist.gov
National Institutes of Health	www.nih.gov
National Historical Publications & Records Commission	www.archives.gov
National Academy of Science	www.nas.edu
National Gallery of Art	www.nga.gov
National Science Foundation	www.nsf.gov
Office of Naval Research	www.onr.navy.mil
Smithsonian Institution	www.si.edu
U.S. Agency for International Development	www.info.usaid.gov
U.S. Information Agency	usinfo.state.gov
U.S. Institute of Peace	www.usip.org
White House Fellowships	www.whitehousefellows.gov/fellows